D1104902

WEST ACADEMIC PUBLISHING'S EMERITUS ADVISORY BOARD

Global Issues in Civil Procedure
Second Edition

Paul Schiff Berman
Walter S. Cox Professor of Law
The George Washington University Law School

Margaret Y.K. Woo
Professor of Law
Northeastern University School of Law

GLOBAL ISSUES SERIES®

WEST
ACADEMIC
PUBLISHING

The publisher is not engaged in rendering legal or other professional advice, and this publication is not a substitute for the advice of an attorney. If you require legal or other expert advice, you should seek the services of a competent attorney or other professional.

Global Issues Series is a trademark registered in the U.S. Patent and Trademark Office.

ISBN: 978-1-64242-854-4

Acknowledgments

This book is designed to provide the reader with an introduction to the comparative, transnational, and international dimensions of various aspects of civil procedure law and policy. It can usefully supplement either a first-year or upper-level course focusing on procedure, or it could be used in conjunction with courses in comparative law, transnational litigation, or international law and dispute resolution. We wish to acknowledge Professor Thomas Main, the author of an earlier 2006 volume with the same title. We have retained some of his original materials and are grateful for his enthusiastic support of our effort to reconceptualize (and of course update) the volume.

In the preparation of this book, Alix M. Meardon and Olivia Sacks, students at The George Washington University Law School, and Adam Aguirre, Steve Kreager, Disha Patel, Kevin Hoesley, and Kelly Cooke, students at Northeastern University Law School, provided invaluable research assistance.

A Note on the Editing: We have omitted citations and footnotes within court opinions and commentary without so specifying; other omissions or alterations are indicated by asterisks or brackets. We have not indicated omissions at the beginning or the end of an excerpt or where the omission is otherwise obvious from context. We have altered paragraph structure to facilitate readability.

Finally, we are grateful to the following sources for their permission to reprint excerpts from their work:

Oscar G. Chase, *American "Exceptionalism" and Comparative Procedure*, 50 AM. J. COMP. L. 277 (2002). A version of this article appears as a chapter in OSCAR G. CHASE, LAW, CULTURE, AND RITUAL: DISPUTING IN CROSS-CULTURAL CONTEXT (2005). Reprinted by permission.

William V. Dorsaneo, III, *The Decline of Anglo-American Civil Jury Practice*, 71 SMU L. REV. 353 (2018). Reprinted by permission.

Robert W. Emerson, *Judges as Guardian Angels: The German Practice of Hints and Feedback*, 48 VAND. J. OF TRANSNAT'L L. 707 (2015). Reprinted by permission.

Valerie P. Hans, *Jury Systems Around the World*, 4 ANN. REV. OF L. & SOC. SCI. 276 (2008). Reprinted by permission.

Geoffrey C. Hazard, Jr., *From Whom No Secrets Are Hid*, 76 TEXAS L. REV. 1665 (1998). Reprinted by permission.

Deborah R. Hensler, *The Globalization of Class Actions: An Overview*, 622 ANNALS AM. ACAD. POL. & SOC. SCI. 7 (2009). Reprinted by permission.

HERBERT JACOB ET AL., COURTS, LAW & POLITICS IN COMPARATIVE PERSPECTIVE (1996). Reprinted by permission.

Maggie Gardner, *Parochial Procedure*, 69 STAN L. REV. 941 (2017). Reprinted by permission.

Alan Paterson, *Financing Legal Services: A Comparative Perspective*, *in* THE OPTION OF LITIGATING IN EUROPE (D.L. Carey Miller & Paul R. Beaumont, eds. 1993). Reprinted by permission (with alterations reflecting updated information authorized by the author).

Stephen N. Subrin, *Discovery in Global Perspective: Are We Nuts?*, 52 DEPAUL L. REV. 299 (2002). Reprinted by permission.

Summary of Contents

Table of Contents

Table of Cases

The principal cases are in bold type.

Table of Authorities

If excerpts have been taken, the authority
appears in bold; all others are roman.

Global Issues in Civil Procedure

Second Edition

Chapter 1

INTRODUCTORY CASE STUDIES OF LEGAL PLURALISM

In the first year of law school, your Civil Procedure course introduces you to the American civil litigation system. In this course, you learn about some of the provisional compromises that the U.S. system has reached as it seeks to balance competing interests and build a fair system of justice. Those compromises have changed over time, as developments in transportation, communication, technology, corporate activity, and the prevailing political climate have repeatedly challenged the existing set of compromises and made a new set of compromises seem more appropriate. Law and society are forever intertwined, and the law is never static; it shifts in response to societal circumstances, and the new legal compromises themselves shape social relations going forward.

If law is not simply a predetermined set of rules, but instead reflects social reality, then it is not sufficient only to know the U.S. legal system. As scholars have long observed, we live in a world of global legal pluralism, where many different overlapping communities may wish to assert their legal norms over a single act or actor. Even if you think you plan to be a local lawyer within the United States, inevitably your clients will create websites that can be viewed abroad, or they will interact with partners or employees from other jurisdictions, or they will be injured by products designed, built, or modified elsewhere. And so, you must be aware of international legal norms as well as the legal regimes of other countries around the world. Studying these regimes also helps you gain perspective on the choices embedded in the U.S. system. And it will help you to think clearly about how to address situations when a single dispute can implicate multiple jurisdictions. Moreover, the problem of managing legal pluralism arises not only in international and transnational disputes; it also arises within the United States because our federalist system requires negotiation among state and federal legal regimes (as well as the legal regimes of tribal sovereignties and territories such as the District of Columbia, Puerto Rico, Guam, the Northern Mariana Islands, and so on). Therefore, again and again in the first year of law school you will need to

1

consider the multiple legal systems and legal norms that might be relevant to a dispute, as well as how best to negotiate and manage the legal pluralism that results.

Consider the following scenario. A British physicist, participating in a Facebook group, denigrates people of Canadian descent. In response, a Canadian graduate student at a French university posts a message to the group, using the university's computer system. This message falsely implies that the physicist is a pedophile. The physicist, enraged, wishes to bring a suit against the student, the university, and Facebook for defamation. Leaving aside the physicist's likelihood of success on the merits of his claim, the first question to be answered is: where can the suit be brought? In the United Kingdom, where the physicist resides? In Canada, where the student is a citizen? In France, where the student now resides and where the allegedly infringing post originated? Or in the United States, where Facebook's corporate headquarters is located? Second, even assuming we know where the suit can be brought, which country's law of defamation should be used? And, third, if the physicist should win a judgment in the United Kingdom, or the United States, or France, can that judgment be enforced in Canada?

Interestingly enough, the problem is not much easier if we transplant this dispute so that it occurs entirely within the United States. Indeed, if our physicist were from California, our student from Maine, and our university located in New York, we still would be hard-pressed to determine in which *state* the suit could be brought, which state's law applied, and how to enforce the judgment of one state elsewhere (though here the U.S. Constitution might help).

These questions are not new, of course. For as long as human beings have traveled from place to place, such issues have arisen. But in the past century (and perhaps even more in the past three decades) the rise of international business activity, the increasing speed of transportation, the globalization of systems of communication, and the deterritorialization of electronically stored data have made these questions both more important and more difficult. Indeed, some have even begun to question whether a set of jurisdictional rules based on physical geography is still the most appropriate way of constructing an international legal system.

A world of legal pluralism requires us to address three types of questions: (1) Where can a lawsuit be brought? (2) What law will be applied? and (3) What is the effect of a judgment? Each of these questions, in turn, asks us to consider to what degree one jurisdiction may have its own law applied beyond its physical borders. And, although courts (and to a lesser degree legislatures) have attempted to fashion rules on the subject, one cannot fully grasp these so-called conflict-of-laws questions without also thinking about the fundamental philosophical dilemmas that underlie these rules. What allows a political entity to exercise "sovereignty"? What does it mean for a community to assert jurisdiction over a lawsuit? How does one define the relevant community that has legal authority over a claim? In an era of inevitable global interconnection, is the nation-state the appropriate entity to be defining legal rules?

Thus, a Civil Procedure course has at least three aims. Certainly, you should become acquainted with the procedural rules governing the U.S. legal system and the provisional compromises that we have struck among the various competing values at stake. But procedural law is constantly changing, and you as future lawyers will be in a position to help determine how our procedural rules develop in the future. Therefore, you must attend to the theoretical foundations underlying our procedural system. You should consider which values you believe a legal system should protect and whether our current system adequately protects those values. After all, if a society's dispute processing system reflects the embedded beliefs, assumptions, and imperatives of the culture, then our choices with regard to civil procedure offer a framework for considering who we are and what we deem important as a people. And finally, you should consider systems beyond our own and begin to think about strategies for dealing with the legal pluralism that exists all around us.

We begin with three case studies that illustrate the sort of legal pluralism that arises because online communication and data storage tend to defy jurisdictional reliance on territorial location given that electronic data crosses territorial borders so easily. As a result, activity that is legal in one location may well create an impact somewhere else, where it may be illegal. In such circumstances, how should we resolve the conflict of laws that inevitably arises? Is it ever justified for a court to assert jurisdiction over those outside of its physical borders and, if so, why and under what circumstances? We will also ask whether it is legitimate for a court to apply its own law in a case involving outsiders. And, if it is, should other legal systems be bound to enforce that judgment, even if their legal norms are different? In general, do you think there are better or worse ways to respond to legal pluralism?

LA LIGUE CONTRE LE RACISME ET L'ANTISÉMITISME V. YAHOO!, INC.

Superior Court of Paris, 2000

[The Yahoo.com website included an auctions page through which various private parties could purchase items from each other.

Among other items available on the auctions page were Nazi relics, insignias, emblems, flags, and other objects. Yahoo.com also provided links to other pages on which various Nazi texts—such as *Mein Kampf* and *The Protocols of the Elders of Zion*—were available for sale. These same sites also included "Holocaust revisionist" material, such as photographs purporting to "prove" that reports of gas chambers were fictitious. L'Union des Etudiants Juif de France (Jewish Students' Union of France, or UEJF) and La Ligue Contre le Racisme et l'Antisémitisme (League Against Racism and Antisemitism, or LICRA) sued Yahoo!, alleging violations of article R. 645–1 of the French Penal Code, which prohibits the public display of Nazi-related objects.]

JEAN-JACQUES GOMEZ, PRESIDING JUSTICE.

Whereas it is not contested that a surfer who accesses Yahoo.com from French territory, directly or by virtue of the link that Yahoo.fr provides, can view on his computer screen pages, services, and sites to which Yahoo.com gives access, in particular the auction service (Auctions) hosted by Geocities.com, Yahoo! Inc.'s hosting service, notably its listings of Nazi items;

Whereas the exhibition of Nazi items for sale constitutes a violation of French law (Article R. [645–1] of the Penal Code) but even more an insult to the collective memory of a country deeply wounded by the atrocities that were committed by and in the name of the Nazi criminal organization against its nationals, and especially against its Jewish nationals;

Whereas by allowing the viewing of these items in France and by allowing the eventual participation of a surfer in France in such an exhibition-sale, Yahoo! Inc. commits a wrong on French territory—the unintentional nature of which is apparent, but which causes the damage to LICRA and the UEJF, both of which have as their mission to pursue in France any form of trivialization of Nazism—notwithstanding that the activity at issue is marginal in relation to the general activity of the auction service that Yahoo.com offers on its site;

Whereas the damage was suffered in France, and we are therefore competent to exercise jurisdiction over the present dispute * * *;

Whereas Yahoo! Inc. argues that it is technically impossible for it to control access to the auction service or to other services and, as a result, to prevent a surfer accessing the Internet from France from viewing these services on his screen;

Whereas Yahoo! Inc. wishes to emphasize that it warns any visitor against using its services for purposes "worthy of reprobation for any reason whatsoever," notably for purposes of racial or ethnic discrimination (see its users' charter);

But whereas Yahoo! Inc. has the capability to identify the geographical origin of the site that accesses its services, based on the [Internet Protocol] address of the surfer, which should allow Yahoo! Inc. to use appropriate means to prevent surfers in France from accessing services and sites the viewing of which on a screen in France * * * can be considered [punishable under French law], as is obviously the case with the display of uniforms, badges, and emblems that recall the ones worn or displayed by the Nazis;

Whereas with regard to surfers who access its services through sites that ensure anonymity, Yahoo! Inc. has less ability to control access, but nevertheless can do so, for example, by systematically refusing access to any visitor who does not reveal his geographical origin;

Whereas the real difficulties encountered by Yahoo! Inc. thus do not constitute insurmountable obstacles; * * *

[We order] Yahoo! Inc. to take all such measures as would dissuade and prevent any access through Yahoo.com to the auction service for Nazi items or any other site or service that constitutes an apology for Nazism or questions Nazi crimes[.]

Notes and Questions

1.   Yahoo! claimed that it could not, as a technological matter, selectively block access to prohibited sites based on the geographical location of the user. Should that matter to the French court? And if service providers are now much better able to identify user location than they were in 2000, should they be required to use that technology to comply with the demands of the French court? Does it matter that users can thwart efforts to identify their locations?

2.   Why do you think there was no dispute that the French court could order the removal of offensive material from Yahoo.fr? Why do you think such removal was insufficient from the point of view of the French complainants?

3.   It is worth noting that, under French jurisdictional law, the French court could have asserted jurisdiction based on a (then-existing) provision that extended jurisdiction over anyone, anywhere in the world, so long as there was a French plaintiff. Because of the controversial nature of such a jurisdictional assertion, however, this provision has rarely been invoked and was not discussed by the court in this case (and the provision has since been struck down by France's highest court).

Nevertheless, Yahoo!'s argument was essentially that even the court's more limited assertion of jurisdiction was tantamount to an assertion of universal jurisdiction over any website viewable in France. Do you agree?

4. Should the mere fact that Yahoo!'s servers are not located in France be sufficient to deny the French court jurisdiction? What criteria should be used for determining whether a company such as Yahoo! should face liability in France? Yahoo! at the time was a multinational operator, with a business plan aimed at reaching web users worldwide, a marketing strategy touting its "global footprint," and a French subsidiary in which it owned a seventy-percent ownership stake. *See* Joel R. Reidenberg, *Yahoo and Democracy on the Internet*, 42 JURIMETRICS J. 261 (2002). Moreover, Yahoo! routinely profiled French users in order to target them with advertisements written in French. Is that sufficient to justify France's assertion of jurisdiction over Yahoo?

5. Should we be concerned that if websites are subject to the laws of *all* jurisdictions from which they can be accessed, the legal norms of the *most restrictive* community will prevail? Or should we be more concerned about the opposite problem: If foreign courts cannot reach websites located in other jurisdictions, will the legal norms of the *least restrictive* community prevail? In the context of the *Yahoo!* case, if foreign courts cannot reach U.S.-based entities, has the United States then imposed its (relatively unrestrictive) First Amendment on global Internet speech? If so, is that problematic? As other countries impose their own restrictions on Internet content, is this a healthy "democratizing" of online regulation, or a recipe for chaos? Or both?

6. Suppose the plaintiffs in the *Yahoo!* case could have obtained, under French law, an order requiring French Internet Service Providers (ISPs) to block French subscribers' access to the offending content on Yahoo!'s auction site (rather than an injunction against the foreign website itself). Wouldn't that "solve" the extraterritoriality problem (while still serving the law's purpose of eliminating the "public display" of Nazi-related material) inasmuch as French law would be applied to the conduct of French, rather than foreign, entities? In February 2002, the Commonwealth of Pennsylvania enacted the Internet Child Pornography Act, 18 PA. CONS. STAT. §§ 7621–7630, which took just this approach to the control of unlawful content on the Internet. The Pennsylvania statute required ISPs to "disable access" to "child pornography items"—defined elsewhere in the statute—"residing on or accessible through its service in a manner accessible to persons located within Pennsylvania" after notification from the Pennsylvania Attorney General that there was probable cause to believe such material could be accessed from within Pennsylvania over the ISP's facilities. By its terms, the statute was directed entirely at *within-state* activities; the statute left the offending websites, which might be physically located anywhere

in the world, completely undisturbed, only ISPs *serving Pennsylvania subscribers* were subject to the court's orders, and compliance with the statute only required them to make the offending websites inaccessible to their subscribers *in Pennsylvania*.

Does Pennsylvania's approach successfully avoid the charge that Pennsylvania is attempting to reach out beyond its borders to control the behavior of individuals or entities outside of its jurisdiction? In *Center for Democracy and Technology v. Pappert*, 337 F. Supp. 2d 606 (E.D. Pa. 2004) a federal court struck down the Pennsylvania statute on the grounds that it violated both the First Amendment and the "dormant" Commerce Clause.

7.   If you were a U.S. judge asked to enforce the French court's order, would you do so? Why or why not? Consider the following case:

YAHOO!, INC. V. LA LIGUE CONTRE LE RACISME ET L'ANTISÉMITISME

United States District Court for the Northern District of California, 2001
169 F. Supp. 2d 1181

FOGEL, DISTRICT JUDGE.

I. PROCEDURAL HISTORY

Defendants La Ligue Contre Le Racisme Et l'Antisemitisme ("LICRA") and L'Union Des Etudiants Juifs De France, citizens of France, are non-profit organizations dedicated to eliminating anti-Semitism. Plaintiff Yahoo!, Inc. ("Yahoo!") is a corporation organized under the laws of Delaware with its principal place of business in Santa Clara, California. Yahoo! is an Internet service provider that operates various Internet websites and services that any computer user can access at the Uniform Resource Locator ("URL") *http:// www.yahoo.com*. Yahoo! services ending in the suffix, ".com," without an associated country code as a prefix or extension (collectively, "Yahoo!'s U.S. Services") use the English language and target users who are residents of, utilize servers based in and operate under the laws of the United States. Yahoo! subsidiary corporations operate regional Yahoo! sites and services in twenty other nations, including, for example, Yahoo! France, Yahoo! India, and Yahoo! Spain. Each of these regional web sites contains the host nation's unique two-letter code as either a prefix or a suffix in its URL (e.g., Yahoo! France is found at *http://www.yahoo.fr* and Yahoo! Korea at *http://www. yahoo.kr*). Yahoo!'s regional sites use the local region's primary language, target the local citizenry, and operate under local laws.

Yahoo! provides a variety of means by which people from all over the world can communicate and interact with one another over the Internet. Examples include an Internet search engine, e-mail, an automated auction site, personal web page hostings, shopping services, chat rooms, and a listing of clubs that individuals can create or join. Any computer user with Internet access is able to post materials on many of these Yahoo! sites, which in turn are instantly accessible by anyone who logs on to Yahoo!'s Internet sites. As relevant here, Yahoo!'s auction site allows anyone to post an item for sale and solicit bids from any computer user from around the globe. Yahoo! records when a posting is made and after the requisite time period lapses sends an e-mail notification to the highest bidder and seller with their respective contact information. Yahoo! is never a party to a transaction, and the buyer and seller are responsible for arranging privately for payment and shipment of goods. Yahoo! monitors the transaction through limited regulation by prohibiting particular items from being sold (such as stolen goods, body parts, prescription and illegal drugs, weapons, and goods violating U.S. copyright laws or the Iranian and Cuban embargos) and by providing a rating system through which buyers and sellers have their transactional behavior evaluated for the benefit of future consumers. Yahoo! informs auction sellers that they must comply with Yahoo!'s policies and may not offer items to buyers in jurisdictions in which the sale of such item violates the jurisdiction's applicable laws. Yahoo! does not actively regulate the content of each posting, and individuals are able to post, and have in fact posted, highly offensive matter, including Nazi-related propaganda and Third Reich memorabilia, on Yahoo!'s auction sites.

On or about April 5, 2000, LICRA sent a "cease and desist" letter to Yahoo!'s Santa Clara headquarters informing Yahoo! that the sale of Nazi and Third Reich related goods through its auction services violates French law. LICRA threatened to take legal action unless Yahoo! took steps to prevent such sales within eight days. Defendant subsequently * * * filed a civil complaint against Yahoo! in the Tribunal de Grande Instance de Paris (the "French Court").

The French Court found that approximately 1,000 Nazi and Third Reich related objects, including Adolf Hitler's *Mein Kampf*, *The Protocol of the Elders of Zion* (an infamous anti-Semitic report produced by the Czarist secret police in the early 1900's), and purported "evidence" that the gas chambers of the Holocaust did not exist were being offered for sale on Yahoo.com's auction site. Because any French citizen is able to access these materials on Yahoo.com directly or through a link on Yahoo.fr, the French Court concluded that the Yahoo.com auction site violates Section R645–1 of the French Criminal Code, which prohibits exhibition of Nazi propaganda and artifacts for sale. On [May 22, 2000], the French Court entered an order requiring Yahoo! to (1) eliminate French citizens' access to any material on the Yahoo.com auction site that offers for sale any Nazi objects, relics, insignia, emblems, and flags; (2) eliminate French citizens' access to web pages on Yahoo.com displaying text, extracts, or quotations from *Mein Kampf* and *Protocol of the Elders of Zion*; (3) post a warning to French citizens on Yahoo.fr that any search through Yahoo.com may lead to sites containing material prohibited by Section R645–1 of the French Criminal Code, and that such viewing of the prohibited material may result in legal action against the Internet user; (4) remove from all browser directories accessible in the French Republic index headings entitled "negationists" and from all hypertext links the equation of "negationists" under the heading "Holocaust." The order subjects Yahoo! to a penalty of 100,000 [Francs] for each day that it fails to comply with the order. The order concludes:

> We order the Company YAHOO! Inc. to take all necessary measures to dissuade and render impossible any access via Yahoo.com to the Nazi artifact auction service and to any other site or service that may be construed as constituting an apology for Nazism or a contesting of Nazi crimes.

The French Court set a return date in July 2000 for Yahoo! to demonstrate its compliance with the order.

Yahoo! asked the French Court to reconsider the terms of the order, claiming that although it easily could post the required warning on Yahoo.fr, compliance with the order's requirements with respect to Yahoo.com was technologically impossible. The French Court sought expert opinion on the matter and on November 20, 2000 "reaffirmed" its order of May 22. The French Court ordered Yahoo! to comply with the May 22 order within three (3) months or face a penalty of 100,000 Francs (approximately U.S. $13,300) for each day of non-compliance. The French Court also provided that penalties assessed against Yahoo! Inc. may not be collected from Yahoo! France. * * *

Yahoo! subsequently posted the required warning and prohibited postings in violation of Section R645–1 of the French Criminal Code from appearing on Yahoo.fr. Yahoo! also amended the auction policy of Yahoo.com to prohibit individuals from auctioning:

> Any item that promotes, glorifies, or is directly associated with groups or individuals known principally for hateful or violent positions or acts, such as Nazis or the Ku Klux Klan. Official government-issue stamps and coins are not prohibited under this policy. Expressive media, such as books and films, may be subject to more permissive standards as determined by Yahoo! in its sole discretion.

Yahoo Auction Guidelines (visited Oct. 23, 2001) <http://user. auctions.Yahoo.com/html/guidelines.html>. Notwithstanding these actions, the Yahoo.com auction site still offers certain items for sale (such as stamps, coins, and a copy of *Mein Kampf*) which appear to violate the French Order. While Yahoo! has removed the *Protocol of the Elders of Zion* from its auction site, it has not prevented access to numerous other sites which reasonably "may be construed as constituting an apology for Nazism or a contesting of Nazi crimes."

Yahoo! claims that because it lacks the technology to block French citizens from accessing the Yahoo.com auction site to view materials which violate the French Order or from accessing other Nazi-based content of websites on Yahoo.com, it cannot comply with the French order without banning Nazi-related material from Yahoo.com altogether. Yahoo! contends that such a ban would infringe impermissibly upon its rights under the First Amendment to the United States Constitution. Accordingly, Yahoo! filed a complaint in this Court seeking a declaratory judgment that the French Court's orders are neither cognizable nor enforceable under the laws of the United States. * * *

II. OVERVIEW

As this Court and others have observed, the instant case presents novel and important issues arising from the global reach of the Internet. Indeed, the specific facts of this case implicate issues of policy, politics, and culture that are beyond the purview of one nation's judiciary. Thus it is critical that the Court define at the outset what is and is not at stake in the present proceeding.

This case is *not* about the moral acceptability of promoting the symbols or propaganda of Nazism. Most would agree that such acts are profoundly offensive. By any reasonable standard of morality, the Nazis were responsible for one of the worst displays of inhumanity in recorded history. This Court is acutely mindful of the emotional pain reminders of the Nazi era cause to Holocaust survivors and deeply respectful of the motivations of the French Republic in enacting the underlying statutes and of the defendant organizations in seeking relief under those statutes. Vigilance is the key to preventing atrocities such as the Holocaust from occurring again.

Nor is this case about the right of France or any other nation to determine its own law and social policies. A basic function of a sovereign state is to determine by law what forms of speech and conduct are acceptable within its borders. In this instance, as a nation whose citizens suffered the effects of Nazism in ways that are incomprehensible to most Americans, France clearly has the right to

enact and enforce laws such as those relied upon by the French Court
here.

What *is* at issue here is whether it is consistent with the
Constitution and laws of the United States for another nation to
regulate speech by a United States resident within the United States
on the basis that such speech can be accessed by Internet users in
that nation. In a world in which ideas and information transcend
borders and the Internet in particular renders the physical distance
between speaker and audience virtually meaningless, the
implications of this question go far beyond the facts of this case. The
modern world is home to widely varied cultures with radically
divergent value systems. There is little doubt that Internet users in
the United States routinely engage in speech that violates, for
example, China's laws against religious expression, the laws of
various nations against advocacy of gender equality or
homosexuality, or even the United Kingdom's restrictions on freedom
of the press. If the government or another party in one of these
sovereign nations were to seek enforcement of such laws against
Yahoo! or another U.S.-based Internet service provider, what
principles should guide the court's analysis?

The Court has stated that it must and will decide this case in
accordance with the Constitution and laws of the United States. It
recognizes that in so doing, it necessarily adopts certain value
judgments embedded in those enactments, including the
fundamental judgment expressed in the First Amendment that it is
preferable to permit the non-violent expression of offensive
viewpoints rather than to impose viewpoint-based governmental
regulation upon speech. The government and people of France have
made a different judgment based upon their own experience. In
undertaking its inquiry as to the proper application of the laws of the
United States, the Court intends no disrespect for that judgment or
for the experience that has informed it. * * *

IV. LEGAL ISSUES

* * *

3. *Abstention*

Defendants * * * argue that this Court should abstain from
deciding the instant case because Yahoo! simply is unhappy with the
outcome of the French litigation and is trying to obtain a more
favorable result here. * * *

In the present case, the French court has determined that
Yahoo!'s auction site and website hostings on Yahoo.com violate
French law. Nothing in Yahoo!'s suit for declaratory relief in this

Court appears to be an attempt to relitigate or disturb the French court's application of French law or its orders with respect to Yahoo!'s conduct in France. Rather, the purpose of the present action is to determine whether a United States court may enforce the French order without running afoul of the First Amendment. The actions involve distinct legal issues, and as this Court concluded in its jurisdictional order, a United States court is best situated to determine the application of the United States Constitution to the facts presented. No basis for abstention has been established.

4.   *Comity*

No legal judgment has any effect, of its own force, beyond the limits of the sovereignty from which its authority is derived. However, the United States Constitution and implementing legislation require that full faith and credit be given to judgments of sister states, territories, and possessions of the United States. U.S. CONST. art. IV, § 1, cl. 1; 28 U.S.C. § 1738. The extent to which the United States, or any state, honors the judicial decrees of foreign nations is a matter of choice, governed by "the comity of nations." *Hilton v. Guyot*, 159 U.S. 113, 163 (1895). Comity "is neither a matter of absolute obligation, on the one hand, nor of mere courtesy and good will, upon the other." *Id.* at 163–64. United States courts generally recognize foreign judgments and decrees unless enforcement would be prejudicial or contrary to the country's interests.

As discussed previously, the French order's content and viewpoint-based regulation of the web pages and auction site on Yahoo.com, while entitled to great deference as an articulation of French law, clearly would be inconsistent with the First Amendment if mandated by a court in the United States. What makes this case uniquely challenging is that the Internet in effect allows one to speak in more than one place at the same time. Although France has the sovereign right to regulate what speech is permissible in France, this Court may not enforce a foreign order that violates the protections of the United States Constitution by chilling protected speech that occurs simultaneously within our borders. * * * Absent a body of law that establishes international standards with respect to speech on the Internet and an appropriate treaty or legislation addressing enforcement of such standards to speech originating within the United States, the principle of comity is outweighed by the Court's obligation to uphold the First Amendment.

Notes and Questions

1.   Although the district court ultimately declined to enforce the French order, it did *not* rule that the French court had acted without proper jurisdiction in the first place. Why not? Is there any advantage to

allowing the French jurisdictional assertion but disagreeing with the substantive rule articulated by the French court?

2.   Should the district court have considered international standards regarding hate speech and not just the First Amendment? If so, how would it have gone about determining precisely what those standards are? To the extent that the First Amendment is in tension with those standards, should that be relevant in a case involving the enforcement of a foreign judgment?

3.   Judge Fogel appears to assume that it would actually be *unconstitutional* for a U.S. court to enforce the French judgment simply because that judgment could not constitutionally have been issued by a U.S. court. But does that necessarily follow? After all, the concerns involved in simply enforcing another jurisdiction's judgment are quite different from those involved when a court is ruling in the first instance. Indeed, the whole idea of full faith and credit in the domestic context rests on the premise that there is a value in states enforcing other states' judgments even if those judgments are contrary to the public policies of the enforcing state. *See, e.g., Baker v. General Motors,* 522 U.S. 222, 233 (1998) (describing the full faith and credit obligation as "exacting"). Mightn't the same be true internationally? *See, e.g.,* Mark Rosen, *Exporting the Constitution,* 53 EMORY L.J. 171 (2004) (arguing that, even if foreign judgments are " 'Un-American' insofar as they come from non-American polities and reflect political values that are at variance with American constitutional law, neither the foreign judgments themselves nor their enforcement by an American court is unconstitutional").

Moreover, it is unclear whether or not the mere enforcement of a foreign order should be deemed sufficient state action to trigger constitutional scrutiny. In *Shelley v. Kraemer,* 334 U.S. 1 (1948), the U.S. Supreme Court ruled that judicial enforcement of racially restrictive covenants would violate the Equal Protection Clause of the Fourteenth Amendment, U.S. CONST. amend. XIV, § 1. *Shelley,* 334 U.S. at 20–21. On the other hand, *Shelley*'s logic "consistently applied, would require individuals to conform their private agreements to constitutional standards whenever, as almost always, the individuals might later seek the security of potential judicial enforcement." LAURENCE H. TRIBE, AMERICAN CONSTITUTIONAL LAW 1697 (2d ed. 1988). This issue implicates longstanding debates about the coherence of trying to draw a distinction between "private" and "public" action for constitutional purposes.

4.   If the U.S. court refuses to enforce the French judgment, does France have any recourse? And, if not, has the United States then "imposed" the First Amendment on France? On the other hand, if the U.S. court enforces the French judgment, would France then be "imposing" its hate speech laws on the United States?

5.   The district court's opinion was subsequently reversed by the United States Court of Appeals for the Ninth Circuit. *See Yahoo!, Inc. v. La Ligue Contre le Racisme et l'Antisémitisme*, 433 F.3d 1199 (9th Cir. 2006) (en banc). The appeals court declined to reach the First Amendment question, however. Instead, a majority of the *en banc* court agreed that the case should be dismissed, though the judges disagreed on the rationale for the dismissal. Some wanted to dismiss for lack of personal jurisdiction over the French defendants because the defendants had insufficient contact with California. Others perceived a ripeness problem, because part of the reason the French defendants had insufficient contact with California is that they had chosen not to seek an enforcement order in the United States. Whatever the rationale, however, the effect of the ruling was to prevent Yahoo!'s claim from going forward unless and until a U.S. court is actually asked to enforce the French order. At that point, the controversy would become ripe for review, and at the same time jurisdiction would presumably no longer be a problem.

6.   When a court is called upon to enforce a foreign judgment, its task is complicated by the fact that it must decipher precisely what obligations the foreign court has imposed on the party seeking to avoid enforcement. The *Yahoo!* case illustrates the difficulties that a court might face. In the California case, Yahoo! argued that it lacked the means to comply with the obligations the French court had imposed upon it. But what obligations, precisely, did the French court impose? Compare the translation of the concluding paragraph of the French court order that the district court adopts here with the one appearing in the case decision earlier in this chapter. The question is how to interpret the crucial language "Ordonnons à la Société YAHOO! Inc. de prendre toutes les mesures de nature à dissuader et à rendre impossible toute consultation sur Yahoo.com . . . ." Here, the court accepts the translation offered by Yahoo!: "We order the Company YAHOO! Inc. to take *all necessary measures to dissuade and render impossible* any access via Yahoo.com . . . ." The alternative translation would understand the French court to have ordered Yahoo! "to take *all such measures as would dissuade and prevent* any access." The passage might also be translated as "to take *all normal measures to dissuade and prevent* any access." Are there substantive differences between these formulations? How might the choice of one translation or another affect the court's decision whether to enforce the judgment?

MATUSEVITCH V. TELNIKOFF

United States District Court for the District of Columbia, 1995
877 F. Supp. 1

[Matusevitch published a letter in a London newspaper, responding to an article written in that same newspaper by Telnikoff. Telnikoff subsequently sued Matusevitch in London for libel, arguing that the letter was defamatory under British law. The U.K. courts ultimately issued judgment against Matusevitch. By that time, Matusevitch was a Maryland citizen, and Telnikoff therefore sought enforcement of the British judgment in Maryland. Matusevitch, in turn, argued that the British judgment was not enforceable in Maryland.]

URBINA, DISTRICT JUDGE.

The court finds that there is no genuine issue as to any material fact as 1) Maryland statutory law indicates that the defendant holds an unrecognized foreign judgment and 2) plaintiff's statement is considered by the Supreme Court to be protected speech under the First Amendment. Because recognition and enforcement of a foreign judgment, based on libel standards that are repugnant to the public policies of the State of Maryland and the United States, would deprive the plaintiff of his First and Fourteenth Amendment rights, the court grants summary judgment for the plaintiff as a matter of law.

I.   Recognition of a Foreign Judgment

Before a party can enforce a judgment from a foreign country in the United States, the moving party must have the foreign judgment recognized by the state in which he is seeking to enforce the judgment. In the State of Maryland, the Uniform Foreign-Money Judgments Recognition Act of 1962 (the "Recognition Act") and the Uniform Enforcement of Foreign Judgments Act of 1964 (the "Enforcement Act") govern the procedure for the recognition and enforcement of a foreign judgment.

The Recognition Act in MD. CODE ANN., CTS. & JUD. PROC. section 10–703 states that:

> [e]xcept as provided in section 10–704, a foreign judgment meeting the requirements of section 10–702 is conclusive between the parties to the extent that it grants or denies recovery of a sum of money. The foreign judgment is enforceable in the same manner as the judgment of a sister state which is entitled to full faith and credit.

Section 10–704 lists a number of grounds for non-recognition of a foreign judgment, four which are mandatory grounds and five which are discretionary grounds for non-recognition. Therefore, before a party can enforce a foreign-country judgment, the Recognition Act requires a proceeding to determine preliminarily whether the court should recognize the foreign-country judgment.

Once the court recognizes the foreign-country judgment, the moving party can simply file that judgment in order to enforce it. Section 11–802 states that:

(a)   Generally (1) (i) Except as provided in subparagraphs (ii) and (iii) of this paragraph, a copy of any foreign judgment authenticated in accordance with an act of Congress or statutes of this State may be filed in the office of the clerk of a circuit court.

(2)   The clerk shall treat the foreign judgment in the same manner as a judgment of the court in which the foreign judgment is filed.

Filing a foreign-country judgment for enforcement purposes, however, remains contingent on the judgment's initial recognition. * * * *

[T]he Recognition Act lists mandatory and discretionary grounds for non-recognition. Section 10–704(b)(2) states that a foreign judgment need not be recognized if "the cause of action on which the judgment is based is repugnant to the public policy of the State."

Case law illustrates that United States courts have refused to recognize foreign judgments based on public policy grounds. In *Laker Airways v. Sabena Belgian World Airlines,* 731 F.2d 909, 931 (D.C.Cir.1984), the court stated that it "is not required to give effect to foreign judicial proceedings grounded on policies which do violence to its own fundamental interests." In *Tahan v. Hodgson,* 662 F.2d 862, 864 (D.C.Cir.1981), the court stated that the "requirements for enforcement of a foreign judgment expressed in *Hilton v. Guyot,* 159 U.S. 113 (1895), are that . . . the original claim not violate American public policy . . . that it not be repugnant to fundamental notions of what is decent and just in the State where enforcement is sought."

Although principles of comity, defined by the Supreme Court as "the recognition which one nation allows within its territory to the legislative, executive, or judicial acts of another nation, having due regard both to international duty and convenience, and to the rights of its own citizens or of other persons who are under the protection of its laws," are taken under consideration, the Supreme Court has ruled that comity "does not require, but rather forbids [recognition] where such a recognition works a direct violation of the policy of our laws, and does violence to what we deem the rights of our citizens." *Hilton,* 159 U.S. at 164. * * * *

In this case, libel standards that are contrary to U.S. libel standards would be repugnant to the public policies of the State of

Maryland and the United States. Therefore, pursuant to section 10–704(b)(2) of the Recognition Act, this court declines to recognize the foreign judgment.

II. Deprivation of First and Fourteenth Amendment rights to the Constitution.

A. *British Libel Law v. U.S. Libel Law*

British law on libel differs from U.S. law. In the United Kingdom, the defendant bears the burden of proving allegedly defamatory statements true and the plaintiff is not required to prove malice on the part of the libel defendant. As a result, a libel defendant would be held liable for statements the defendant honestly believed to be true and published without any negligence. In contrast, the law in the United States requires the plaintiff to prove that the statements were false and looks to the defendant's state of mind and intentions. In light of the different standards, this court concludes that recognition and enforcement of the foreign judgment in this case would deprive the plaintiff of his constitutional rights.

B. *Protected Speech*

Speech similar to the plaintiff's statements have received protection under the First Amendment to the Constitution and are thereby unactionable in U.S. courts. In *Hustler Magazine, Inc. v. Falwell,* 485 U.S. 46 (1988), the Supreme Court held that hyperbole is not actionable. Plaintiff contends that his statements were plainly hyperbolic because they were stated in an attempt to portray defendant's extremist position.

In addition, in the United States, courts look to the context in which the statements appeared when determining a First Amendment question.* * * * In the case at hand, the court notes that the British judgment was based on jury instructions which asked the jury to ignore context. Therefore, this court finds that if the statements were read in context to the original article or statement and in reference to the location of the statements in the newspaper, a reader would reasonably be alerted to the statements' function as opinion and not as an assertion of fact.

C. *Limited Public Figure*

The Supreme Court in *New York Times Co. v. Sullivan,* 376 U.S. 254 (1964), explained that a public figure must show by clear and convincing evidence that the libel defendant published defamatory statements with actual malice. The defendant in this case has described himself as a prominent activist for Human Rights in the Soviet Union since 1955. Therefore, for purposes of his article about the composition of Russian personnel hired by Radio Free Europe/Radio Liberty, the court finds that the defendant was a limited public figure. In light of defendant's status as a limited public figure, the plaintiff is entitled to all the constitutional safeguards concerning speech used against public figures.

During the trial in England, because of British libel standards for the defense of "fair comment", the court never looked to the degree of fault or the accused party's intentions. * * * * As a result, since there appears to be no proof that the plaintiff made the statements with actual malice, the plaintiff enjoys the constitutional protection for speech directed against public figures.

For the reasons stated herein, the court grants summary judgment in favor of the Plaintiff.

Notes and Questions

1.   In what ways is this case similar to, or different from, the *Yahoo!* case? Should those differences lead to a different result with regard to the judgment enforcement decision?

2.   Should legal jurisdiction be based on community affiliation? If so, what were the relevant community affiliations for this dispute? Is the First Amendment truly implicated?

3.   In response to defamation suits abroad against U.S. individuals and publishers, Congress enacted, in 2010, a statute seeking to block enforcement of such suits. The statute reads in relevant part:

[A] domestic court shall not recognize or enforce a foreign judgment for defamation unless the domestic court determines that—

(A) the defamation law applied in the foreign court's adjudication provided at least as much protection for freedom of speech and press in that case as would be provided by the first amendment to the Constitution of the United States and by the constitution and law of the State in which the domestic court is located; or

(B) even if the defamation law applied in the foreign court's adjudication did not provide as much protection for freedom of speech and press as the first amendment to the Constitution of the United States and the constitution and law of the State, the party opposing recognition or enforcement of that foreign judgment would have been found liable for defamation by a domestic court applying the first amendment to the Constitution of the United States and the constitution and law of the State in which the domestic court is located.

If you had been in Congress at the time, would you have voted for this statute? Why or why not? By its terms, the statute would equally block enforcement against Yahoo! and against Matusevitch. Is that the correct result, or are these two cases distinguishable?

4.   Does the United States have an interest in having its judgments enforced by courts abroad? If so, might statutes like this cause other legal systems to retaliate? How do we best balance the need for an interlocking legal system against the reality that different systems have different norms and procedures?

Chapter 2

UNDERSTANDING THE U.S. LEGAL SYSTEM IN COMPARATIVE CONTEXT

Every society has disputes. With disputes comes the need for dispute resolution. And one key to resolving disputes is the set of rules delineating how to decide such disputes. Indeed, often it is as much the process of resolution as the resolution itself that legitimizes the outcome. Like substantive law, the process of disputing can be described as "cultural behavior, informed by participants' moral views about how to fight." Sally Engle Merry, *Disputing Without Culture*, 100 HARV. L. REV. 2057, 2063 (1987). Legal procedure is then not simply a practical way of ensuring the enforcement of substantive rights; it also reflects our collective sense of justice.

Determining who, what, where and how legal facts are constructed from a messy dispute is the crux of civil procedure. While some nations believe that the role of litigation is limited to resolving individual disputes, other nations carry the view that litigation can serve to restructure broader social norms. Where a country stands in this spectrum is often a product of historical, political and social forces, which in turn determine how civil litigation rules are structured. Civil procedure rules, such as who is best to take charge of a lawsuit—the disputants, the lawyers or the judges—or how easy it is to file a complaint, will vary accordingly. In light of these possible similarities or differences, a comparative study of even one other system's civil procedure rules adds to our understanding of how norms are established and enforced, as well as the role of courts and legal systems in society more generally.

When considering legal rules and legal disputes beyond the United States, it is important to distinguish among three types of legal categories: transnational, comparative, and international:

- "Transnational" refers to litigation that takes place in the domestic legal system of one country that ends up having an impact on an act or actor from another country.

- "Comparative" involves thinking about the similarities and differences among various domestic legal systems regarding how those systems resolve domestic disputes. Thus, one can compare two legal systems without needing to consider a case that involves both systems, unlike in transnational litigation, where multiple systems are necessarily implicated.

- Finally, "international" refers to systems, treaties, and reform efforts that transcend national boundaries, such as international courts, arbitral bodies, harmonization regimes, and so on. Here, the applicable legal regime does not belong to any particular domestic system, but instead is developed with the goal of applying globally.

In order to see the differences among these three concepts, imagine that you are general counsel to a U.S. company that does global business on the internet. If you are sued by a plaintiff from another country in that country's courts, that is a transnational litigation. You will therefore need to think about whether you want to challenge the foreign court's jurisdiction, whether U.S. or foreign law should apply, what rules of procedure should be used, whether a U.S. court would recognize and enforce any judgment issued against you by the foreign court, and so on.

But even absent transnational litigation, you may wish to understand comparatively the legal systems of other jurisdictions where you do business, both to anticipate possible consequences and to see if perhaps there are aspects of those legal systems that you may wish to argue should be adopted in the United States.

Finally, to the extent that it is complicated for your company to be subject to multiple, possibly conflicting, legal regimes, you may wish to advocate for an international regulatory approach that would harmonize the various different national laws or that would provide a separate adjudicative body where transnational disputes involving your company could be decided.

A. COMMON LAW V. CIVIL LAW SYSTEMS

Given that the world is so full of different legal systems, it is worth considering some fundamental differences between the U.S. civil procedure system and the systems of other countries around the world. The following excerpts introduce the two dominant legal traditions: the common law and the civil law traditions.

HERBERT JACOB ET AL., COURTS, LAW & POLITICS IN COMPARATIVE PERSPECTIVE (1996)

Western law has conventionally been divided into two distinct categories: a civil code tradition and a common-law tradition. The civil code finds its ancient roots in Roman law but is also the product of the French revolution. Where French armies conquered, they imposed the Napoleonic civil code. Thus, the legal systems of almost the entire continent of Europe can be traced to this common ancestor. In the intervening years, each country has added or subtracted details, but the common parentage remains apparent. A distinctive feature of the civil code was its design as a seamless body of legal prescriptions, based on simple principles that could best be understood by lay people. Scholars were its principal drafters, and they considered law as a science rather than as a political art. In keeping with the contempt with which French revolutionaries held judges of the old regime and the revolutionaries' commitment to popular sovereignty, the drafters of the civil code granted little authority to the judiciary. Judges were to apply the law, but their decisions were not given authority as precedents. At the same time, lawyers remained overshadowed by magistrates and judges in the conduct of trials. Courts were *state* institutions rather than a battleground for attorneys sponsored by private interests.

The second category of Western legal systems is those based on what is described as the common law. Its origins lie in England with the gradual development of legal authority as interpreted by the monarchy's judges. In the English version, however, parliamentary authority became supreme; no written constitution provided opportunities to declare Acts of Parliament unconstitutional. However, Parliament did not begin to write comprehensive legal codes until the twentieth century, and many gaps existed in the law. Courts filled that vacuum by decisions in disputes brought to them. By citing their earlier decisions as precedent, courts built up a large body of case law without challenging the authority of Parliament. English settlers brought this common law to the American colonies. However, the adoption of a written constitution in the United States quickly allowed judges to exercise judicial review in a manner unknown to nineteenth-century England. In addition, both in England and in the United States the principal drafters of law have been judges, lawyers, and politicians rather than academic scholars. Law is not considered a science, but rather a pragmatic endeavor. Moreover, lawyers play a central role in litigation. Courts (and judges) sit passively until activated by private interests as represented by lawyers.

These two types of law, however, no longer are as distinct as they were during the nineteenth and early twentieth centuries. In the 1970s judges began to cite their own decisions as precedent in many civil code countries and even dispute the authority of legislatures. Over time the seamless structure of the civil code showed ruptures as new laws addressed novel social and economic problems. At the same time, common law countries—particularly the United States— codified segments of their law, though not with the same single-minded attentiveness to basic principles as the civil code. Common law judges have become somewhat more active although not yet equaling their civil code peers; civil code lawyers have become more aggressive although not yet matching their common law counterparts.

While common law and civil code legal systems demarcate significant variations in national legal practices, one must also take into account national differences in the willingness of people to employ the law to resolve their disputes and in the perceived acceptability of litigation as an alternative to other modes of processing. Some American researchers find that when people in the United States seek to resolve disputes they act "in the shadow of the law." Mnookin and Kornhauser suggest that remedies that might be obtained by litigation lurk in the background during many negotiations and that court action is often viewed as a viable strategic alternative.[8] It is not true, however, that Americans think about law in all their disputes, and abundant evidence exists in other countries that multiple normative orders exist which sometimes push litigation to the periphery of dispute processing. Some scholars argue that social norms and habitual behaviors lead some people away from thinking about legal rights when they confront a dispute; the Japanese are sometimes identified as reflecting such preferences. However, current scholarship has challenged this interpretation and points instead to legal institutions that restrict access to courts and to legal remedies in addition to attitudes toward the law.

The combination of circumstances that lead people to invoke the law, therefore, vary not only with public attitudes toward law but also with institutional arrangements. A willingness to mobilize the law to challenge the actions of government agencies depends not only on the perceived legitimacy of such a challenge but also on such particulars as the availability of legal aid, the willingness of courts to accept jurisdiction, the presence of alternative forums for hearing such complaints, the costs and risk associated with making

---

[8]   Robert H. Mnookin and Lewis Kornhauser, *Bargaining in the Shadow of the Law: The Case of Divorce*, 88 YALE L. J. 950 (1979).

complaints, and the benefits that may be gained by proceeding one way or another. Resort to law for more personal remedies—such as compensation for injuries resulting from auto accidents or damages arising from contractual disputes—also varies with such circumstances, which are the product of government policy as well as social customs.

GEOFFREY C. HAZARD, JR., *FROM WHOM NO SECRETS ARE HID*
76 TEX. L. REV. 1665 (1998)

The fundamental differences in civil procedural systems are, along one division, differences between the common-law and civil-law systems. * * * *

The common-law systems all derive from England and include the United States, Canada, Australia, New Zealand, South Africa and India, as well as other smaller regimes such as Israel, Singapore, and Bermuda. The civil-law systems originated on the European continent and include systems derived more or less from Roman law (the law of the Roman Empire codified in the Justinian Code) and canon law (the law of the Roman Catholic Church, itself substantially derived from Roman law). The civil-law systems include those of France, Germany, Italy, and Spain and virtually all other European countries and, in a borrowing or migration of legal systems, those of Latin America and Japan.

There are many significant differences between common-law and civil-law systems. First, the judge in civil-law systems rather than the advocates in common-law systems, has responsibility for development of the evidence and exposition of the legal concepts that should govern decision. However, there is great variance among civil-law systems in the manner and degree to which this responsibility is exercised, and no doubt variance among the judges in any given system.

In general, however, in the civil-law systems the final selection of witnesses to be examined and the examination itself are done by the judge and only indirectly by the advocates, who nominate the witnesses and who may suggest questions that should be asked. Second, civil-law litigation proceeds through a series of short hearing sessions—sometimes less than an hour each—focused on development of evidence. The products of this are then consigned to the case file until an eventual final stage of analysis and decision. In contrast, common-law litigation has one or more preliminary or pretrial stages, and then a trial at which all the evidence is received consecutively, including all "live" testimony. Third, a civil-law final hearing usually takes less time than a common-law trial of a similar case. This is partly due to a difference in the role of judge and advocates, but it also results from the different character of a common-law trial and a civil-law final hearing. Fourth, a civil-law judgment in the court of first instance (i.e., trial court) is generally subject to a more searching reexamination in the court of second instance (i.e., appellate court) than a common-law judgment. Also, re-examination in the civil-law systems extends to facts as well as law. Fifth, a judge in a civil-law system serves his entire professional career as a judge, whereas the judges in common-law systems are almost entirely selected from the ranks of the bar. Thus, civil-law judges lack the experience of having been a lawyer, which may affect their views. These are important differences, but not worlds of difference.

The American common-law system, however, has differences from most other common-law systems that are of equally great if not greater significance. The American system is unique in many respects. First, jury trial is a broadly available right in the American federal courts and, more or less to the same extent, in the state court systems. No other country routinely uses juries in civil cases. Second, the American version of the adversary system generally affords the advocates far greater latitude in the form and style of the case's presentation than in other common-law systems. This is in part because of our use of juries. Third, in the American system, each party, including a winning party, pays his own lawyer and cannot recover that cost from a losing opponent. This rule has been changed by statute for specific types of cases but almost invariably in the direction of allowing recovery of litigation costs only by a successful plaintiff. In most all other countries the winning party, whether plaintiff or defendant, recovers at least a substantial portion of his litigation costs. Fourth, American rules of discovery give wide latitude for exploration of potentially relevant evidence * * *. Fifth, American judges are selected in a variety of ways in which political affiliation plays an important part. In most of the other common-law countries, judges are selected on the basis of professional standards.

B. THE ROLE OF COMPARATIVE LAW IN CIVIL PROCEDURE

How much should foreign legal materials matter to U.S. courts? Or, to put it another way, how much should comparative law matter to a U.S. judge making a decision regarding U.S. law? U.S. Supreme Court Justices Stephen Breyer and Antonin Scalia famously clashed on these questions. *A Conversation Between U.S. Supreme Court Justices*, 3 INT'L J. CONST. L. 519, 523 (2005). Justice Breyer argued that in deciding U.S. constitutional cases he is looking for the best answer and therefore he takes into account the views of other judges throughout the world, not as binding upon him, but as useful resources in understanding how other smart people have tackled similar problems elsewhere in the world. Justice Scalia meanwhile maintained that, when interpreting the American Constitution, the goal should always be "to try to understand what it meant, what it was understood by the society to mean when it was adopted," *id.* at 525, and not "to selectively choose foreign law when it agrees with what the justices would like the case to say, but not use it when it doesn't agree," *id.* at 521. Some states have added to their laws provisions that prohibit the use of foreign law in their courts.

Consider the following two perspectives on the appropriate role of comparative law in our thinking about civil procedure.

MARGARET Y.K. WOO, *COMPARATIVE LAW IN A TIME OF NATIVISM*
41 HASTINGS INT'L & COMP. L. REV. 1 (2018)

* * * * Historically, comparative law is challenged as a discipline. Critics point to the body of existing scholarship that is mostly descriptive of foreign law, with or without explicit comparison, and [argue] that this body remains "random, unconnected, and thus inconsequential." At its strongest, it is argued, this body of scholarship contributes to the categorization and world mapping of legal families, traditions, or cultures but has yet to develop any overarching theoretical basis or framework towards a better understanding of legal systems. * * * [T]his critique would like to see the development of broader theories to explain certain functional legal phenomena underlying different legal systems.

On the other extreme, there are those comparativists who caution against the pronouncement of such "grand theories." Particularly those who study non-western legal systems point to the danger of speculating broadly across cultures and across times, and the possibility that efforts at engaging in broad theoretical work may unwittingly lead us to believe that we are considering foreign legal cultures in universal or value-free terms when, in fact, we are examining them through conceptual frameworks that are products of our own values and traditions, and that are often applied merely to see what foreign societies have to tell us about ourselves.

These comparativists emphasize our responsibilities to appreciate more fully the importance of "descriptions" and, particularly, the type of textured, reflective examination that Clifford Geertz terms "thick description." Not wishing to run the risk of cultural relativism, these critics recognize that the effort to understand a different legal system necessarily entails the formation of judgments. But these critics argue for more thoughtful and careful comparisons and particular and modest, rather than grand, guidelines for our endeavor and conclusions.

By contrast, there are those who voice concerns as to whether comparative law is even possible since law is so rooted in national traditions. These theorists * * * point to the different legal traditions as the root of national economic development and of indelible distinctions. They reject projects of unification because minds of continental and common lawyers follow incommensurable patterns of thought.

But notably, more recent critics have taken the critique beyond a methodological objection to voice an objection based more on fear that unification would erase traditions and national legal cultures. On a more philosophical level, recent critics [argue] not that it is impossible to do comparative methodology but rather that it is not normatively desirable.

Thus, while U.S. Chief Justice John Roberts voiced a methodological objection to reference to [comparative] law by U.S. courts because consulting how other countries treat particular legal questions pending in the United States is like "looking out over a crowd and picking out your friends," Justice Samuel Alito, during his confirmation hearing, emphasized a more philosophical objection that "the Framers of the U.S. Constitution did not want Americans to have the rights of people in France or the rights of people in Russia, or any of the other countries on the continent of Europe at the time. They wanted them to have the rights of Americans, and. . .I don't think it's appropriate to look at foreign law."

These recent changes present challenges to comparativists. But comparative law and reference to foreign legal materials are more important than ever. There is certainly no single answer, but rather, there are a number of cautionary guidelines to keep in mind in our comparative work. This might mean adjusting our perspective, methodology and goals.

A. Law is National Identity

Whether or not we like it, we must keep in mind and acknowledge that law is sovereign identity. While in the past, we have recognized that law may be rooted in tradition, history and culture, we have not fully appreciated the constitutive aspect of law in creating national identity. Where previous institutions of religion

and tribes defined a particular state, today, it is the institution of law
* * *.

But unlike history or tradition or cultural identity * * *, national
identity is one that can be adopted, created and shed. And law, as
both reflective and constitutive of this national identity, draws
physical as well as political boundaries. Thus, for example, civil
procedure laws define the overall parameters of a court's authority,
and jurisdiction rules delineate the political power of any given state.
Jurisdiction rules define where a court sits in the political division of
governance and draws a metaphysical border in authorizing a state's
right to exercise coercive power over an individual or dispute within
and without its physical border. Thus, the growth of a court's
jurisdiction often coincides with state expansion. As enactments of
the state, procedural requirements are symbolic and physical
messages as to the power of the state. Tensions between states often
morph into more technical disputes over jurisdiction of the courts.

Prominent political geographer Richard Hartshorne argued that
the integration of a state's territory involves two competing types of
forces: centrifugal forces that pull populations apart (away from the
center), and centripetal forces that pull populations together.
Centrifugal forces can include geographic divisions such as water
bodies, mountain ranges or sheer areal size and distances that limit
interaction by the state's population. Human dimensions such as
differences in religious belief, culture, and economic activity can also
act as centrifugal forces. These forces can limit interaction, producing
regionalism and creating dissimilarity among groups of citizens
within a state. Under such circumstances, what stops a state from
falling apart? If a state is to exist in a stable form, there must be
centripetal forces of greater magnitude than the existing centrifugal
forces. Law can act both as a centrifugal or centripetal force.

If recent events demonstrate the persistence of nation states and
borders, then, we must find ways to delineate national identity
through law without insisting on the exclusivity of a national legal
regime. Or in other words, how can we use law as a centripetal force
(pulling populations together) and use comparative law without
turning the exercise into one that is a centrifugal force (pulling
populations apart). Comparative studies have the potential to
promote law as a centripetal force. Law is adaptive and the very act
of comparative studies in recognizing differences and yet drawing out
commonalities allows law to be adaptive in selective ways. Yet,
fundamental to comparative law's success must be an assurance that
law is part and parcel of national identity and that the comparative
gaze is not an erasure of national identity. By recognizing that law is
part and parcel of national identity, comparative law can reassure

populations and combat their fears of change and the rise of nationalism as an exclusionary banner.

B.   Law is not "Neutral"

One type of centrifugal force is inequality and so, one of our tasks must be to recognize the inherent power disparity in any legal reform efforts and that the failure to recognize power imbalances can lead to hegemonic imposition of supposedly objective values by more economically developed countries onto less developed countries. This is often the case with the at times messianic route of the U.S. with its many "rule of law" projects. Such comparative law projects without recognizing inequality effects could act as a centrifugal force. * * * *

The criticism is that comparativists downplay distributional consequences in assessing similarities and differences among legal regimes, and instead investigate and highlight technical similarities or cultural differences. Yet, not only is this "objectivity" intellectually impossible, this "objective" perspective also limits the impact and contributions that comparative law can make. The "objectively" neutral position would limit comparative law to societies that are comparatively similar, and to areas of law that are decidedly "apolitical" such as private and commercial law. An emphasis only on private law would be in contradiction to the changed understanding of private law in the 20th century which re-orients private law as a political tool of regulation, and which views constitutional and administrative law as the dominant areas of a country's legal system superseding private law.

[For example,] * * * comparisons between Chinese legal traditions and European ones are * * * often one sided with the comparisons done by those from more developed countries of legal systems in "less developed countries." Rarely are these works focused on better understanding European institutions. Using European institutions as the benchmark risks "Eurocentricism" in which "other parts of the world must become like Europe to 'develop' or 'modernize.'" More problematically, "There is always the danger that something is "lost in translation"—some subtle but perhaps significant aspect of Chinese law actually becomes harder to understand once we explain them via comparison to European ones. As such, comparative methods encourage us to overemphasize the differences, or overlook deeper distinctions that course beneath facial similarities.

We cannot ignore the reality of power disparities among the legal systems we study and the distributional effects of whatever solution we suggest. * * * Whenever we propose that the model from one country be applied in another country, we must always consider the comparative power structures of the two countries. But if legal reform is to be achieved, the political context, the power differential between systems, and the recognition of distributional effects cannot be ignored.

C.   Localization/Synchronization

These ideas are also in line with present comparative law debates in China on the nature and aim of legal transplantation. [For example,] * * * Lijun Wang * * * * reminds us that the development of law is driven by social realities that have their own character of autonomy. * * * * Wang's position urges recognition of the determinants presented by social realities, and a study of the interconnectedness among these determinants.

In the area of civil procedure, for example, while class actions can be used to funnel social discontent into courts as in the U.S., in countries such as China which values harmony above rights, class actions are seen as instigators in times of social instability. Or, for example, it is difficult to apply the concept of burden of proof in a society with limited [numbers of] lawyers, particularly where substantive law has not adapted accordingly. Similarly, a local preference for substantive justice may mean resistance to the concept of res judicata. There must therefore be synchronization based on local conditions.

* * * * Globalization does not mean "de-nationalization." In the diverse legal order that can result from globalization, the sovereign state can maintain the independence and autonomy of its domestic laws even as it participates in comparative studies and understanding. As comparativists, we understand law, not only as the rules and how they operate in practice, but also from where these rules derive, the choices they represent, and the principles they encompass; that is, information and values that come from local synchronization.

D.   Overlapping Rather than Convergence

Finally, we may want to recognize the limitations of harmonization and convergence as the sole goals of comparative law. * * * * [T]he pressure for harmonization of domestic civil procedural rules is particularly strong today to prevent parties from forum shopping in transnational disputes. As international economic transactions aided by technology increasingly lead to complex legal problems without borders, efforts were made to draft transnational rules such as the completion by the American Law Institute and UNIDROIT of the proposed "Principles of Transnational Civil

Procedure." While this work has substantial descriptive value as a source of comparative analysis of civil procedure, it also has a normative objective, which is to promote international "harmonization"—in this context, apparently meaning uniformity or near-uniformity of procedural law.

But an undue focus on harmonization looking for single answers is problematic in a number of ways. On the one hand, harmonization/convergence can funnel one into a view that only the state can make law and neglect other sources of legal norms. Theorists, such as those within the legal pluralism school, have pointed out that legal orders may be rooted in different sources of legitimacy, such as tradition, religion, or the will of the people, and that such legal norms often co-exist in the same field as state promulgated norms. Also, the reality of pluralism between state and non-state legal orders inevitably takes the comparative focus away from western legal systems and towards the customary law of developing countries, and the laws of groups and communities such as the Quakers, Romani, Native Americans and religious organizations.

Furthermore, harmonization as a sole goal also understates the undeniable task of law as a source of sovereign identity. Brexit may be the strongest recent rejection of harmonization. A single-minded push to harmonization may neglect to recognize the continued pull of distinct but equal spheres legal spheres defined by national borders. Harmonization and convergence, if at all, can only occur in the context of the overlapping normative orders of national legal systems, whether in Europe or elsewhere. This preserves national identity, lessens resistance, even as it allows for each nation state's participation in the global order.

MAGGIE GARDNER, *PAROCHIAL PROCEDURE*
69 STAN. L. REV. 941 (2017)

* * * The need for reciprocity is integral to international trade, which requires systems for resolving cross-border disputes. The rules of private international law, as they coalesced in the late nineteenth century, have grown into one such system that is based in domestic courts and managed through principles of international comity.

"Comity" is a notoriously slippery term, taking on different meanings in different contexts. This Article understands comity to mean the accommodation of other countries' jurisdictional interests in return for reciprocal treatment over the long run. Especially since the communication and transportation revolutions in the late nineteenth century, multiple countries may have an interest in adjudicating a given dispute, whether based on the location of the relevant conduct, the nationality of the parties, or some other nexus. This is both good and bad from a governance perspective. Overlapping pools of jurisdiction reduce the risk of unintended regulatory gaps. But they increase the risk of conflict between nation-states, as well as uncertainty for private parties as to which rules will govern (and which courts will do the governing). Overreaching by one state can, in turn, prompt the unaccommodated state to retaliate, in particular by refusing to accommodate the overreaching state's interests in future cases. This general concern for reciprocity encourages states and their courts to exercise some restraint in displacing foreign law in transnational disputes, whether in terms of personal jurisdiction, choice of law, or recognition of a foreign court's prior judgment.

Under this cooperative conception of comity, the institutions of one state may help give effect to the laws or interests of another state. It is important to keep this traditional, affirmative conception of comity in mind, as comity in the twentieth century has increasingly come to be associated with restraint or abstention: in the modern era, U.S. courts concerned about their "inability . . . to gauge the precise implications of their decisions for the delicate subject of foreign relations" more often invoke comity as a reason to avoid deciding cases with international elements. But focusing on comity-as-abstention misses that foreign states' interests—and thus U.S. foreign relations—are often better protected through judicial accommodation than through judicial abdication. Thus, throughout the nineteenth century, U.S. courts routinely invoked and applied foreign law in transnational disputes regarding contracts, property, and corporate organization. As early as the 1850s, Congress explicitly authorized the federal courts to assist foreign judicial proceedings, at least in some circumstances, by compelling witness testimony. And in 1895, the U.S. Supreme Court famously invoked comity in *Hilton v. Guyot* to justify a presumption in favor of enforcing foreign judgments.

Starting in the late eighteenth century, countries sought to codify aspects of this affirmative comity, first through bilateral agreements and then through multilateral conferences. In 1888 and 1889, South American states convened in Montevideo, Uruguay to adopt several conventions on private international law, and continental European states gathered for the First Hague Conference on Private International Law in 1893 to discuss standardizing conflict-of-laws rules, family law, and civil procedure for transnational cases. Today, more than 140 countries across multiple continents are involved in the Hague Conference, which is responsible for thirty-eight multinational private law conventions now in force. These conventions help regulate comity by formalizing countries' commitments to providing judicial assistance and access to courts in transnational disputes.

The United States, however, did not join the Hague Conference until 1964. By that time, growing transnational litigation in U.S. courts—reflecting increased global trade after World War II—was becoming a source of international friction. U.S. judges were interpreting U.S. laws, particularly antitrust laws, to reach extraterritorial conduct based on its effects within the United States, triggering rounds of diplomatic protests starting in the 1950s. And as U.S. courts heard more transnational cases, "[i]t was soon evident that the rest of the world was not willing to accept some of the American legal procedures." In particular, U.S. court orders compelling broad American-style discovery from foreign litigants provoked much hostility. In response, France (followed by other states) adopted "blocking statutes" in the 1970s and 1980s that prohibited the production of certain types of evidence located within its territory for use in U.S. litigation. * * * *

The Service Convention and the Evidence Convention were adopted during this postwar era to ease tensions and improve the efficiency of cross-border cases, in particular by providing some common ground between civil and common law traditions. For example, in many civil law jurisdictions, "local judicial authorities supervise all evidence-taking." For foreigners to take depositions or gather documents in the territory of such a civil law state, then, can trespass on that state's exclusive enforcement jurisdiction. The Evidence Convention sought to address this problem by channeling requests for evidence through a government agency, which allows the concerned government some nominal oversight of the evidence collection. Similarly, many countries consider service of process a governmental function. Foreigners thus raise jurisdictional sensitivities when they attempt to serve judicial documents within other countries' territories. Like the Evidence Convention, the Service Convention provides a default procedure whereby cross-border service is channeled through a government agency that is in turn obliged to ensure that the service is completed.

The Conventions' success in reconciling these cultural differences, however, has been mixed. While some of the fault lies with those who wrote and implemented the treaties on behalf of the United States, judges have largely borne the blame for parochial results in transnational cases. It is the scope and tenor of that blame that I hope to temper. * * * *

Across a range of debates, scholars have worried that U.S. judges are insufficiently sensitive to the dynamic effects their decisions may have on this system of private international law. These critiques are united by the concern that the courts' myopia is hurting the international order and with it the long-term interests of the United States. For shorthand, I call this common theme the "parochial critique." * * * *

The parochial critique surfaces primarily in two lines of scholarship. On the one hand, some scholars have criticized U.S. courts for closing their doors to transnational litigation, particularly through heavy use of forum non conveniens but also through other prudential doctrines like standing, abstention, and act of state. Pamela Bookman recently labeled this practice "litigation isolationism" and tied it to broader antilitigation trends in U.S. courts. "Isolationists" worry that judges, in declining jurisdiction over transnational cases, are aggravating trading partners and creating access-to-justice gaps—whether because plaintiffs may not be able to continue litigation in the foreign forum due to mounting litigation costs, because they may find the foreign forum closed to them due to retaliatory legislation, or because they may not be able to enforce the resulting foreign judgment in U.S. courts. Some scholars also argue that dismissals for forum non conveniens run counter to U.S. treaty commitments to provide access to U.S. courts. * * * *

On the other hand, some scholars worry that when judges *do* keep transnational cases, they are insensitive to conflicts of adjudicative and prescriptive jurisdiction. This judicial imperialism manifests in the courts' willingness to compel discovery located in foreign states despite those states' objections; their general avoidance of foreign or international law; and their use of antisuit injunctions to prevent parties from initiating cases or seeking conflicting relief in foreign courts—injunctions that, while targeted at private parties, have the effect of encroaching on the adjudicative jurisdiction of foreign states.

"Imperialists" link this U.S.-centrism to a breakdown in reciprocity that traps litigants in the middle. In the discovery context, for example, foreign states have enacted "blocking statutes" to counter the perceived overreaching of U.S. courts. Foreign parties in U.S. litigation often argue that they should not be forced to comply with U.S. discovery orders when doing so would violate those blocking statutes or other foreign laws, such as data privacy or bank secrecy laws, but U.S. courts have been unreceptive to such arguments. More generally, the reluctance of U.S. courts to apply international or foreign law can undermine the reciprocal recognition of rights, leaving U.S. citizens and corporations at a disadvantage when they need to seek recourse before foreign courts.

In both lines of scholarship, the common assumption has been that this parochialism stems from judges and their provincial views. The solution, then, is to educate judges to use foreign or international law or perhaps to show them how parochial procedure hurts U.S. interests in the long run. Even when scholars take a more structural view, they urge new statutes or rules meant to constrain parochial judges.

That story of parochial judges, however, is not a fully satisfying explanation for parochial doctrines. * * * *

[Instead,] parochialism might still result even if most judges hold neutral or positive views about transnational cases, foreign litigants, or international law. Transnational litigation differs from purely domestic litigation in important, if relatively self-evident, respects. When those differences are set against the constraints within which judges work, unguided discretion will predictably build to parochial results. * * * * [C]onstraints on judging intersect with the transnational context to encourage three doctrinal trends: *the search for rubrics*, as judges seek to structure and simplify decisionmaking in unfamiliar areas of law; *miscalibration*, as judges' focus on the specific and concrete leads them to overemphasize case management concerns while marginalizing more abstract systemic interests; and *ossification*, as judges fill in harder-to-ascertain factors—typically those intended to protect comity interests—by relying on prior judicial opinions. The accumulated weight of these three trends creates path dependence toward parochial outcomes, even in the absence of binding authority.

Notes and Questions

1.   Some scholars have argued that because of globalization the common law and civil law systems have converged. They note the trend towards codification in common law countries and by contrast, the increasingly active role of judges in filling gaps in statutory provisions in civil law countries. They also note the role of conventions and model laws in creating greater uniformity. *See* Ugo Mattel & Luca G. Pes, *Common Law and Civil Law: A Convergence*, in THE OXFORD HANDBOOK OF LAW AND POLITICS (Gregory A. Caldeira, R. Daniel Kelemen, & Keith E. Whittington eds., 2008). If this convergence is real, what are the pros and cons of such convergence? What may be the best of both worlds?

2.   Professor Woo attributes some of the antagonism to the use of comparative law materials in American courts to the cultural fact that law is basically national identity. On this theory, adopting another country's law may be seen as a compromise in one's national identity.

Professor Gardner attributes the same reluctance to various institutional and procedural constraints. What do you think? Is the resistance more cultural or institutional? Or do those two types of constraint perhaps derive from similar concerns?

3.   Consider the fights over judicial reference by U.S. judges to non-U.S. law. Professor Martha Minow argues that antagonism to using foreign law stems from a fear that "we risk being taken over, or losing what we are by engaging with others and to a desire to protect American exceptionalism." Martha Minow, *The Controversial Status of International and Comparative Law in the United States*, 52 HARV. INT'L L.J. ONLINE 1 (2010). Minow emphasizes, however, that neglecting developments in international and comparative law could vitiate the vitality, nimbleness, and effectiveness of American law or simply leave us without the best tools and insights as we design and run institutions, pass legislation, and work to govern ourselves. Given the challenges of both cultural and institutional barriers, what solutions might you develop that would aid greater exchange of views and use of comparative law materials in U.S. courts?

Chapter 3

JURISDICTION AND FORUM SELECTION CLAUSES

A. PERSONAL JURISDICTION IN FOREIGN COURTS

In the United States the Constitution determines the scope of a court's jurisdiction over parties to a case. Beginning in the nineteenth century, the U.S. Supreme Court has repeatedly invoked the Due Process Clause of the Fourteenth Amendment as the touchstone for the jurisdictional inquiry. In the current formulation of that Due Process inquiry, a court has *general* jurisdiction over a defendant in the defendant's state of citizenship and has *specific* jurisdiction over a defendant who has "minimum contacts" sufficiently related to the claim. The Due Process Clause further demands that the exercise of jurisdiction not offend what the Supreme Court has called "traditional notions of fair play and substantial justice."

In most other countries the doctrine of personal jurisdiction is not constitutional, but statutory. Moreover, the doctrine tends to focus on the competence of a court to hear a case, rather than the rights of a particular defendant. Finally, instead of using abstract phrases requiring judicial interpretation, such as "minimum contacts" and "traditional notions of fair play and substantial justice," code-based jurisdictional schemes purport to provide straight-forward rules to enumerate the permissible bases for exercise of a court's authority over a defendant.

For many years, differences among the codes of the various European countries created tension, and they also interfered with the free movement of people, goods, services, and capital. The six founding members of the European Community (Belgium, France, Germany, Holland, Italy and Luxembourg) initiated an effort to reduce these barriers and to harmonize national laws on a broader scale. This effort led to the Brussels Convention on Jurisdiction and the Recognition and Enforcement of Judgments, which was ratified in 1973. Other countries joined upon their accession to the European Community. A parallel convention, called the Lugano Convention, expanded the reach to Member States of the European Free Trade Association. Accession to the Conventions required countries to abandon those forms of jurisdiction that were not part of the common ground set forth in the Conventions. These Conventions, in turn, were incorporated into the Council Regulation on Jurisdiction and the Recognition and Enforcement of Judgments in Civil and Commercial Matters, which came into effect on March 1, 2002 (the "Brussels I Regulation"). The Brussels I Regulation, excerpted below, is binding on all Member States (except Denmark, which is bound by the Brussels Convention).

REGULATION (EU) NO 1215/2012 OF THE EUROPEAN PARLIAMENT AND OF THE COUNCIL OF 12 DECEMBER 2012

On Jurisdiction and the Recognition and Enforcement
of Judgments in Civil and Commercial Matters

Preamble

* * * *

(15) The rules of jurisdiction should be highly predictable and founded on the principle that jurisdiction is generally based on the defendant's domicile. Jurisdiction should always be available on this ground save in a few well-defined situations in which the subject-matter of the dispute or the autonomy of the parties warrants a different connecting factor. The domicile of a legal person must be defined autonomously so as to make the common rules more transparent and avoid conflicts of jurisdiction.

(16) In addition to the defendant's domicile, there should be alternative grounds of jurisdiction based on a close connection between the court and the action or in order to facilitate the sound administration of justice. The existence of a close connection should ensure legal certainty and avoid the possibility of the defendant being sued in a court of a Member State which he could not reasonably have foreseen. This is important, particularly in disputes concerning non-contractual obligations arising out of violations of privacy and rights relating to personality, including defamation.

* * * *

CHAPTER II: JURISDICTION

* * * *

Section 1: General Provisions

Article 4

1.   Subject to this Regulation, persons domiciled in a Member State shall, whatever their nationality, be sued in the courts of that Member State.

2.   Persons who are not nationals of the Member State in which they are domiciled shall be governed by the rules of jurisdiction applicable to nationals of that Member State.

Article 5

1.   Persons domiciled in a Member State may be sued in the courts of another Member State only by virtue of the rules set out in Sections 2 to 7 of this Chapter.

* * * *

Section 2: Special Jurisdiction

Article 7

A person domiciled in a Member State may be sued in another Member State:

(1)   (a) in matters relating to a contract, in the courts for the place of performance of the obligation in question;

(b) for the purpose of this provision and unless otherwise agreed, the place of performance of the obligation in question shall be:

— in the case of the sale of goods, the place in a Member State where, under the contract, the goods were delivered or should have been delivered,

— in the case of the provision of services, the place in a Member State where, under the contract, the services were provided or should have been provided;

(c) if point (b) does not apply then point (a) applies;

(2) in matters relating to tort, delict or quasi-delict, in the courts for the place where the harmful event occurred or may occur;

These sorts of mechanical rules are thought to increase predictability and minimize controversy. However, the seemingly simple rules can lead to the same sorts of ambiguities and interpretive problems you may already have encountered in studying U.S. Supreme Court jurisdiction cases. And sometimes those ambiguities are resolved very differently from their resolution in U.S. jurisprudence.

Consider, for example, *World-Wide Volkswagen Corp. v. Woodson,* 444 U.S. 286 (1980), in which the U.S. Supreme Court held it unconstitutional for an Oklahoma court to exercise jurisdiction over a New York car dealership and regional distributor, even though the allegedly defective car crashed and caused harm in Oklahoma. According to the Court, because the car entered Oklahoma only through the unilateral act of the consumer, jurisdiction in Oklahoma was inappropriate. Compare the Supreme Court's reasoning in that case to a possibly analogous case decided by the European Court of Justice:

ZUID-CHEMIE BV V PHILIPPO'S MINERALENFABRIEK NV/SA
European Court of Justice, 2009

* * * *

Article 5 of Regulation No 44/2001, which features in Section 2 ('Special jurisdiction') of Chapter II, provides:

'A person domiciled in a Member State may, in another Member State, be sued:

. . .

3.   in matters relating to tort, delict or quasi-delict, in the courts for the place where the harmful event occurred or may occur;*

. . .'

Zuid-Chemie is an undertaking manufacturing fertiliser which, in July 2000, purchased two consignments of a product called 'micromix' from HCI Chemicals Benelux BV ('HCI'), an undertaking established in Rotterdam (Netherlands).

HCI, which is itself unable to manufacture micromix, ordered it from Philippo's and provided the latter with all the raw materials—except for one—necessary for the manufacture of that product. In

---

*   The provision of the Brussels Convention referred to in this case is the precursor provision to Article 7(2) of the Brussels I regulation excerpted above.

consultation with HCI, Philippo's purchased the outstanding raw material, namely zinc sulphate, from G.J. de Poorter, trading under the name Poortershaven, in Rotterdam.

Philippo's manufactured the micromix in its factory in Belgium, to which Zuid-Chemie came to take delivery of that product.

Zuid-Chemie processed the micromix in its factory in the Netherlands in order to produce various consignments of fertiliser. It sold and dispatched a number of those consignments to its customers.

It subsequently transpired that the cadmium content of the zinc sulphate purchased from Poortershaven was too high, with the result that the fertiliser was rendered unusable or of limited utility. Zuid-Chemie claims that this has caused it to suffer loss.

On 17 January 2003, Zuid-Chemie instituted proceedings against Philippo's before the Rechtbank (Local Court) Middleburg (Netherlands) in which it sought a declaration that Philippo's was liable for the damage which Zuid-Chemie had sustained and an order requiring that undertaking to pay it various sums in respect of the loss which it claimed to have suffered, in addition to payment of compensation plus interest and costs. * * * *

By its first question, the referring court seeks essentially to ascertain whether * * * the words 'place where the harmful event occurred' designate the place where the defective product was delivered to the purchaser or whether they refer to the place where the initial damage occurred following normal use of the product for the purpose for which it was intended. * * * *

[I]t is necessary to bear in mind that the Court has already held, when interpreting [this provision], that the system of common rules of conferment of jurisdiction laid down in [the regulation] is based on the general rule * * * that persons domiciled in a Contracting State are to be sued in the courts of that State, irrespective of the nationality of the parties.

It is only by way of derogation from that fundamental principle attributing jurisdiction to the courts of the defendant's domicile that [the regulation] makes provision for certain special jurisdictional rules * * *.

The Court has also held that those rules of special jurisdiction must be interpreted restrictively and cannot give rise to an interpretation going beyond the cases expressly envisaged by that convention.

Nevertheless, it is settled case-law that, where the place in which the event which may give rise to liability in tort, delict or quasi-delict occurs and the place where that event results in damage are not identical, the expression 'place where the harmful event occurred' * * * must be understood as being intended to cover both the place where the damage occurred and the place of the event giving rise to it, so that the defendant may be sued, at the option of the claimant, in the courts for either of those places.

In that connection, the Court has stated that the rule of special jurisdiction * * * is based on the existence of a particularly close connecting factor between the dispute and the courts of the place where the harmful event occurred, which justifies the attribution of jurisdiction to those courts for reasons relating to the sound administration of justice and the efficacious conduct of proceedings. The courts for the place where the harmful event occurred are usually the most appropriate for deciding the case, in particular on the grounds of proximity and ease of taking evidence.

Although it is common ground between the parties * * * that Essen is the place of the event giving rise to the damage, they disagree as regards the determination of the place where the damage occurred.

The place where the damage occurred is, according to the case-law, the place where the event which may give rise to liability in tort, delict or quasi-delict resulted in damage.

The place where the damage occurred must not, however, be confused with the place where the event which damaged the product itself occurred, the latter being the place of the event giving rise to the damage. By contrast, the 'place where the damage occurred' is the place where the event which gave rise to the damage produces its harmful effects, that is to say, the place where the damage caused by the defective product actually manifests itself.

It must be recalled that the case-law distinguishes clearly between the damage and the event which is the cause of that damage, stating, in that connection, that liability in tort, delict or quasi-delict can arise only on condition that a causal connection can be established between those two elements.

Regard being had to the foregoing, the place where the damage occurred cannot be any other than Zuid-Chemie's factory in the Netherlands where the micromix, which is the defective product, was processed into fertiliser, causing substantial damage to that fertiliser which was suffered by Zuid-Chemie and which went beyond the damage to the micromix itself.

It must also be observed that the choice of the Netherlands courts which is thereby available to Zuid-Chemie makes it possible

* * * for the court which is most appropriate to deal with the case and, therefore, enables the rule of special jurisdiction * * * to have practical effect.

In that connection, it is worth pointing out that the Court has held * * * that that provision covers not only the place of the event giving rise to the damage, but also the place where the damage occurred, and that to decide in favour only of the place of the event giving rise to the damage would, in a significant number of cases, cause confusion between the heads of jurisdiction laid down by [the regulation], with the result that the latter provision would, to that extent, lose its effectiveness. Such a consideration relating to confusion between the heads of jurisdiction is likely to apply in the same way with regard to the failure to take account, where appropriate, of a place where damage occurred which differs from the place of the event which gave rise to that damage.

It follows from the foregoing that [the jurisdictional provision] must be interpreted as meaning that, in the context of a dispute such as that in the main proceedings, the words 'place where the harmful event occurred' designate the place where the initial damage occurred as a result of the normal use of the product for the purpose for which it was intended. * * * *

Notes and Questions

1.   Are there any ways to distinguish *Zuid-Chemie* from *World-Wide Volkswagen*? Do you think such differences would have mattered to the European Court of Justice?

2.   Do you find the European Court's approach more or less satisfying than the U.S. Supreme Court's approach in *World-Wide Volkswagen*?

3.   The U.S. Supreme Court has at times based its jurisdictional inquiry on a conception of fairness to the defendant, but at other times it has focused on the sovereign power of the state. Which approach does the European Court of Justice use? Do you think jurisdiction is best thought of as a rule about fairness to the defendant or as a rule protecting the sovereign power of a state vis a vis other states?

B. FOREIGN FORUM SELECTION CLAUSES

Often the issue of jurisdiction will be addressed by the parties long before any dispute has developed. Indeed, provisions limiting the jurisdiction in which an action may be brought are commonplace in a variety of contracts—and especially those with multinational connections. Forum-selection clauses were once widely disfavored by many courts on the theory that such provisions operated to improperly divest all other courts of jurisdiction. But now it is well-recognized that parties to a contract may, in general, freely select a forum of their choosing to resolve a dispute arising from that contract.

The Hague Convention on Choice of Court Agreements came into force in 2015 and has thus far been signed by 32 countries, though both China and the United States have signed but not ratified the Convention. The Convention is meant to establish rules for enforcing private party forum selection clauses by requiring that judgments resulting from jurisdiction exercised in accordance with a forum selection clause be recognized and enforced in the courts of other Contracting States.

Significantly, the Convention applies only to international business-to-business agreements that contain exclusive forum selection clauses and therefore does not apply to consumer contracts, employment relationships, family law matters, insolvency proceedings, nuclear damage, and personal injury claims, among others. In addition, even in the business-to-business context, the Convention allows courts not to recognize or enforce the judgment of a court chosen pursuant to a forum selection clause if it "would be manifestly incompatible with the public policy of the requested State."

Despite the fact that the United States has not ratified the Convention, courts in the United States generally treat forum-selection clauses as *prima facie* valid unless the party seeking to avoid the enforcement of a forum-selection clause makes a "strong showing" that it should be set aside.

In practice, this standard means that in the United States a party challenging a forum-selection clause must show that:

- Enforcement of the clause would be *unreasonable and unjust*, or *in contravention of public policy*;

- The clause is invalid because of *fraud or overreaching*; or

- A trial in the contractual forum would be *so gravely difficult and inconvenient* that the challenging party would, for all practical purposes, be deprived of its day in court.

The Bremen v. Zapata Off-Shore Co., 407 U.S. 1 (1973). In *Carnival Cruise Lines, Inc. v. Shute*, 499 U.S. 585 (1991), however, the Court determined that it could also consider the "fundamental fairness" of the clause. In the following case, the Ninth Circuit had to reconcile these well-settled principles with a pre-determined Congressional mandate that appears to prohibit the enforcement of forum selection clauses in cases seeking enforcement of federal securities laws.

RICHARDS V. LLOYD'S OF LONDON

United States Court of Appeals for the Ninth Circuit, 1998
135 F.3d 1289

GOODWIN, CIRCUIT JUDGE.

The primary question this case presents is whether the antiwaiver provisions of the Securities Act of 1933 and the Securities Exchange Act of 1934 void choice of law and choice of forum clauses in an international transaction. The district court found that they do not. * * * * [W]e affirm the district court.

Appellants, all citizens or residents of the United States, are more than 600 "Names" who entered into underwriting agreements. The Names sued four defendants: the Corporation of Lloyd's, the Society of Lloyd's, the Council of Lloyd's, (collectively, "Lloyd's") and Lloyd's of London, (the "unincorporated association").

Lloyd's is a market in which more than three hundred Underwriting Agencies compete for underwriting business. Pursuant to the Lloyd's Act of 1871–1982, Lloyd's oversees and regulates the competition for underwriting business in the Lloyd's market. The market does not accept premiums or insure risks. Rather, Underwriting Agencies, or syndicates, compete for the insurance business. Each Underwriting Agency is controlled by a Managing Agent who is responsible for the financial status of its agency. The Managing Agent must attract not only underwriting business from brokers but also the capital with which to insure the risks underwritten.

The Names provide the underwriting capital. The Names become Members of the Society of Lloyd's through a series of agreements, proof of financial means, and the deposit of an irrevocable letter of credit in favor of Lloyd's. To become a Name, one must travel to England to acknowledge the attendant risks of participating in a syndicate and sign a General Undertaking. The General Undertaking is a two page document containing choice of forum and choice of law clauses (collectively the "choice clauses"), which form the basis for this dispute. The choice clauses read:

2.1 The rights and obligations of the parties arising out of or relating to the Member's membership of, and/or underwriting of insurance business at, Lloyd's and any other matter referred to in this Undertaking shall be governed by and construed in accordance with the laws of England.

2.2   Each party hereto irrevocably agrees that the courts of England shall have exclusive jurisdiction to settle any dispute and/or controversy of whatsoever nature arising out of or relating to the Member's membership of, and/or underwriting of insurance business at, Lloyd's. . . .

By becoming a Member, the Names obtain the right to participate in the Lloyd's Underwriting Agencies. The Names, however, do not deal directly with Lloyd's or with the Managing Agents. Instead, the Names are represented by Members' Agents who, pursuant to agreement, stand in a fiduciary relationship with their Names. Upon becoming a Name, an individual selects the syndicates in which he wishes to participate. In making this decision, the individual must rely to a great extent on the advice of his Members' Agent. The Names generally join more than one underwriting agency in order to spread their risks across different types of insurance. When a Name undertakes an underwriting obligation, that Name is responsible only for his share of an agency's losses; however, his liability is unlimited for that share.

In this case, the risk of heavy losses has materialized and the Names now seek shelter under United States securities laws and the Racketeer Influenced and Corrupt Organizations Act ("RICO"), 18 U.S.C. § 1961 et seq. The Names claim that Lloyd's actively sought the investment of United States residents to fill an urgent need to build up capital. According to the Names, Lloyd's concealed information regarding the possible consequences of the risks undertaken and deliberately and disproportionately exposed the Names to massive liabilities for which sufficient underwriting capital or reinsurance was unavailable. * * * *

I

We analyze the validity of the choice clause under *The Bremen v. Zapata Off-Shore Co.,* 407 U.S. 1 (1972), where the Supreme Court stated that courts should enforce choice of law and choice of forum clauses in cases of "freely negotiated private international agreement[s]." *Bremen,* 407 U.S. at 12–13.

A

The Names dispute the application of *Bremen* to this case. They contend that *Bremen* does not apply to cases where Congress has spoken directly to the immediate issue—as they claim the antiwaiver provisions do here.

The Securities Act of 1933 provides that:

Any condition, stipulation, or provision binding any person acquiring any security to waive compliance with any provision of this subchapter or of the rules and regulations of the Commission shall be void.

15 U.S.C. § 77n. The 1934 Securities Exchange Act contains a substantially similar provision. 15 U.S.C. § 78cc(a). The Names seize on these provisions and claim that they void the choice clauses in their agreement with Lloyd's.

Certainly the antiwaiver provisions are worded broadly enough to reach this case. They cover "*any* condition, stipulation, or provision binding any person acquiring *any* security to waive compliance with any provision of this subchapter. . . ." Indeed, this language is broad enough to reach any offer or sale of anything that could be alleged to be a security, no matter where the transaction occurs.

Nevertheless, this attempt to distinguish *Bremen* fails. In *Bremen* itself, the Supreme Court contemplated that a forum selection clause may conflict with relevant statutes. *Bremen*, 407 U.S. at 15 ("A contractual choice-of-forum clause should be held unenforceable if enforcement would contravene a strong public policy of the forum in which suit is brought, whether declared *by statute* or by judicial decision.") (emphasis added).

Moreover, in *Scherk v. Alberto-Culver Co.*, 417 U.S. 506 (1974), the Supreme Court explicitly relied on *Bremen* in a case involving a securities transaction. Echoing the language of *Bremen*, the Court found that "[a] contractual provision specifying in advance the forum in which disputes shall be litigated and the law to be applied is . . . an almost indispensable precondition to achievement of the orderliness and predictability essential to any international business transaction." *Id.* at 516. *See Bremen*, 407 U.S. at 13–14 ("[A]greeing in advance on a forum acceptable to both parties is an indispensable element in international trade, commerce, and contracting.") * * * *

Indeed, were we to find that *Bremen* did not apply, the reach of United States securities laws would be unbounded. The Names simply prove too much when they assert that "*Bremen*'s judicially-created policy analysis under federal common law is not controlling when Congress has expressed its will in a statute." This assertion, if true, expands the reach of federal securities law to any and all such transactions, no matter how remote from the United States. We agree with the Fifth Circuit that "we must tread cautiously before expanding the operation of U.S. securities law in the international arena." *Haynsworth v. The Corporation*, 121 F.3d 956, 966 (5th Cir. 1997).

B

Having determined that *Bremen* governs international contracts specifying forum and applicable law, we turn to the question whether the contract between Lloyd's and the Names is international. Not surprisingly, the Names contend that these were purely domestic securities sales. They claim that Lloyd's solicited the Names in the United States and that the trip the Names made to England was a mere ritual without legal significance.

We disagree. The Names signed a contract with English entities to participate in an English insurance market and flew to England to consummate the transaction. That the Names received solicitations in the United States does not somehow erase these facts. Moreover, Lloyd's insistence that individuals travel to England to become a Name does not strike us as mere ritual. Lloyd's likely requires this precisely so that those who choose to be the Names understand that English law governs the transaction. Entering into the Lloyd's market in the manner described is plainly an international transaction.

II

We now apply *Bremen* to this case. *Bremen* emphasized that "in the light of present-day commercial realities and expanding international trade we conclude that the forum clause should control absent a strong showing that it should be set aside." *Bremen*, 407 U.S. at 15. The Court reasoned that "[t]he elimination of all [ ] uncertainties [regarding the forum] by agreeing in advance . . . is an indispensable element in international trade, commerce, and contracting." *Id*. at 13–14. Thus, "absent some compelling and countervailing reason [a forum selection clause] should be honored by the parties and enforced by the courts." *Id*. at 12. The party seeking to avoid the forum selection clause bears "a heavy burden of proof." *Id*. at 17.

The Supreme Court has identified three grounds for repudiating a forum selection clause: first, if the inclusion of the clause in the agreement was the product of fraud or overreaching; second, if the party wishing to repudiate the clause would effectively be deprived of his day in court were the clause enforced; and third, "if enforcement would contravene a strong public policy of the forum in which suit is brought." *Id*. at 12–13, 15, 18. The Names contend that the first and third grounds apply in this case.

A

The Names' strongest argument for escaping their agreement to litigate their claims in England is that the choice clauses contravene a strong public policy embodied in federal and state securities law and RICO. [But] we follow our six sister circuits that have ruled to enforce the choice clauses. We do so because we apply *Scherk* and because English law provides the Names with sufficient protection.

In *Scherk*, the Supreme Court was confronted with a contract that specified that all disputes would be resolved in arbitration before the International Chamber of Commerce in Paris, France. The arbitrator was to apply the law of the state of Illinois. The Court enforced the forum selection clause despite then hostile precedent.[4] *Id.* at 520–21. *See Wilko v. Swan*, 346 U.S. 427 (1953), *overruled by Rodriguez de Quijas v. Shearson/American Express, Inc.*, 490 U.S. 477, 485 (1989).

The Court's treatment of *Wilko* leaves little doubt that the choice clauses in this case are enforceable. In *Wilko*, the Supreme Court ruled that "the right to select the judicial forum is the kind of 'provision' that cannot be waived under § 14 of the Securities Act." *Wilko*, 346 U.S. at 435. In *Scherk*, the Court had before it a case where both the District Court and the Seventh Circuit found a forum selection clause invalid on the strength of *Wilko*. *Scherk*, 417 U.S. at 510.

In distinguishing *Wilko*, the Supreme Court stated that there were "significant and, we find, crucial differences between the agreement involved in *Wilko* and the one signed by the parties here." *Scherk*, 417 U.S. at 515. The first and primary difference that the Court relied upon was that "Alberto-Culver's contract . . . was a truly international agreement." *Id.* The Court reasoned that such a contract needs, as "an almost indispensable precondition," a "provision specifying in advance the forum in which disputes shall be litigated *and the law to be applied.*" *Id.* at 516 (emphasis added).

Moreover, the Supreme Court has explained that, in the context of an international agreement, there is "no basis for a judgment that only United States laws and United States courts should determine this controversy in the face of a solemn agreement between the parties that such controversies be resolved elsewhere." *Id.* at 517 n. 11. To require that " 'American standards of fairness' must . . . govern the controversy demeans the standards of justice elsewhere in the

---

[4]   The court recognized that an agreement to arbitrate "is, in effect, a specialized kind of forum-selection clause." *Scherk*, 417 U.S. at 519.

world, and unnecessarily exalts the primacy of United States law over the laws of other countries." *Id.*

These passages from *Scherk*, we think, resolve the question whether public policy reasons allow the Names to escape their "solemn agreement" to adjudicate their claims in England under English law. *Scherk* involved a securities transaction. The Court rejected *Wilko*'s holding that the antiwaiver provision of the '34 Act prohibited choice clauses. It also recognized that enforcing the forum selection clause would, in some cases, have the same effect as choosing foreign law to apply. Yet the Court did not hesitate to enforce the forum selection clauses. It believed that to rule otherwise would "reflect a 'parochial concept that all disputes must be resolved under our laws and in our courts.' " *Id.* at 519 (quoting *Bremen*, 407 U.S. at 9). As the Supreme Court has explained, " '[w]e cannot have trade and commerce in world markets and international waters exclusively on our terms, governed by our laws, and resolved in our courts.' " *Id.* (quoting *Bremen*, 407 U.S. at 9).

Relying on *Mitsubishi Motors Corp. v. Soler Chrysler-Plymouth, Inc.*, 473 U.S. 614, 634 (1985), the Names argue that federal and state securities laws are of "fundamental importance to American democratic capitalism." They claim that enforcement of the choice clauses will deprive them of important remedies provided by our securities laws. The Supreme Court disapproved of such an outcome, the Names contend, when it stated that "in the event the choice-of-forum and choice-of-law clauses operated in tandem as a prospective waiver of a party's right to pursue statutory remedies for antitrust violations, we would have little hesitation in condemning the agreement as against public policy." *Id.* at 637 n. 19.

Without question this case would be easier to decide if this footnote in Mitsubishi had not been inserted. Nevertheless, we do not believe dictum in a footnote regarding antitrust law outweighs the extended discussion and holding in *Scherk* on the validity of clauses specifying the forum and applicable law. The Supreme Court repeatedly recognized in *Scherk* that parties to an international securities transaction may choose law other than that of the United States, yet it never suggested that this affected the validity of a forum selection clause. *See also Bremen*, 407 U.S. at 13 n.15 (recognizing that a forum selection clause also acts to select applicable law).

B

Of course, were English law so deficient that the Names would be deprived of any reasonable recourse, we would have to subject the choice clauses to another level of scrutiny. *See Carnival Cruise Lines*,

Inc. v. Shute, 499 U.S. 585, 595 (1991) ("It bears emphasis that forum-selection clauses contained in form passage contracts are subject to judicial scrutiny for fundamental fairness."). In this case, however, there is no such danger. *See Haynsworth*, 121 F.3d at 969 ("English law provides a variety of protections for fraud and misrepresentations in securities transactions."). *Cf. British Midland Airways Ltd. v. International Travel*, Inc., 497 F.2d 869, 871 (9th Cir. 1974) (This court is "hardly in a position to call the Queen's Bench a kangaroo court.").

We disagree with the dramatic assertion that "[t]he available English remedies are not adequate substitutes for the firm shields and finely honed swords provided by American securities law." *Richards v. Lloyd's of London*, 107 F.3d 1422, 1430 (9th Cir. 1997). The Names have recourse against both the Member and Managing Agents for fraud, breach of fiduciary duty, or negligent misrepresentation. Indeed, English courts have already awarded substantial judgments to some of the other Names. *See Arubuthnott v. Fagan and Feltrim Underwritings Agencies Ltd.*, 3 Re LR 145 (H.L. 1994). * * * *[6]

While it is true that the Lloyd's Act immunizes Lloyd's from many actions possible under our securities laws, Lloyd's is not immune from the consequences of actions committed in bad faith, including fraud. The Names contend that entities using the Lloyd's trade name willfully and fraudulently concealed massive long tail liabilities in order to induce them to join syndicates. If so, we have been cited to no authority that Lloyd's partial immunity would bar recovery.

C

* * * * The Names also argue that the choice clauses were the product of fraud. They claim that at the time of signing the General Undertaking, Lloyd's knew that the Names were effectively sacrificing valid claims under United States law by signing the choice clauses and concealed this fact from the Names. Had the Names known this fact, they contend, they never would have agreed to the choice clauses. The Names never allege, however, that Lloyd's misled them as to the legal effect of the choice clauses. Nor do they allege that Lloyd's fraudulently inserted the clauses without their knowledge. Accordingly, we view the allegations made by the Names

---

[6] The Names complain that the Member and Managing Agents are insolvent. If so, this is truly unfortunate. It does not, however, affect our analysis of the adequacy of English law.

as going only to the contract as a whole, with no allegations as to the inclusion of the choice clauses themselves.

Absent such allegations, these claims of fraud fail. The Supreme Court has noted that simply alleging that one was duped into signing the contract is not enough. *Scherk*, 417 U.S. at 519 n.14 (The fraud exception in Bremen "does not mean that any time a dispute arising out of a transaction is based upon an allegation of fraud . . . the clause is unenforceable."). For a party to escape a forum selection clause on the grounds of fraud, it must show that "*the inclusion of that clause in the contract* was the product of fraud or coercion." *Id.* (citing *Prima Paint Corp. v. Flood & Conklin Mfg. Co.*, 388 U.S. 395 (1967)) (emphasis in original). *See also Prima Paint*, 388 U.S. at 404 ("[T]he statutory language [of the United States Arbitration Act] does not permit the federal court to consider claims of fraud in the inducement of the contract generally.") * * * *

Notes and Questions

1.   In *Richards* the Ninth Circuit enforced the forum selection clause, emphasizing the need for "orderliness and predictability" in international business transactions. Is the need for orderliness and predictability less compelling in domestic transactions? (Would the clause have been enforced if this had been a domestic transaction and a domestic forum selected by the parties?)

2.   How does the court distinguish *Mitsubishi*?

3.   In this case the plaintiffs were relatively sophisticated commercial actors. Should the outcome be different if the plaintiffs were ordinary consumers or investors? Or should the sophistication of the parties be irrelevant?

4.   Likewise, should it matter whether the forum selection clause was part of a true bargained-for exchange or was, instead, part of a take-it-or-leave-it "contract of adhesion"? Or is the proviso from *Carnival Cruise* that forum selection clauses are scrutinized for fundamental fairness sufficient to protect those interests?

5.   If the court *had* applied *Carnival Cruise* and determined that the forum selection clause was fundamentally unfair, would that ruling itself undermine the whole point of the forum selection clause? After all, then the court would be applying U.S. law in contravention of the clause. Is there any way out of this problem?

C. FORUM SELECTION CLAUSES AND MANDATORY LAW

If a forum selection clause has the practical effect of allowing the parties to contract around a mandatory law, should the clause still control? The *Richards* decision enforces a forum selection clause even though doing so would mean that U.S. securities law will not be applied. Is that the right result? On the one hand, as the court notes, U.S. securities law should not apply extraterritorially, but on the other it may be problematic if a forum selection clause allows parties to contract around important public policies. This problem is exacerbated if the contract in question is not a true bargained-for exchange but is instead a take-it-or-leave-it contract between parties of disparate bargaining power, as for example in most employment or consumer contracts.

Consider a 2012 case, decided by the courts of Germany. In November 2005 an American company headquartered in Virginia entered into an agency agreement with a German sales agent. Under the contract the German agent was responsible for sales not only in Germany, but also throughout the European Union. Both parties agreed to resolve all disputes exclusively in courts within the Western District of Virginia. Moreover, the contract contained a choice-of-law clause designating Virginia law as governing law.

The German Commercial Code (GCC) provides sales agents with a right to demand a substantial settlement after the principal terminates the agency relationship, and under German law parties may not contractually exclude the agent's right to this post-termination payment. Importantly, the contract in this case did in fact expressly exclude the agent's German-law right to the payment.

In April 2009 the American principal terminated its German sales agent. The agent filed suit in the District Court of Heilbronn, Germany, for the payment. When the American company moved to dismiss on the basis of the exclusive forum-selection clause, the German agent countered that the court had jurisdiction in spite of the clause under § 23 of the German Civil Procedure Code (GCPC), which gives courts jurisdiction if the defendant owns assets located within the court's geographical district. Because the American company had founded a subsidiary in the District of Heilbronn, the agent argued that it owned assets (i.e. the subsidiary's stock) located within the court's § 23 GCPC jurisdiction. The German Supreme Court agreed and asserted jurisdiction over the American company. German Supreme Court, Sep. 5, 2012—VII ZR 25/12 = 2013 Internationales Handelsrecht (IHR), 35, https://perma.cc/9VY6-KPWB.

What made this case remarkable was that the court asserted jurisdiction despite a perfectly valid forum-selection agreement. The court ruled, however, that using Virginia courts and Virginia law would result in the German agent losing his right to the post-termination payment. Because this right is a mandatory rule within the European Union and cannot be abrogated by contract, the court ruled that the company could not avoid the rule through application of the choice-of-forum clause.

Do you agree with the court's result? Does it effectively mean that E.U. law applies extraterritorially just as the *Richards* court feared? Or does the fact that the corporation employed a German citizen and had a subsidiary in Germany make the decision reasonable?

Does the nature of the bargain matter? What if the employee had negotiated a higher salary in return for the forum selection clause? Does that mean the employee is now receiving an unfair windfall? Does the result in this case therefore depend on the degree of bargaining power enjoyed by the two parties? Should a jurisdictional rule depend on such factors?

D. ONLINE FORUM SELECTION CLAUSES

Forum selection clauses are commonly included as a part of online terms-of-service agreements. In order to access or use a website or online service, the user assents to a large number of contractual provisions that few users actually read. Are these true contracts at all? If so, should they be deemed to be unconscionable contracts because of the inherent disparity of bargaining power between the parties to the contract and the lack of any opportunity for negotiation? Or would that render online services potentially subject to too many different legal rules? With regard to forum selection clauses in particular, should the provisions of these clauses be enforced even if they deprive other courts of jurisdiction? Consider the following case, in which the Canadian Supreme Court split 4–3 on the enforceability of an online forum selection clause.

DOUEZ V FACEBOOK, INC.
Supreme Court of Canada, 2017

Facebook, an American corporation headquartered in California, operates one of the world's leading social networks and generates most of its revenues from advertising. D is a resident of British Columbia and has been a member of Facebook since 2007. In 2011, Facebook created a new advertising product called "Sponsored Stories", which used the name and picture of Facebook members to advertise companies and products to other members. D brought an action in British Columbia against Facebook alleging that it used her name and likeness without consent for the purposes of advertising, in contravention to British Columbia's *Privacy Act*. D also seeks certification of her action as a class proceeding under the Class Proceedings Act. The proposed class includes all British Columbia residents who had their name or picture used in Sponsored Stories. The estimated size of the class is 1.8 million people.

Under the *Privacy Act*, actions under the Act must be heard in the British Columbia Supreme Court. However, as part of the registration process, all potential users of Facebook must agree to its terms of use which include a forum selection and choice of law clause requiring that disputes be resolved in California according to California law.

Facebook brought a preliminary motion to stay the action on the basis of this forum selection clause. * * * *

Held: * * * * The forum selection clause is unenforceable.

Opinion of JUSTICES KARAKATSANIS, WAGNER AND GASCON:

In the absence of legislation to the contrary, the common law test for forum selection clauses established in *Z.I. Pompey Industrie v. ECU-Line N.V.*, 2003 SCC 27, [2003] 1 S.C.R. 450, continues to apply and provides the analytical framework for this case. * * * *.

Forum selection clauses serve a valuable purpose and are commonly used and regularly enforced. However, forum selection clauses divert public adjudication of matters out of the provinces, and court adjudication in each province is a public good. Because forum selection clauses encroach on the public sphere of adjudication, Canadian courts do not simply enforce them like any other clause. Where no legislation overrides the forum selection clause, the two-step approach set out in *Pompey* applies to determine whether to enforce a forum selection clause and stay an action brought contrary to it. At the first step, the party seeking a stay must establish that the clause is valid, clear and enforceable and that it applies to the cause of action before the court. If this party succeeds, the onus shifts to the plaintiff who must show strong cause why the court should not enforce the forum selection clause and stay the action. At this second step of the test, a court must consider all the circumstances, including the convenience of the parties, fairness between the parties and the interests of justice. Public policy may also be a relevant factor at this step. The strong cause factors have been interpreted and applied restrictively in the commercial context, but commercial and consumer relationships are very different. Irrespective of the formal validity of the contract, the consumer context may provide strong reasons not to enforce forum selection clauses. Thus, the *Pompey* strong cause factors should be modified in the consumer context to account for the different considerations relevant to this context.

When considering whether it is reasonable and just to enforce an otherwise binding forum selection clause in a consumer contract, courts should take account of all the circumstances of the particular case, including public policy considerations relating to the gross inequality of bargaining power between the parties and the nature of the rights at stake. * * * *

With respect to the first step of the *Pompey* test, the forum selection clause contained in Facebook's terms of use is enforceable. At the second step of the test, however, D has met her burden of establishing that there is strong cause not to enforce the forum selection clause. A number of different factors, when considered cumulatively, support a finding of strong cause. Most importantly, the claim involves a consumer contract of adhesion between an individual consumer and a large corporation and a statutory cause of action implicating the quasi-constitutional privacy rights of British Columbians. It is clear from the evidence that there was gross inequality of bargaining power between the parties. Individual consumers in this context are faced with little choice but to accept Facebook's terms of use. Additionally, Canadian courts have a greater interest in adjudicating cases impinging on constitutional and quasi-constitutional rights because these rights play an essential role in a free and democratic society and embody key Canadian values. This matter requires an interpretation of a statutory privacy tort and only a local court's interpretation of privacy rights under the *Privacy Act* will provide clarity and certainty about the scope of the rights to others in the province. Overall, these public policy concerns weigh heavily in favour of strong cause.

Two other secondary factors also suggest that the forum selection clause should not be enforced. First, even assuming that a California court could or would apply the *Privacy Act*, the interests of justice support having the action adjudicated by the British Columbia Supreme Court. The lack of evidence concerning whether a California court would hear D's claim is not determinative. The British Columbia Supreme Court, as compared to a California one, is better placed to assess the purpose and intent of the legislation and to decide whether public policy or legislative intent prevents parties from opting out of rights created by the *Privacy Act* through a choice of law clause in favour of a foreign jurisdiction. Second, the expense and inconvenience of requiring British Columbian individuals to litigate in California, compared to the comparative expense and inconvenience to Facebook, further supports a finding of strong cause. The chambers judge found it would be more convenient to have Facebook's books and records made available for inspection in British

Columbia than requiring D to travel to California to advance her claim. There is no reason to disturb this finding.

Concurring Opinion of JUSTICE ABELLA:

This is an online consumer contract of adhesion. To become a member of Facebook, a consumer must accept all the terms stipulated in the terms of use, including the forum selection clause. No bargaining, no choice, no adjustments. The automatic nature of the commitments made with online contracts intensifies the scrutiny for clauses that have the effect of impairing a consumer's access to potential remedies.

The operative test in *Pompey* for determining whether to enforce a forum selection clause engages two distinct inquiries. The first is into whether the clause is enforceable under contractual doctrines like public policy, duress, fraud, unconscionability or grossly uneven bargaining positions. If the clause is enforceable, the onus shifts to the consumer to show "strong cause" why the clause should not be enforced because of factors typically considered under *the forum non conveniens doctrine*. Keeping the two *Pompey* inquiries distinct means that before the onus shifts, the focus starts where it should, namely on whether the contract or clause itself is enforceable based on basic contractual principles.

In this case, the forum selection clause is unenforceable under the first step of the *Pompey* test applying contractual principles.

The burdens of forum selection clauses on consumers and their ability to access the court system range from added costs, logistical impediments and delays, to deterrent psychological effects. When online consumer contracts of adhesion contain terms that unduly impede the ability of consumers to vindicate their rights in domestic courts, particularly their quasi-constitutional or constitutional rights, public policy concerns outweigh those favouring enforceability of a forum selection clause.

Public policy concerns relating to access to domestic courts are especially significant in this case given that it deals with a fundamental right: privacy. Section 4 of British Columbia's *Privacy Act* states that the particular protections in the *Act* "must be heard and determined by the Supreme Court" despite anything contained in another Act. This is statutory recognition that privacy rights under the *Act* are entitled to protection in British Columbia by judges of the British Columbia Supreme Court. It would be contrary to public policy to enforce a forum selection clause in a consumer contract that has the effect of depriving a party of access to a statutorily mandated court.

Tied to the public policy concerns is the "grossly uneven bargaining power" of the parties. Facebook is a multi-national corporation which operates in dozens of countries. D is a private citizen who had no input into the terms of the contract and, in reality, no meaningful choice as to whether to accept them given Facebook's undisputed indispensability to online conversations.

The doctrine of unconscionability also applies in this case to render the forum selection clause unenforceable. Both elements required for the doctrine of unconscionability to apply—inequality of bargaining power and unfairness—are met in this case. The inequality of bargaining power between Facebook and D in an online contract of adhesion gave Facebook the unilateral ability to require that any legal grievances D had could not be vindicated in British Columbia where the contract was made, but only in California where Facebook has its head office. This gives Facebook an unfair and overwhelming procedural—and potentially substantive—benefit.

Dissenting Opinion of JUSTICES MCLACHLIN, MOLDAVER and CÔTÉ:

When parties agree to a jurisdiction for the resolution of disputes, courts will give effect to that agreement, unless the claimant establishes strong cause for not doing so. In this case, D has not shown strong cause for not enforcing the forum selection clause to which she agreed. Therefore, the action must be tried in California, as the contract requires, and a stay of the underlying claim should be entered.

* * * * Pursuant to *Pompey*, where the parties have agreed in advance to a choice of forum, there is no need to inquire into which of the two forums is the more convenient; the parties have settled the matter by their contract, unless the contractual clause is invalid or inapplicable or should not be applied because the plaintiff has shown strong cause not to do so. * * * *

With respect to the first step of the *Pompey* test, Facebook has discharged the burden of establishing that the forum selection clause is enforceable and applies in the circumstances: it is established that an enforceable contract may be formed by clicking an appropriately designated online icon; the contract on its face is clear and there is no inconsistency between a commitment to strive to apply local laws and an agreement that disputes will be tried in California; and finally, s. 4 of the *Privacy Act* grants the Supreme Court of British Columbia subject matter jurisdiction over *Privacy Act* claims to the exclusion of other British Columbia courts but nothing in the language of s. 4 suggests that it can render an otherwise valid contractual term unenforceable.

While the court can refuse to enforce otherwise valid contractual provisions that offend public policy, the party seeking to avoid enforcement of the clause must prove the existence of an overriding public policy that outweighs the very strong public interest in the enforcement of contracts. No such overriding public policy is found on the facts of this case. Forum selection clauses, far from being unconscionable or contrary to public policy, are supported by strong policy considerations. They serve an important role of increasing certainty and predictability in transactions that take place across borders. And, the fact that a contract is in standard form does not affect the validity of such a clause. That is not to say that forum selection clauses will always be given effect by the courts. Burdens of distance or geography may render the application of a forum selection clause unfair in the circumstances. However, those considerations are relevant at the second step of *Pompey*, not the first. Here, the forum selection clause is valid and applicable and the first step of *Pompey* test has been met.

As to the second step of the *Pompey* test, requiring the plaintiff to demonstrate strong cause is essential for upholding certainty, order and predictability in private international law, especially in light of the proliferation of online services provided across borders. In this case, none of the circumstances relied on by D show strong cause why the forum selection clause should not be enforced. She has not shown that the facts in the case and the evidence to be adduced shifts the balance of convenience from the contracted state of California to British Columbia. Further, the British Columbia tort created by the *Privacy Act* does not require special expertise and the courts of California have not been shown to be disadvantaged in interpreting the *Privacy Act* as compared with the Supreme Court of British Columbia. Nothing in D's situation suggests that the class action she wishes to commence could not be conducted in California just as easily as in British Columbia. There is also no suggestion that Facebook does not genuinely wish all litigation with users to take place in California. Finally, D has not shown that application of the forum selection clause would deprive her of a fair trial.

Applying the strong cause test in a nuanced manner or modifying the test to place the burden on the defendant in the context of consumer contracts of adhesion would amount to inappropriately overturning the Court's decision in *Pompey* and substituting new and different principles. Nuancing the strong cause test by considering the factor of the consumer's lack of bargaining power conflates the first step of the test set out in *Pompey* with the second step, in a way that profoundly alters the law endorsed in *Pompey*. It is at the first step that inequality of bargaining power is relevant. Inequality of bargaining power may lead to a clause being declared unconscionable—something not argued by D. In this case, Facebook has demonstrated that the forum selection clause is enforceable and D has failed to establish strong cause why the forum selection clause she agreed to should not be enforced.

Notes and Questions

1.   Can you articulate the arguments in each of the three opinions in this case? Which do you find most persuasive? If you agree with the Court majority, are there *any* circumstances in which you would enforce an online forum selection clause, or do you think they should never be deemed valid?

2.   People sign form contractual agreements all the time, every time they rent a car, or acquire a credit card, or purchase a ticket, or lease a home. Most of these form contracts include forum selection clauses. Moreover, consumers rarely read such contractual provisions before agreeing to them. Yannis Bakos et al., *Does Anyone Read the Fine Print? Consumer Attention to Standard Form Contracts*, 43 J. LEGAL STUD. 1 (2014) (finding "only one or two of every 1,000 retail software shoppers access the [software] license agreement and that most of those who do access it read no more than a small portion"). Do you think that this reality should render all such contracts unenforceable? What do you think the justices in the *Douez* majority would say? Does it matter if the forum selected is in a different country from the country where the plaintiff is a citizen?

3.   Does the online context in this case make it distinguishable from the other sorts of form contracts mentioned above? If so, why?

4.   Is it relevant precisely *how* the user assents to the terms of service? For example, if a website requires a user to scroll through the contractual terms and then affirmatively click "I agree," does that render a contract more enforceable? Or do you think the mechanism is irrelevant given the inequality of bargaining power and the lack of real back-and-forth negotiation?

5.   Should courts think of these contracts through the prism of contract law at all? Should judges instead treat the terms as part of the actual product being sold and then examine those terms for compliance with fundamental fairness and consumer protection norms? But then how do we determine *which* jurisdiction's conceptions of fairness and *which* jurisdiction's consumer protection rules should apply?

6.   For an extended critique of the way in which form contractual provisions (including forum selection clauses) displace public law, *see* MARGARET JANE RADIN, BOILERPLATE: THE FINE PRINT, VANISHING RIGHTS AND THE RULE OF LAW (Princeton Univ. Press 2013).

Chapter 4

CHOICE OF LAW

When a dispute potentially implicates the law of two or more different legal communities, which community's law should govern that dispute? Courts find this a perennially vexing problem. The task is further complicated by the need to select a *method* to use in choosing the appropriate law. It is not surprising, therefore, that the search for a system of choice of law has occupied a great deal of judicial and scholarly time and effort. If you take a Conflicts of Law course later in law school you will address these issues in great detail. Here, we just provide a taste of the complexities.

Of course, the so-called *Erie* doctrine, encountered in most first-year Civil Procedure courses, wrestles with a set of choice-of-law problems between federal and state law. This is a *vertical* choice-of-law problem. The European Union also addresses vertical choice-of-law problems in determining when to apply E.U. law and when to apply the law of individual nation-states to various matters of governance.

In contrast, *horizontal* choice-of-law problems arise in the United States (and other federal systems, such as Canada, Australia, Germany, and Brazil) when there is no applicable federal law and the question is whether the law of one state (or province) or another should apply. Horizontal choice-of-law problems also arise in transnational cases when the laws of multiple countries might apply. This chapter focuses on such horizontal transnational choice-of-law questions.

We begin with perhaps the two simplest ways to resolve the choice of law problem: internationalism and localism.

By internationalism, we mean an international law rule that would dictate a choice-of-law approach in all multijurisdictional cases. Such a rule could be adopted by treaty. However, public international law has historically been focused on relationships among nation-states and on what nation-state governments are permitted to do. Thus, public international law has largely addressed wars, diplomatic relations, and, more recently, human rights that individuals possess against their governments. However, there are very few international rules governing the relationships among private actors in civil suits. And even though the courts adjudicating these cases (and choosing the applicable legal rules) are in most circumstances formal, state-sanctioned bodies, these choice-of-law decisions are often viewed as outside the ambit of public international law. To be sure, the Hague Conference on Private International Law has produced treaties on choice of law in commercial contracts and family law matters. Yet, although many additional efforts to harmonize civil procedure rules have been attempted, they have generally run aground because of the deep-seated differences in rules among countries. Thus, international law to date provides few over-arching choice-of-law rules. Therefore, the decision of which law to apply is usually itself decided by courts applying domestic law.

But *which* domestic law should apply? Or, to go back one step, which domestic choice-of-law rule should be used to determine which domestic substantive law should be applied? One answer is to rely on extreme localism: always apply forum law (the law of the court hearing the case). This is known as *lex fori*, the law of the forum, and it has much to recommend it. After all, if a state has territorial sovereignty and can exercise complete control over activities and persons within its physical boundaries, then perhaps there is no reason ever to consider non-forum law. Indeed, one could go even farther and say that as a matter of democratic legitimacy *lex fori* is the *only* legitimate choice-of-law rule because a judge elected or appointed by a community must of necessity apply the norms of that community. In addition, it is undoubtedly the case that judges have more familiarity in applying their own jurisdiction's law. They know the language, the legal style, the databases to search, and so on. Accordingly, they are less likely to make basic errors than when applying foreign law to a dispute. Given these advantages, do you think this is a viable methodology to resolve choice-of-law problems?

For better or worse, a purely forum-based approach has proved unsatisfying. First, if all courts necessarily apply their own law, then the law to be applied in a multijurisdictional dispute may depend solely on which party files a lawsuit first. For example, under *lex fori*, if a dispute arises between a German company and a U.S. company, German law would apply if the suit is first filed in Germany, and U.S. law would apply if the suit is first filed in the United States. This seems to be an arbitrary way to choose the relevant law, and it can result in a race to the courthouse to be the first to file. Second, and relatedly, the same dispute would be resolved using completely different law depending only on where it was filed. Third, such a system might thwart party expectations if a suit ends up being adjudicated based on the law of a jurisdiction only tangentially related to the suit. Finally, cases might be decided based on the law of a jurisdiction that has no real interest in the dispute. Certainly a *lex fori* approach would, at the very least, put pressure on the law of personal jurisdiction and forum non conveniens, perhaps reining in broad assertions of legal authority.

If there are no universal rules for choice of law and if *lex fori* is unsatisfying, then the choice-of-law decision becomes a variable question of local law in which legislatures or judges decide under what circumstances to apply their own law and under what circumstances to apply foreign law. This question too is in some sense impossible to resolve satisfactorily. After all, by definition we are considering a case with multijurisdictional elements. Choosing any single law to apply to that dispute will therefore necessarily be "jurispathic", to use the famous phrased coined by legal scholar Robert Cover: it will anoint one law the law of the case and "kill off" any other law that might have been applied. Short of constructing an amalgam of the various possibly applicable laws, one law will always be chosen, and that law will always be unsuitable in at least some respects.

Thus, there is no truly right answer to a choice-of-law question. The best we can do is try a variety of imperfect attempts, while recognizing that each approach is in fact imperfect and has differing strengths and weaknesses. As noted above, choice-of-law problems arise domestically in any case that involves acts or actors in multiple states or provinces. Generally, such domestic choice-of-law questions are decided by each state according to its own choice-of-law rules, though in the United States the American Law Institute's First and Second Restatements of Conflict of Laws have been extremely influential. But as difficult as those cases are to resolve, a transnational dispute raises additional concerns. Not surprisingly, some commenters have argued that the proposed Third Restatement of Conflict of Laws explicitly take into account the transnational context in fashioning proposed choice-of-law rules. *See, e.g.*, Ralf Michaels & Christopher A. Whytock, *Internationalizing the New Conflict of Laws Restatement*, 27 DUKE J. OF COMP. & INT'L L. 349 (2017). The following two cases offer a taste of the complexities that can arise in transnational choice-of-law questions.

LAURITZEN V. LARSEN
Supreme Court of the United States, 1953
345 U.S. 571

JACKSON, J.

The key issue in this case is whether statutes of the United States should be applied to this claim of maritime tort. Larsen, a Danish seaman, while temporarily in New York, joined the crew of the *Randa*, a ship of Danish flag and registry, owned by petitioner, a Danish citizen. Larsen signed ship's articles, written in Danish, providing that the rights of crew members would be governed by Danish law and by the employer's contract with the Danish Seamen's Union, of which Larsen was a member. He was negligently injured aboard the *Randa* in the course of employment, while in Havana harbor.

Respondent brought suit under the Jones Act[1] * * *. Petitioner contended that Danish law was applicable and that, under it, respondent had received all of the compensation to which he was entitled. * * * * Entertaining the cause, the court ruled that American rather than Danish law applied, and the jury rendered a verdict of $ 4,267.50. The Court of Appeals, Second Circuit, affirmed. * * * *

Denmark has enacted a comprehensive code to govern the relations of her shipowners to her seagoing labor which by its terms and intentions controls this claim. Though it is not for us to decide, it is plausibly contended that all obligations of the owner growing out of Danish law have been performed or tendered to this seaman. The shipowner, supported here by the Danish Government, asserts that the Danish law supplies the full measure of his obligation and that maritime usage and international law as accepted by the United States exclude the application of our incompatible statute.

That allowance of an additional remedy under our Jones Act would sharply conflict with the policy and letter of Danish law is plain from a general comparison of the two systems of dealing with shipboard accidents. Both assure the ill or injured seafaring worker the conventional maintenance and cure at the shipowner's cost, regardless of fault or negligence on the part of anyone. But, while we limit this to the period within which maximum possible cure can be

---

[1] "Any seaman who shall suffer personal injury in the course of his employment may, at his election, maintain an action for damages at law, with the right of trial by jury, and in such action all statutes of the United States modifying or extending the common-law right or remedy in cases of personal injury to railway employees shall apply . . . ." 46 U.S.C. § 688.

effected, the Danish law limits it to a fixed period of twelve weeks, and the monetary measurement is different. The two systems are in sharpest conflict as to treatment of claims for disability, partial or complete, which are permanent, or which outlast the liability for maintenance and cure, to which class this claim belongs. Such injuries Danish law relieves under a state-operated plan similar to our workmen's compensation systems. Claims for such disability are not made against the owner but against the state's Directorate of Insurance Against the Consequences of Accidents. They may be presented directly or through any Danish Consulate. They are allowed by administrative action, not by litigation, and depend not upon fault or negligence but only on the fact of injury and the extent of disability. Our own law, apart from indemnity for injury caused by the ship's unseaworthiness, makes no such compensation for such disability in the absence of fault or negligence. But, when such fault or negligence is established by litigation, it allows recovery for elements such as pain and suffering not compensated under Danish law and lets the damages be fixed by jury. In this case, since negligence was found, United States law permits a larger recovery than Danish law. If the same injury were sustained but negligence was absent or not provable, the Danish law would appear to provide compensation where ours would not.

Respondent does not deny that Danish law is applicable to his case. The contention as stated in his brief is rather that "A claimant may select whatever forum he desires and receive the benefits resulting from such choice" and "A ship owner is liable under the laws of the forum where he does business as well as in his own country." This contention that the Jones Act provides an optional cumulative remedy is not based on any explicit terms of the Act, which makes no provision for cases in which remedies have been obtained or are obtainable under foreign law. Rather he relies upon the literal catholicity of its terminology. If read literally, Congress has conferred an American right of action which requires nothing more than that plaintiff be "any seaman who shall suffer personal injury in the course of his employment." It makes no explicit requirement that either the seaman, the employment or the injury have the slightest connection with the United States. Unless some relationship of one or more of these to our national interest is implied, Congress has extended our law and opened our courts to all alien seafaring men injured anywhere in the world in service of watercraft of every foreign nation—a hand on a Chinese junk, never outside Chinese waters, would not be beyond its literal wording.

But Congress in 1920 wrote these all-comprehending words, not on a clean slate, but as a postscript to a long series of enactments governing shipping. All were enacted with regard to a seasoned body of maritime law developed by the experience of American courts long accustomed to dealing with admiralty problems in reconciling our own with foreign interests and in accommodating the reach of our own laws to those of other maritime nations.

The shipping laws of the United States, set forth in Title 46 of the United States Code, comprise a patchwork of separate enactments, some tracing far back in our history and many designed for particular emergencies. While some have been specific in application to foreign shipping and others in being confined to American shipping, many give no evidence that Congress addressed itself to their foreign application and are in general terms which leave their application to be judicially determined from context and circumstance. By usage as old as the Nation, such statutes have been construed to apply only to areas and transactions in which American law would be considered operative under prevalent doctrines of international law. * * * *

This doctrine of construction is in accord with the long-heeded admonition of Mr. Chief Justice Marshall that "an act of congress ought never to be construed to violate the law of nations if any other possible construction remains . . . ." *The Charming Betsy,* 2 Cranch 64, 118. * * * * This is not, as sometimes is implied, any impairment of our own sovereignty, or limitation of the power of Congress. * * * * On the contrary, we are simply dealing with a problem of statutory construction rather commonplace in a federal system by which courts often have to decide whether "any" or "every" reaches to the limits of the enacting authority's usual scope or is to be applied to foreign events or transactions.[7] * * * *

---

[7] Cheatham and Reese, *Choice of the Applicable Law,* 52 COL. L. REV. 959, 961, dealing with state statutes, puts the problem in this fashion:

"There is one rule or policy which, wherever applicable, takes precedence over others and, to a large extent, saves the courts from further pain of decision. That controlling policy, obvious as it may be, is that a court must follow the dictates of its own legislature to the extent that these are constitutional. But, although choice of law constitutes no exception to this fundamental rule, rarely can the principle be applied in practice. The vast run of statutes are enacted with only the intrastate situation in mind. The application of a statute to out-of-state occurrences, therefore, must generally be determined in accordance with ordinary conflict of laws rules. And this is so even if, as is frequently the case, the statute employs such sweeping terms as 'every contract' or 'every decedent.' Unless it appears that the draftsmen so intended, language of this sort is not to be taken literally to mean that the statute is applicable to every transaction wherever occurring or to every case brought in the forum. Where, on the other hand, it is clear that the legislature has actually addressed itself to the choice of law problem, the courts, subject to the limitation of constitutionality, must give effect to its intentions."

Congress could not have been unaware of the necessity of construction imposed upon courts by such generality of language and was well warned that in the absence of more definite directions than are contained in the Jones Act it would be applied by the courts to foreign events, foreign ships and foreign seamen only in accordance with the usual doctrine and practices of maritime law.

Respondent places great stress upon the assertion that petitioner's commerce and contacts with the ports of the United States are frequent and regular, as the basis for applying our statutes to incidents aboard his ships. But the virtue and utility of sea-borne commerce lies in its frequent and important contacts with more than one country. If, to serve some immediate interest, the courts of each were to exploit every such contact to the limit of its power, it is not difficult to see that a multiplicity of conflicting and overlapping burdens would blight international carriage by sea. Hence, courts of this and other commercial nations have generally deferred to a nonnational or international maritime law of impressive maturity and universality. It has the force of law, not from extraterritorial reach of national laws, nor from abdication of its sovereign powers by any nation, but from acceptance by common consent of civilized communities of rules designed to foster amicable and workable commercial relations.

International or maritime law in such matters as this does not seek uniformity and does not purport to restrict any nation from making and altering its laws to govern its own shipping and territory. However, it aims at stability and order through usages which considerations of comity, reciprocity and long-range interest have developed to define the domain which each nation will claim as its own. Maritime law, like our municipal law, has attempted to avoid or resolve conflicts between competing laws by ascertaining and valuing points of contact between the transaction and the states or governments whose competing laws are involved. The criteria, in general, appear to be arrived at from weighing of the significance of one or more connecting factors between the shipping transaction regulated and the national interest served by the assertion of authority. It would not be candid to claim that our courts have arrived at satisfactory standards or apply those that they profess with perfect consistency. But in dealing with international commerce we cannot be unmindful of the necessity for mutual forbearance if retaliations are to be avoided; nor should we forget that any contact which we hold sufficient to warrant application of our law to a foreign transaction will logically be as strong a warrant for a foreign country to apply its law to an American transaction.

In the case before us, two foreign nations can claim some connecting factor with this tort—Denmark, because, among other reasons, the ship and the seaman were Danish nationals; Cuba, because the tortious conduct occurred and caused injury in Cuban waters. The United States may also claim contacts because the seaman had been hired in and was returned to the United States, which also is the state of the forum. We therefore review the several factors which, alone or in combination, are generally conceded to influence choice of law to govern a tort claim, particularly a maritime tort claim, and the weight and significance accorded them.

1. *Place of the Wrongful Act.* The solution most commonly accepted as to torts in our municipal and in international law is to apply the law of the place where the acts giving rise to the liability occurred, the *lex loci delicti commissi.* This rule of locality, often applied to maritime torts, would indicate application of the law of Cuba, in whose domain the actionable wrong took place. The test of location of the wrongful act or omission, however sufficient for torts ashore, is of limited application to shipboard torts, because of the varieties of legal authority over waters she may navigate. * * * *

The locality test, for what it is worth, affords no support for the application of American law in this case and probably refers us to Danish in preference to Cuban law, though this point we need not decide, for neither party urges Cuban law as controlling.

2. *Law of the Flag.* Perhaps the most venerable and universal rule of maritime law relevant to our problem is that which gives cardinal importance to the law of the flag. Each state under international law may determine for itself the conditions on which it will grant its nationality to a merchant ship, thereby accepting responsibility for it and acquiring authority over it. Nationality is evidenced to the world by the ship's papers and its flag. The United States has firmly and successfully maintained that the regularity and validity of a registration can be questioned only by the registering state.

This Court has said that the law of the flag supersedes the territorial principle, even for purposes of criminal jurisdiction of personnel of a merchant ship, because it "is deemed to be a part of the territory of that sovereignty [whose flag it flies], and not to lose that character when in navigable waters within the territorial limits of another sovereignty." On this principle, we concede a territorial government involved only concurrent jurisdiction of offenses aboard our ships. Some authorities reject, as a rather mischievous fiction, the doctrine that a ship is constructively a floating part of the flag-state, but apply the law of the flag on the pragmatic basis that there must be some law on shipboard, that it cannot change at every change of waters, and no experience shows a better rule than that of the state that owns her.

It is significant to us here that the weight given to the ensign overbears most other connecting events in determining applicable law. As this Court held in *United States v. Flores,* and iterated in *Cunard Steamship Co. v. Mellon*:

> "And so by comity it came to be generally understood among civilized nations that all matters of discipline and all things done on board which affected only the vessel or those belonging to her, and did not involve the peace or dignity of the country, or the tranquillity of the port, should be left by the local government to be dealt with by the authorities of the nation to which the vessel belonged as the laws of that nation or the interests of its commerce should require. . . ."

This was but a repetition of settled American doctrine.

These considerations are of such weight in favor of Danish and against American law in this case that it must prevail unless some heavy counterweight appears.

3. *Allegiance or Domicile of the Injured.* Until recent times there was little occasion for conflict between the law of the flag and the law of the state of which the seafarer was a subject, for the long-standing rule, as pronounced by this Court after exhaustive review of authority, was that the nationality of the vessel for jurisdictional purposes was attributed to all her crew. * * * * In some later American cases, courts have been prompted to apply the Jones Act by the fact that the wrongful act or omission alleged caused injury to an American citizen or domiciliary. We need not, however, weigh the seaman's nationality against that of the ship, for here the two coincide without resort to fiction. Admittedly, respondent is neither citizen nor resident of the United States. While on direct examination he answered leading questions that he was living in New York when he joined the *Randa*, the articles which he signed recited, and on cross-examination he admitted, that his home was Silkeburg, Denmark. His presence in New York was transitory and created no such national interest in, or duty toward, him as to justify intervention of the law of one state on the shipboard of another.

4. *Allegiance of the Defendant Shipowner.* A state "is not debarred by any rule of international law from governing the conduct of its own citizens upon the high seas or even in foreign countries when the rights of other nations or their nationals are not infringed." *Skiriotes v. Florida,* 313 U.S. 69, 73. Until recent times this factor

was not a frequent occasion of conflict, for the nationality of the ship was that of its owners. But it is common knowledge that in recent years a practice has grown, particularly among American shipowners, to avoid stringent shipping laws by seeking foreign registration eagerly offered by some countries. Confronted with such operations, our courts on occasion have pressed beyond the formalities of more or less nominal foreign registration to enforce against American shipowners the obligations which our law places upon them. But here again the utmost liberality in disregard of formality does not support the application of American law in this case, for it appears beyond doubt that this owner is a Dane by nationality and domicile.

5. *Place of Contract.* Place of contract, which was New York, is the factor on which respondent chiefly relies to invoke American law. It is one which often has significance in choice of law in a contract action. But a Jones Act suit is for tort * * * *. [T]his action does not seek to recover anything due under the contract or damages for its breach.

The place of contracting in this instance, as is usual to such contracts, was fortuitous. A seaman takes his employment, like his fun, where he finds it; a ship takes on crew in any port where it needs them. The practical effect of making the *lex loci contractus* govern all tort claims during the service would be to subject a ship to a multitude of systems of law, to put some of the crew in a more advantageous position than others, and not unlikely in the long run to diminish hirings in ports of countries that take best care of their seamen.

But if contract law is nonetheless to be considered, we face the fact that this contract was explicit that the Danish law and the contract with the Danish union were to control. Except as forbidden by some public policy, the tendency of the law is to apply in contract matters the law which the parties intended to apply. * * * *

6. *Inaccessibility of Foreign Forum.* It is argued, and particularly stressed by an *amicus* brief, that justice requires adjudication under American law to save seamen expense and loss of time in returning to a foreign forum. This might be a persuasive argument for exercising a discretionary jurisdiction to adjudge a controversy; but it is not persuasive as to the law by which it shall be judged. * * * * [W]e do not find this seaman disadvantaged in obtaining his remedy under Danish law from being in New York instead of Denmark. The Danish compensation system does not necessitate delayed, prolonged, expensive and uncertain litigation. It is stipulated in this case that claims may be made through the

Danish Consulate. There is not the slightest showing that to obtain any relief to which he is entitled under Danish law would require his presence in Denmark or necessitate his leaving New York. And, even if it were so, the record indicates that he was offered and declined free transportation to Denmark by petitioner.

7.   *The Law of the Forum.* It is urged that, since an American forum has perfected its jurisdiction over the parties and defendant does more or less frequent and regular business within the forum state, it should apply its own law to the controversy between them. The "doing business" which is enough to warrant service of process may fall quite short of the considerations necessary to bring extraterritorial torts to judgment under our law. Under respondent's contention, all that is necessary to bring a foreign transaction between foreigners in foreign ports under American law is to be able to serve American process on the defendant. We have held it a denial of due process of law when a state of the Union attempts to draw into control of its law otherwise foreign controversies, on slight connections, because it is a forum state. The purpose of a conflict-of-laws doctrine is to assure that a case will be treated in the same way under the appropriate law regardless of the fortuitous circumstances which often determine the forum. Jurisdiction of maritime cases in all countries is so wide and the nature of its subject matter so far-flung that there would be no justification for altering the law of a controversy just because local jurisdiction of the parties is obtainable. * * * *

This review of the connecting factors which either maritime law or our municipal law of conflicts regards as significant in determining the law applicable to a claim of actionable wrong shows an overwhelming preponderance in favor of Danish law. The parties are both Danish subjects, the events took place on a Danish ship, not within our territorial waters. Against these considerations is only the fact that the defendant was served here with process and that the plaintiff signed on in New York, where the defendant was engaged in our foreign commerce. The latter event is offset by provision of his contract that the law of Denmark should govern. We do not question the power of Congress to condition access to our ports by foreign-owned vessels upon submission to any liabilities it may consider good American policy to exact. But we can find no justification for interpreting the Jones Act to intervene between foreigners and their own law because of acts on a foreign ship not in our waters.

In apparent recognition of the weakness of the legal argument, a candid and brash appeal is made by respondent and by *amicus* briefs to extend the law to this situation as a means of benefiting seamen and enhancing the costs of foreign ship operation for the competitive advantage of our own. We are not sure that the interest of this foreign seaman, who is able to prove negligence, is the interest of all seamen or that his interest is that of the United States. Nor do we stop to inquire which law does whom the greater or the lesser good. The argument is misaddressed. It would be within the proprieties if addressed to Congress. Counsel familiar with the traditional attitude of this Court in maritime matters could not have intended it for us.[29]

The judgment below is reversed and the cause remanded to District Court for proceedings consistent herewith.

Reversed and remanded.

MR. JUSTICE BLACK agrees with the Court of Appeals and would affirm its judgment.

MR. JUSTICE CLARK, not having heard oral argument, took no part in the consideration or decision of this case.

Notes and Questions

1.   This case is made easier by the fact that the ship owner, the flag of the ship, and the employee were all Danish. Thus, one might think that applying New York law just because of the territorial location of the contract is an arbitrary way of resolving the choice-of-law dispute. Nevertheless, many choice-of-law doctrines emphasize territoriality in precisely that way and therefore would apply the place of the tort, the place of the contracting, the place where property is located, and so on. This purely territorialist focus can create odd results. For example, in *Kyle v. Kyle*, 128 So. 2d 427 (Fla. Dist. Ct. App. 1961), a couple married in Canada signed a prenuptial agreement in Canada regarding ownership of their property, lived in Canada, and divorced in Canada, but their agreement was invalidated by a Florida court using Florida law solely because the property subject to the Canadian prenuptial agreement was located in Florida.

2.   We can make the *Lauritzen* case more difficult if we change the facts and posit a New York employee. Under such circumstances should Danish law still apply? What if the ship owner were Swiss but chose to register the ship in Denmark because the owner preferred Danish law? Then does the ship become a floating piece of Denmark, subject always to Danish law? If so, would it matter whether the contract was signed off the ship on New York land versus on board the ship docked in the harbor?

---

[29] *Cf. The Peterhoff*, 5 Wall. 28, 57: "In cases such as that now in judgment, we administer the public law of nations, and are not at liberty to inquire what is for the particular advantage or disadvantage of our own or another country."

3.   Should a ship owner be able to artificially determine the law to be applied on board the ship simply by choosing where to register? Might this give corporations too much power to determine the law to be applied? Corporations often try to manipulate the law to be applied to them by choosing where to incorporate. Should choice-of-law rules require a more substantive connection to the place of incorporation? Or is it important to honor flag rules or place-of-incorporation rules so that moveable ships and national and multinational corporations are not potentially subjected to the laws of every jurisdiction they impact?

4.   To explore these issues, consider *Barcelona.com v. Excelentisimo Ayuntamiento de Barcelona*, 330 F.3d 617 (4th Cir. 2003). In that case, a citizen of Spain set up a corporation in the United States solely to register the domain name Barcelona.com with a U.S. domain name registrar corporation. When the City Council of Barcelona sued for trademark violation, the question was whether Spanish law should apply or instead U.S. law (under which place names cannot be trademarked). What factors do you think should matter in making this determination? From the perspective of community affiliation, this was a dispute between a Spanish citizen and a Spanish city concerning a domain name associated with that Spanish city. Thus, it might seem reasonable that Spanish law would apply. On the other hand, the domain name was registered by a (nominally) U.S. corporation using a U.S. domain name registrar. In the end, the U.S. court decided that U.S. trademark law should apply and therefore rejected the City's claim. Is this the correct result? Is it required under *Lauritzen*?

5.   How much deference should a U.S. court give to a foreign government's interpretation of its own law? In *Animal Sci. Prods., Inc. v. Hebei Welcome Pharm. Co.*, 138 S. Ct. 1865 (2018), U.S. purchasers of Vitamin C claimed that four Chinese vitamin manufacturers had colluded to fix prices in violation of U.S. antitrust law. The manufacturers argued in response that Chinese law actually *required* that they fix the price and quantity of Vitamin C exports, and the Chinese government submitted a brief supporting the manufacturers. The U.S. Supreme Court unanimously held that, in determining the content of foreign law under Federal Rule of Civil Procedure 44, a U.S. court "should accord respectful consideration to a foreign government's submission, but is not bound to accord conclusive effect to the foreign government's statements." Thus, the Court remanded the case so that the trial judge could conduct an independent inquiry as to the precise content of Chinese law. Is this the correct result? It seems odd for a U.S. judge to be able to second-guess a foreign government as to the correct interpretation of its own law. Yet, to the extent a foreign government might simply be trying to protect its own corporations, perhaps some skepticism is warranted.

6.   If you were the trial judge in this case, how would you go about determining what Chinese law required? Further, even if you

determined that Chinese law did in fact require the price fixing at issue, should that provide a valid defense to the antitrust lawsuit, or should U.S. antitrust law apply regardless, given that the Chinese manufacturers were attempting to sell in the United States? Is the argument of the Chinese manufacturers analogous to Yahoo! claiming that the First Amendment of the U.S. Constitution immunizes the company from a hate speech suit in France as in the case we encountered in Chapter One?

7.   In *Spector v. Norwegian Cruise Line Ltd.*, 545 U.S. 119 (2005), the U.S. Supreme Court applied the Americans with Disabilities Act (ADA) to a claim brought by a U.S. passenger against a non-U.S. cruise line based in part on the fact that the boat operated in U.S. waters. The majority opinion does not cite Lauritzen, but is its logic in tension with *Lauritzen*? Or is the fact that the passenger is a U.S. citizen relevant? If so, does that suggest *Lauritzen* would have been decided differently if the seaman had been American? But then the flag issue may be doing less work than it seems from the opinion. As the dissent in *Spector* pointed out, applying the ADA to foreign ships may require them to make major changes despite not being U.S. entities. If you agree that the ADA should apply to foreign entities serving U.S. customers, then should foreign law also apply to U.S. companies that serve foreign customers? In this regard, again consider the *Yahoo!* case in Chapter One, as well as the following case, which raises similar issues.

GOOGLE SPAIN, SL & GOOGLE, INC. V. AGENCIA ESPAÑOLA DE PROTECCIÓN DE DATOS (AEPD)
European Court of Justice, 2014

On 5 March 2010, Mr Costeja González, a Spanish national resident in Spain, lodged with the AEPD a complaint against La Vanguardia Ediciones SL, which publishes a daily newspaper with a large circulation, in particular in Catalonia (Spain) ("La Vanguardia"), and against Google Spain and Google Inc. The complaint was based on the fact that, when an internet user entered Mr Costeja González's name in the search engine of the Google group ("Google Search"), he would obtain links to two pages of La Vanguardia's newspaper, of 19 January and 9 March 1998 respectively, on which an announcement mentioning Mr Costeja González's name appeared for a real-estate auction connected with attachment proceedings for the recovery of social security debts.

By that complaint, Mr Costeja González requested, first, that La Vanguardia be required either to remove or alter those pages so that the personal data relating to him no longer appeared or to use certain tools made available by search engines in order to protect the data. Second, he requested that Google Spain or Google Inc. be required to remove or conceal the personal data relating to him so that they ceased to be included in the search results and no longer appeared in the links to La Vanguardia. Mr Costeja González stated in this context that the attachment proceedings concerning him had been fully resolved for a number of years and that reference to them was now entirely irrelevant.

By decision of 30 July 2010, the AEPD rejected the complaint in so far as it related to La Vanguardia, taking the view that the publication by it of the information in question was legally justified as it took place upon order of the Ministry of Labour and Social Affairs and was intended to give maximum publicity to the auction in order to secure as many bidders as possible.

On the other hand, the complaint was upheld in so far as it was directed against Google Spain and Google Inc. The AEPD considered in this regard that operators of search engines are subject to [European Union] data protection legislation given that they carry out data processing for which they are responsible and act as intermediaries in the information society. The AEPD took the view that it has the power to require the withdrawal of data and the prohibition of access to certain data by the operators of search engines when it considers that the locating and dissemination of the data are liable to compromise the fundamental right to data protection and the dignity of persons in the broad sense, and this would also encompass the mere wish of the person concerned that such data not be known to third parties. The AEPD considered that that obligation may be owed directly by operators of search engines, without it being necessary to erase the data or information from the website where they appear, including when retention of the information on that site is justified by a statutory provision. * * *

[We must] examine first * * * whether Article 2(b) of [European Union] Directive 95/46 is to be interpreted as meaning that the activity of a search engine as a provider of content which consists in finding information published or placed on the internet by third parties, indexing it automatically, storing it temporarily and, finally, making it available to internet users according to a particular order of preference must be classified as "processing of personal data" within the meaning of that provision when that information contains personal data. If the answer is in the affirmative, [then the question is] whether Article 2(d) of Directive 95/46 is to be interpreted as meaning that the operator of a search engine must be regarded as the "controller" in respect of that processing of the personal data, within the meaning of that provision.

According to Google Spain and Google Inc., the activity of search engines cannot be regarded as processing of the data which appear on third parties' web pages displayed in the list of search results, given that search engines process all the information available on the internet without effecting a selection between personal data and other information. Furthermore, even if that activity must be classified as "data processing", the operator of a search engine cannot be regarded as a "controller" in respect of that processing since it has no knowledge of those data and does not exercise control over the data. * * *

Article 2(b) of [European Union] Directive 95/46 defines "processing of personal data" as "any operation or set of operations which is performed upon personal data, whether or not by automatic means, such as collection, recording, organisation, storage, adaptation or alteration, retrieval, consultation, use, disclosure by transmission, dissemination or otherwise making available, alignment or combination, blocking, erasure or destruction".

As regards in particular the internet, the Court has already had occasion to state that the operation of loading personal data on an internet page must be considered to be such "processing" within the meaning of Article 2(b) of Directive 95/46.

So far as concerns the activity at issue in the main proceedings, it is not contested that the data found, indexed and stored by search engines and made available to their users include information relating to identified or identifiable natural persons and thus "personal data" within the meaning of Article 2(a) of that directive.

Therefore, it must be found that, in exploring the internet automatically, constantly and systematically in search of the information which is published there, the operator of a search engine "collects" such data which it subsequently "retrieves", "records" and "organises" within the framework of its indexing programmes, "stores" on its servers and, as the case may be, "discloses" and "makes available" to its users in the form of lists of search results. As those operations are referred to expressly and unconditionally in Article 2(b) of Directive 95/46, they must be classified as "processing" within the meaning of that provision, regardless of the fact that the operator of the search engine also carries out the same operations in respect of other types of information and does not distinguish between the latter and the personal data.

Nor is the foregoing finding affected by the fact that those data have already been published on the internet and are not altered by the search engine. * * * [I]ndeed, * * * a general derogation from the application of Directive 95/46 in such a case would largely deprive the directive of its effect. * * *

As to the question whether the operator of a search engine must be regarded as the "controller" in respect of the processing of personal data that is carried out by that engine in the context of an activity such as that at issue in the main proceedings, it should be recalled that Article 2(d) of Directive 95/46 defines "controller" as "the natural or legal person, public authority, agency or any other body which alone or jointly with others determines the purposes and means of the processing of personal data".

It is the search engine operator which determines the purposes and means of that activity and thus of the processing of personal data that it itself carries out within the framework of that activity and which must, consequently, be regarded as the "controller" in respect of that processing pursuant to Article 2(d).

Furthermore, it would be contrary not only to the clear wording of that provision but also to its objective—which is to ensure, through a broad definition of the concept of "controller", effective and complete protection of data subjects—to exclude the operator of a search engine from that definition on the ground that it does not exercise control over the personal data published on the web pages of third parties. * * *

Moreover, it is undisputed that that activity of search engines plays a decisive role in the overall dissemination of those data in that it renders the latter accessible to any internet user making a search on the basis of the data subject's name, including to internet users who otherwise would not have found the web page on which those data are published. * * *

It follows from all the foregoing considerations that Article 2(b) and (d) of Directive 95/46 are to be interpreted as meaning that, first, the activity of a search engine consisting in finding information published or placed on the internet by third parties, indexing it automatically, storing it temporarily and, finally, making it available to internet users according to a particular order of preference must be classified as "processing of personal data" within the meaning of Article 2(b) when that information contains personal data and, second, the operator of the search engine must be regarded as the "controller" in respect of that processing, within the meaning of Article 2(d). * * *

[C]oncerning the territorial scope of Directive 95/46:

Google Search is offered worldwide through the website "www. google.com". In numerous States, a local version adapted to the national language exists. The version of Google Search in Spanish is offered through the website "www.google.es", which has been registered since 16 September 2003. Google Search is one of the most used search engines in Spain.

Google Search is operated by Google Inc., which is the parent company of the Google Group and has its seat in the United States.

Google Search indexes websites throughout the world, including websites located in Spain. The information indexed by its "web crawlers" or robots, that is to say, computer programmes used to locate and sweep up the content of web pages methodically and automatically, is stored temporarily on servers whose State of location is unknown, that being kept secret for reasons of competition.

Google Search does not merely give access to content hosted on the indexed websites, but takes advantage of that activity and includes, in return for payment, advertising associated with the internet users' search terms, for undertakings which wish to use that tool in order to offer their goods or services to the internet users.

The Google group has recourse to its subsidiary Google Spain for promoting the sale of advertising space generated on the website "www.google.com". Google Spain, which was established on 3 September 2003 and possesses separate legal personality, has its seat in Madrid (Spain). Its activities are targeted essentially at undertakings based in Spain, acting as a commercial agent for the Google group in that Member State. Its objects are to promote, facilitate and effect the sale of on-line advertising products and services to third parties and the marketing of that advertising. * * *

Directive 95/46 states that "establishment on the territory of a Member State implies the effective and real exercise of activity through stable arrangements" and that "the legal form of such an establishment, whether simply [a] branch or a subsidiary with a legal personality, is not the determining factor".

It is not disputed that Google Spain engages in the effective and real exercise of activity through stable arrangements in Spain. As it moreover has separate legal personality, it constitutes a subsidiary of Google Inc. on Spanish territory and, therefore, an "establishment" within the meaning of Article 4(1)(a) of Directive 95/46.

In order to satisfy the criterion laid down in that provision, it is also necessary that the processing of personal data by the controller be "carried out in the context of the activities" of an establishment of the controller on the territory of a Member State.

Google Spain and Google Inc. dispute that this is the case since the processing of personal data at issue in the main proceedings is carried out exclusively by Google Inc., which operates Google Search without any intervention on the part of Google Spain; the latter's activity is limited to providing support to the Google group's advertising activity which is separate from its search engine service.

Nevertheless, as the Spanish Government and the Commission in particular have pointed out, Article 4(1)(a) of Directive 95/46 does not require the processing of personal data in question to be carried out "by" the establishment concerned itself, but only that it be carried out "in the context of the activities" of the establishment.

Furthermore, in the light of the objective of Directive 95/46 of ensuring effective and complete protection of the fundamental rights and freedoms of natural persons, and in particular their right to privacy, with respect to the processing of personal data, those words cannot be interpreted restrictively. * * * * [T]he European Union legislature sought to prevent individuals from being deprived of the protection guaranteed by the directive and that protection from being circumvented, by prescribing a particularly broad territorial scope.

In the light of that objective of Directive 95/46 and of the wording of Article 4(1)(a), it must be held that the processing of personal data for the purposes of the service of a search engine such as Google Search, which is operated by an undertaking that has its seat in a third State but has an establishment in a Member State, is carried out "in the context of the activities" of that establishment if the latter is intended to promote and sell, in that Member State, advertising space offered by the search engine which serves to make the service offered by that engine profitable.

In such circumstances, the activities of the operator of the search engine and those of its establishment situated in the Member State concerned are inextricably linked since the activities relating to the advertising space constitute the means of rendering the search engine at issue economically profitable and that engine is, at the same time, the means enabling those activities to be performed. * * *

[C]oncerning the extent of the responsibility of the operator of a search engine under Directive 95/46:

* * * Google Spain and Google Inc. submit that, by virtue of the principle of proportionality, any request seeking the removal of information must be addressed to the publisher of the website concerned because it is he who takes the responsibility for making the information public, who is in a position to appraise the lawfulness of that publication and who has available to him the most effective and least restrictive means of making the information inaccessible. Furthermore, to require the operator of a search engine to withdraw

information published on the internet from its indexes would take insufficient account of the fundamental rights of publishers of websites, of other internet users and of that operator itself. * * *

Under Article 6 of Directive 95/46 * * * the controller has the task of ensuring that personal data are processed "fairly and lawfully", that they are "collected for specified, explicit and legitimate purposes and not further processed in a way incompatible with those purposes", that they are "adequate, relevant and not excessive in relation to the purposes for which they are collected and/or further processed", that they are "accurate and, where necessary, kept up to date" and, finally, that they are "kept in a form which permits identification of data subjects for no longer than is necessary for the purposes for which the data were collected or for which they are further processed". In this context, the controller must take every reasonable step to ensure that data which do not meet the requirements of that provision are erased or rectified. * * *

This provision permits the processing of personal data where it is necessary for the purposes of the legitimate interests pursued by the controller or by the third party or parties to whom the data are disclosed, except where such interests are overridden by the interests or fundamental rights and freedoms of the data subject—in particular his right to privacy with respect to the processing of personal data—which require protection under * * * the directive. Application of [the Directive] thus necessitates a balancing of the opposing rights and interests concerned, in the context of which account must be taken of the significance of the data subject's rights. * * *

Requests * * * may be addressed by the data subject directly to the controller who must then duly examine their merits and, as the case may be, end processing of the data in question. Where the controller does not grant the request, the data subject may bring the matter before the supervisory authority or the judicial authority so that it carries out the necessary checks and orders the controller to take specific measures accordingly. * * *

[P]rocessing of personal data * * * carried out by the operator of a search engine is liable to affect significantly the fundamental rights to privacy and to the protection of personal data when the search by means of that engine is carried out on the basis of an individual's name, since that processing enables any internet user to obtain through the list of results a structured overview of the information relating to that individual that can be found on the internet— information which potentially concerns a vast number of aspects of his private life and which, without the search engine, could not have been interconnected or could have been only with great difficulty—and thereby to establish a more or less detailed profile of him. Furthermore, the effect of the interference with those rights of the data subject is heightened on account of the important role played by the internet and search engines in modern society, which render the information contained in such a list of results ubiquitous.

In the light of the potential seriousness of that interference, it is clear that it cannot be justified by merely the economic interest which the operator of such an engine has in that processing. However, inasmuch as the removal of links from the list of results could, depending on the information at issue, have effects upon the legitimate interest of internet users potentially interested in having access to that information, in situations such as that at issue in the main proceedings a fair balance should be sought in particular between that interest and the data subject's fundamental rights * * *. [T]hat balance may * * * depend, in specific cases, on the nature of the information in question and its sensitivity for the data subject's private life and on the interest of the public in having that information, an interest which may vary, in particular, according to the role played by the data subject in public life. * * *

[E]ven initially lawful processing of accurate data may, in the course of time, become incompatible with the directive where those data are no longer necessary in the light of the purposes for which they were collected or processed. That is so in particular where they appear to be inadequate, irrelevant or no longer relevant, or excessive in relation to those purposes and in the light of the time that has elapsed.

Therefore, if it is found, following a request by the data subject pursuant to * * * Directive 95/46, that the inclusion in the list of results displayed following a search made on the basis of his name of the links to web pages published lawfully by third parties and containing true information relating to him personally is, at this point in time, * * * having regard to all the circumstances of the case, * * * inadequate, irrelevant or no longer relevant, or excessive in relation to the purposes of the processing at issue carried out by the operator of the search engine, the information and links concerned in the list of results must be erased. * * *

[These] rights override, as a rule, not only the economic interest of the operator of the search engine but also the interest of the general public in finding that information upon a search relating to the data subject's name. However, that would not be the case if it appeared, for particular reasons, such as the role played by the data subject in public life, that the interference with his fundamental rights is justified by the preponderant interest of the general public in having, on account of inclusion in the list of results, access to the information in question.

As regards a situation such as that at issue in the main proceedings, which concerns the display, in the list of results that the internet user obtains by making a search by means of Google Search on the basis of the data subject's name, of links to pages of the on-line archives of a daily newspaper that contain announcements mentioning the data subject's name and relating to a real-estate auction connected with attachment proceedings for the recovery of social security debts, it should be held that, having regard to the sensitivity for the data subject's private life of the information contained in those announcements and to the fact that its initial publication had taken place 16 years earlier, the data subject establishes a right that that information should no longer be linked to his name by means of such a list. Accordingly, since in the case in point there do not appear to be particular reasons substantiating a preponderant interest of the public in having, in the context of such a search, access to that information, * * * the data subject may * * * require those links to be removed from the list of results.

Notes and Questions

1.   Who has committed an unlawful act? Had Google done anything wrong?

2.   On what basis does the European Court of Justice assert jurisdiction over Google.com, as opposed to Google Spain? Is it the same rationale as in the *Yahoo!* case discussed in Chapter One, or is it different? What role does Google's search term advertising scheme play in the Court's decision?

3.   Why does the Court rule that Google must remove certain sites from certain searches as opposed to requiring the sites themselves to delete material that violates the privacy right articulated?

4.   Notice that in this case the European Court of Justice is in a sense using Google as a way to enforce its privacy ruling beyond Europe. After all, the European authorities would not only have difficulty finding every website owner, but those owners might be outside of Europe. Thus, by focusing on Google, the European Court of Justice is able to more effectively enforce its order even outside its own jurisdiction. Is that a problem? If you think so, then consider what would happen if Europe *cannot* deploy Google in this way: websites that wish to avoid the European Court ruling could simply incorporate (or locate their servers) outside of Europe. And under a *Lauritzen*-type approach such moves might be sufficient to evade European law. If that is so, then is deploying Google simply the best way to enforce territorially-based law in a world

where entities often cause harm regardless of their territorial location? Or maybe the *Lauritzen* approach must be revisited in a less territorially-based world? But even if the European Court of Justice tried to assert jurisdiction directly over a foreign website, would it be effective? Doesn't that depend on whether the country where the website operator is located chooses to enforce the European judgment? In that regard, is this simply a repeat of the *Yahoo!* case from Chapter One, 15 years later?

5.   If you were the General Counsel of Google, what steps would now be required in order to comply with this order? Would altering searches on country-specific sites such as google.es be sufficient, or will Google need to change its search results for all of its websites, including google.com? And how will Google determine if material fits within the scope of the privacy right the Court articulates? Who will decide? Is it appropriate for the Court to place this burden on Google? Or is this precisely the way in which internet regulation *should* work?

6.   If you were operating a website and you found out that Google was no longer listing your site in response to certain search terms, should there be a way for you to object? With whom do you file your complaint? With Google? With your own court system? What if you go to a U.S. court? Should that court follow the parameters of the privacy right articulated by the European Court of Justice? Is this similar to, or different from, the question of whether the *Yahoo!* decision should be enforced in the United States?

Chapter 5

ACCESS TO JUSTICE IN COMPARATIVE CONTEXT

Access to justice is recognized as both a basic human right and a means to protect other universally recognized human rights. While this is true in the criminal context, jurisdictions differ in their treatment of the right to counsel in civil cases. In the United States, the Supreme Court in *Gideon v. Wainwright,* 372 U.S. 335 (1963), found a constitutional right to state-provided counsel in criminal cases. But in *Lassiter v. Dept. of Social Serv. of Durham County*, 452 U.S. 18 (1981), the Court affirmed that due process did not require the state to appoint counsel to represent a mother in a civil proceeding to terminate her parental rights with respect to her infant son. *Lassiter* did leave open the possibility of a right to state-provided counsel in civil cases where personal liberty is at stake. In *Turner v. Rogers*, 564 U.S. 431 (2011), however, the Court rejected even that claim in a case of one-year imprisonment for civil contempt of court for failing to pay child support, although it did suggest it might come to a different conclusion if the government (as opposed to the custodial parent) were pressing the contempt case. State courts, in interpreting their own state constitutions, have frequently taken a more expansive view of due process in recognizing a right to counsel in a number of civil areas.

A. ACCESS TO JUSTICE AS AN INTERNATIONAL HUMAN RIGHT

Despite these U.S. Supreme Court decisions, some have argued that the right to counsel in civil cases is required as a matter of international human rights. Article 10 of the Universal Declaration of Human Rights provides that "[e]veryone is entitled in full equality to a fair and public hearing by an independent and impartial tribunal, in the determination of his rights and obligations and of any criminal charge against him." Universal Declaration of Human Rights, G.A. Res. 217A (III), art. 10, U.N. GAOR, 3d Sess., 1st plen. mtg., U.N. Doc. A/810 (Dec. 10, 1948). Accordingly, the Universal Declaration does seem to extend its statement of procedural fairness to civil as well as criminal matters, though it does not dictate specific requirements beyond equality of treatment and an impartial tribunal. Earlier drafts of the Universal Declaration had gone further and had stated that everyone in both civil and criminal matters "shall have the right to consult with and to be represented by counsel." DAVID WEISSBRODT, ARTICLES 8, 10 AND 11 OF THE UNIVERSAL DECLARATION OF HUMAN RIGHTS: THE RIGHT TO A FAIR TRIAL 13 (2001) (describing early drafts of the Universal Declaration). However, because the national delegations on the drafting committee agreed that such detailed language belonged in a treaty rather than in the Universal Declaration, the General Assembly of the United Nations ultimately adopted the more general, final version of Article 10. *Id.* at 14 (noting that India and the United Kingdom initially proposed the right to counsel language be omitted); *see* David Weissbrodt & Mattias Hallendorff, *Travaux Préparatoires of the Fair Trial Provisions—Articles 8 to 11—of the Universal Declaration of Human Rights*, 21 HUM. RTS. Q. 1061, 1071 (1999).

The right to counsel in civil matters has increasingly become established as a general principle of law in the international community. The European Court of Human Rights has construed the European Convention for the Protection of Human Rights and Fundamental Freedoms to require a right to civil counsel.[1] The Inter-American Court of Human Rights has also recognized the right. *See* Inter-Am. Comm'n on Human Rights, Am. Convention on Human Rights, art. 3, (Jan. 31, 2007) ("Every person has the right to recognition as a person before the law."). Finally, the United Nations Committee on the Elimination of All Forms of Racial Discrimination has advocated that the right to counsel in civil cases be protected. *See* U.N. Comm. on the Elimination of Racial Discrimination [CERD], *International Convention on the Elimination of All Forms of Racial Discrimination: Consideration of Reports Submitted by States Parties Under Article 9 of the Convention*, CERD/C/USA/CO/6 ¶ 22 (Feb. 18, 2008) ("The Committee further recommends that the State part[ies] allocate sufficient resources to ensure legal representation . . . in civil proceedings. . . ."). As Professor Martha Davis has argued, "the wealth of relevant interpretive material combined with the weight of considerable international practice make clear that provision of counsel in civil matters is an emerging human right increasingly

---

[1]   *See* Convention for the Protection of Human Rights and Fundamental Freedoms, art. 6, Nov. 4, 1950, 213 U.N.T.S. 221 [hereinafter European Convention] (providing that "[i]n the determination of his civil rights and obligations . . . everyone is entitled to a fair and public hearing. . . ."). This provision has been construed to require appointment of civil counsel. *Airey v. Ireland*, 32 Eur. Ct. H.R. (ser. A) at para. 21 (1979). More recently, the European Court of Human Rights ruled in *Steel & Morris v. United Kingdom*, (2005) 41 E.H.R.R. 22, that England's legal aid statute denying counsel to indigent defendants in defamation cases violated the right to counsel, and therefore failed to satisfy the European Convention's guarantee of a "fair hearing."

recognized by the law of nations, especially when the civil matter at issue involves fundamental rights." Martha F. Davis, *In the Interests of Justice: Human Rights and the Right to Counsel in Civil Cases*, 25 TOURO L. REV. 147, 156 (2009). Nevertheless, such an emerging international consensus, even if it exists, has not been deemed to create a cognizable due process claim for individual litigants in U.S. courts.

B. ACCESS TO JUSTICE AS A DOMESTIC LEGAL RIGHT

The South African Constitution's Bill of Rights provides mandatory legal aid for criminal cases (Section 35) and for children under seven years of age (Section 28), but it is a statute, the Legal Aid Act, that creates a right of access to legal services in civil matters (with restrictions as to the areas of the law covered). In the case below, Nkuzi and an international public interest litigation organization argued that legal aid reform under that statute had not yet been implemented and that, during this transition period, legal aid was being denied to one of South Africa's most sensitive entitled populations: labor tenants. *Nkuzi* was thus framed as public interest impact litigation aimed at recognizing a constitutional right to legal aid in matters of land tenure security.

NKUZI DEVELOPMENT ASSOCIATION V. SOUTH AFRICA

Land Claims Court of South Africa, 2001

MOLOTO, J.

This is an application for a declaratory order to the effect that persons who have a right to security of tenure in terms of the Extension of Security of Tenure Act ("ESTA") and the Land Reform (Labour Tenants) Act ("Labour Tenants Act") and whose tenure is threatened or has been infringed, have a right to legal representation or legal aid at State expense under certain conditions, and other relief. * * * *

The application is premised on the fact that the right to secure tenure or alternative redress is guaranteed in the Bill of Rights to the Constitution of the Republic of South Africa Act, ("the Constitution"). Section 25(6) of the Constitution reads:

"A person or community whose tenure of land is legally insecure as a result of past racially discriminatory laws or practices is entitled, to the extent provided by an Act of Parliament, either to tenure which is legally secure or to comparable redress."

With a view to giving effect to section 25(6) of the Constitution, the Parliament enacted the Labour Tenants Act and ESTA. These acts define the extent to which a large number of rural and periurban people whose tenure of land is legally insecure, are entitled to legally secure tenure. However, a very large number of the people for whose benefit the Labour Tenants Act and ESTA were enacted, do not enjoy that entitlement when their rights are infringed or threatened with infringement. This is so because they are overwhelmingly poor and vulnerable people with little or no formal education. When their tenure security is threatened or infringed, they do not understand the documents initiating action or the processes to follow in order to defend their rights. On the other hand they cannot afford the fees for a lawyer to represent them because of their poverty. As a result they are quite often unable to defend or enforce their rights and their entitlement under the Constitution, the Labour Tenants Act and ESTA.

The Legal Aid Board is the institution through which the Government provides legal aid to the indigent. However, most of these people or a large number of them are not able to obtain legal services through the Legal Aid Board. Several reasons can be identified for this situation:

(a)   The number of lawyers practising in the rural areas is small. Most attorneys prefer to practise in the cities and towns where there is a pool of reasonably well to do (comparatively speaking) clientele.

(b)   Of the few lawyers practising in the rural areas most have very close social and professional connections with landowners in the district. As a result many of them are reluctant to represent labour tenants and occupiers against the landowners. In its circular no 5 of 1998, the Legal Aid Board states: "[I]n many rural areas local attorneys are unwilling to act against prominent local farmers."

(c)   The Legal Aid Board has always paid very modest fees with the result that very few lawyers have been prepared to do legal work on instructions from the Legal Aid Board. This has had the effect that the pool of lawyers from whom legal aid representation could be sought is small. * * * *

As a result of the above, very many poor, illiterate litigants appear in court unrepresented. Labour tenants and occupiers form a significant portion of such litigants. There is a need to assist labour tenants and occupiers to protect their constitutionally guaranteed rights. One of the ways in which the rights of labour tenants and occupiers, as outlined in section 25 of the Constitution and further expanded upon in the Labour Tenants Act and ESTA, can be protected is to ensure that their right in terms of section 34 of the Constitution is upheld. This means that labour tenants and occupiers are entitled to a fair trial before they can be evicted and for the trial to be fair it is necessary that the labour tenant or occupier understands his or her rights under the law and the complexities of a trial. Where he or she does not understand, there is a need for legal representation, or at the very least, an explanation of his or her rights by the judicial officer. Given the order I intend making it is important that information about the rights of labour tenants and occupiers to a just and fair trial be disseminated as widely as possible.

The issue of judicial officers informing litigants about their rights arose in criminal cases in the period before South Africa was a constitutional state. It is to that field of law that I look for guidance. The rights of an accused were then understood not to include the right to legal aid. The right of the accused was a right to representation, if he or she could afford it and obtain it. The question then arose whether the judicial officer was under a duty to inform the accused of that right to legal representation.

The question arose crisply *in S v Radebe; S v Mbonani*. Goldstone, J. (Van der Merwe, J. concurring) referred to:

"... a general duty on the part of judicial officers to ensure that unrepresented accused fully understand their rights and the recognition that in the absence of such understanding a fair and just trial may not take place."

The court held further as follows:

"If there is a duty upon judicial officers to inform unrepresented accused of their legal rights, then I can conceive of no reason why the right to legal representation should not be one of them ... depending upon the complexity of the charge, or of the legal rules relating thereto, and the seriousness thereof, an accused should not only be told of this right but he should be encouraged to exercise it. He should be given a reasonable time within which to do so. He should also be informed in appropriate cases that he is entitled to apply to the Legal Aid Board for assistance. A failure on the part of the judicial officer to do this, having regard to the circumstances of a particular case, may result in an unfair trial in which there may well be a complete failure of justice. I should make it clear that I am not suggesting that the absence of legal representation per se or the absence of the suggested advice to an accused person per se will necessarily result in such an irregularity or an unfair trial and the failure of justice. Each case will depend upon its own facts and peculiar circumstances."

This approach was followed in a number of cases culminating in the endorsement of the approach by the Supreme Court of Appeal.

Once it is found that there is a right to representation at State expense in certain civil cases, I can conceive of no logical reason why a judicial officer should not inform the person appearing before him/her of that right, and how to exercise it. There is no logical basis for distinguishing between criminal and civil matters. The issues in civil matters are equally complex and the laws and procedures difficult to understand. Failure by a judicial officer to inform these litigants of their rights, how to exercise them and where to obtain assistance may result in a miscarriage of justice.

The following order is made:

1.   It is declared that:

1.1   The persons who have a right to security of tenure in terms of the Extension of Security of Tenure Act, Act 62 of 1997 and the Land Reform (Labour Tenants) Act, Act 3 of 1996, and whose security of tenure is threatened or has been infringed, have a right to legal representation or legal aid at State expense if substantial injustice would otherwise result, and if they cannot reasonably afford the cost thereof from their own resources.

1.2   The State is under a duty to provide such legal representation or legal aid through mechanisms selected by it.

1.3   The cases in which substantial injustice could result include, but are not limited to, cases where

1.3.1   the potential consequences for the person concerned are severe, which will be so if the person concerned might be deprived of a home and will not readily obtain suitable alternative accommodation; and

1.3.2   the person concerned is not likely to be able effectively to present his or her case unrepresented, having regard to the complexity of the case, the legal procedure, and the education, knowledge and skills of the person concerned.

1.4   Legal aid or legal representation need not be provided in cases where there is no reasonable or probable cause.

1.5   The State or its agent is entitled to adopt a screening process to establish whether the person concerned is entitled to legal aid or legal representation, before granting such aid or representation.

2   The Minister of Justice and the Minister of Land Affairs are directed to take all reasonable measures to give effect to this order, so that people in all parts of the country who have rights as set out in this order, are able to exercise those rights effectively.

Notes and Questions

1.   Does the court rule that the right to counsel derives from the statute or from the Constitution? How do the two interrelate in this case?

2.   Why do you think the court does not recognize a right to counsel in all civil cases?

3.   Notice that the court does not extend the right to counsel even to all land cases of this type. What are the limitations on the right? Are they reasonable or do you think they will lead to problems in application?

4.   Are there equivalent circumstances where you think the U.S. Constitution should be interpreted to provide a right to counsel in civil cases?

5.   Imagine that a professor accused you of academic misconduct and a disciplinary tribunal were convened to decide whether you should be expelled from law school. Would you want a lawyer? If you couldn't afford one, do you think the law school should provide one?

C. DIFFERENT MODELS OF CIVIL LEGAL SERVICES

The United States is unique in the world in having a mechanism for so-called contingency fees. Under this model, a lawyer agrees to take on a client's civil case at no charge, but then the lawyer collects a percentage (usually a third to a half) of any resulting judgment or settlement. While the contingency fee model helps to alleviate the problem of right to counsel in civil cases, it operates only as an adequate incentive for lawyers in cases with the promise of large awards and attorney's fees. In the areas of housing, family law, and small claims, legal representation remains elusive to poor litigants who cannot afford counsel. Today, American civil legal aid remains a matter of private charity and public appropriations. A patchwork of pro bono lawyers, community legal aid, and federal- and state-funded legal services organizations partially fills this gap, but huge needs remain unmet.

Consider the following comparative paper from a publication of the United Kingdom National Committee of Comparative Law that examines the four principal legal aid models—charitable, judicare, salaried, and mixed—focusing mainly on Western industrialized countries. What are the strengths and weaknesses of the different models, and what are the implications of seeking legal aid in a particular setting?

ALAN PATERSON, *FINANCING LEGAL SERVICES: A COMPARATIVE PERSPECTIVE, IN* THE OPTION OF LITIGATING IN EUROPE

D.L. Carey Miller & Paul R. Beaumont, eds.
U.K. Compar. L. Series 14, 1993

There are four principal legal aid models: 'charitable', 'judicare', 'salaried' and 'mixed'.

A. The Charitable Model

Under this approach, meeting the legal needs of the impecunious is considered to be a professional obligation—and usually a gratuitous one. Historically its hallmarks have included:

    a.   poor funding and inadequate coverage;

    b.   services provided by 'volunteer' members of the professions, almost invariably (especially in the case of counsel) the youngest and least experienced practitioners, on a part-time basis;

    c.   services provided on a gratuitous basis with no court dues or expenses being [reimbursed]. Even today there are numerous examples of the charitable model operating both within and without the United Kingdom. The former range from the advice clinics staffed by volunteer solicitors to the free initial interview offered by solicitors * * * * and from 24 hour freephone advice lines to representing clients on a speculative basis.

In the United States, though not in the United Kingdom, there has been a longstanding voluntary commitment to 'pro bono' work by the really large firms. [Beginning in the 1980s,] we have seen the emergence of a 'mandatory pro bono' movement in the USA. With the decline in Federal funding for legal aid it is increasingly being suggested that attorneys should undertake on a voluntary or a compulsory basis one or two cases a year or give up 40 hours or so a year to assist in the provision of legal services to the poor. As yet no State has adopted this on a compulsory basis but [some] smaller jurisdictions have, covering more than twelve thousand lawyers. For lawyers who are unwilling to undertake the obligation or whose specialisms are irrelevant to the poor there is provision for the contribution to take the form of a set financial donation to the programme.

Although the objections to such programmes can be overcome, it must be doubted whether in the present climate mandatory pro bono will make the transition to the United Kingdom. In particular solicitors are likely to argue that the fact that legal aid work pays at less than 70% of the private client fee rates, is evidence of a substantial existing pro bono contribution. Certainly, the National Legal Aid Advisory Committee of Australia used this argument (legal aid pays at 80% of private client rates there) in concluding that it would be neither desirable nor practicable that pro bono work should play a significant part in any future strategy for supplying legal services to the poor in Australia. Moreover it is difficult to see how pro bono work would have other than a symbolic role to play in meeting the legal needs of the poor in the United Kingdom. The presence of the charitable model in a jurisdiction is unlikely to predispose litigants to choose to raise their actions there. It might however, predispose them not to do so.

B.   The Legal Aid/Judicare Model

The second model of legal aid is usually referred to under its American title, namely, the 'Judicare Model' in order to distinguish it from other legal aid models. Under this approach the state funds the private profession to provide legal services to individuals. This model exists in most of the leading industrial countries in the Western world. In some (for example, the United Kingdom, * * * Germany, Norway, Sweden, most Canadian provinces, Australia, New Zealand and Hong Kong), it is the dominant mode of providing legal services. In most western countries it took over from the first model in the second half of the twentieth century but in a few, for example, Belgium, Italy and Spain, the first model still prevails de facto if not also de jure.

I.   Primary Characteristics

The primary characteristics of the judicare model owe much to the version of it which developed in the United Kingdom, where the model was first introduced on a large scale (in 1950). Its features include the fact that judiciare is:

1. State Funded: providing access to justice is seen as a State obligation rather than a charitable duty of the profession;

2. Independent: responsibility for the administration and award of legal aid is placed in the hands of an independent body, board or court;

3. Demand-led: expenditure is open-ended although it is subject to constraints and monitoring before, during and after the provision of the service;

4. Broad in scope: much wider than under the charitable model. Nevertheless some restrictions on coverage exist in that certain types of action may be excluded, e.g. defamation, simplified divorces and small claims. In the UK it is not available in tribunals and in most countries it is designed to support individual rather than collective actions;

5. Subject to multiple eligibility criteria: including means and merits testing and an expectation that funding from other sources e.g. a trade union are not available to the applicant;

6. Contributory: assisted persons are often required to contribute towards the cost of their cases, depending on their means. * * * * One of the significant features of the United Kingdom model (as opposed to the position in many other European jurisdictions) is that the Legal Aid Fund is expected to bear the bulk of the risk of loss if assisted parties are unsuccessful in their actions. However, for successful assisted parties legal aid is a loan, not a grant and should they be unable to recover the cost of their lawyer from the other side it will be deducted from their contributions and any winnings through the mechanism of the statutory charge;

7. Provided by Private Practitioners: the overwhelming majority of legal aid and advice and assistance is provided by private practitioners. * * * *

8. Open panel: hitherto assisted parties have had a very wide choice of lawyer to act for them in legal aid cases. This is a major advantage over the charitable model,

in that assisted parties can be represented by some of the best and most experienced court lawyers in the jurisdiction. Commentators have tended to see most of the features outlined above as strengths, stressing particularly the importance of state funding; independence; breadth of coverage; risk protection and choice. Nonetheless, viewed from the standpoint of the profession, consumers and the government there are also a number of weaknesses in the model. * * * *

C. The Salaried Model

There are relatively few jurisdictions in the western world (the United States of America and Quebec being the most prominent) in which the third or 'salaried' model of legal aid provision predominates. Nevertheless the model is to be found in a number of other western countries (including the United Kingdom, * * * Canada, Australia, New Zealand, Sweden and Finland). The essential difference from the judicare model is that the services are provided by publicly salaried lawyers. The latter are usually restricted in the range of services which they can provide. * * * * In Australia and the United Kingdom the limits are enshrined in formal agreements, elsewhere the programmes' own priorities ensure that rarely (except in Sweden) are they in competition with the private profession. In the United States of America the Legal Services Corporation salaried programmes are also banned from taking cases to do with school desegregation, abortion, or engaging in political activities such as picketing, striking, lobbying or working for political campaigns. It follows that the utility of salaried lawyer programmes to foreign applicants will be limited—particularly in damages or divorce cases which are typically left as the preserve of private practitioners. However in those instances where a foreign applicant's case can be dealt with by a law centre there is the added bonus that the service is provided free of charge.

D. The Mixed Model

Even though the experts are divided over the relative cost-effectiveness of the judicare and salaried models of legal aid, there is a remarkable measure of agreement between them that the ideal way forward for western countries is a model that involves a mixture of judicare and salaried elements. In that most of the jurisdictions with salaried programmes also have judicare programmes it might seem that the mixed model exists widely throughout the world. However, in most countries the two types of programme have developed independently in an ad hoc fashion. Genuinely planned and integrated examples of the mixed model, combining the best features of both models with respect to specialist expertise, work styles, client appeal etc., are few and far between. In Sweden, Quebec, [and to some degree Ireland, Ukraine, and Chile] the theoretical integration of the two models (the salaried offices assess all legal aid applications and allocate cases to private practitioners) has not worked in practice, partly because they are to an extent in competition with each other. This, in turn, leads to overlaps in coverage and the costly duplication of expertise. Instead, it is in the United Kingdom, Australia and Ontario that a division of labour has sprung up which emphasises the complementary nature of the two models— particularly where the strategic version of the salaried model is in evidence. But even in these jurisdictions developments have been largely unplanned. * * * *

D. THE ABA MODEL ACCESS TO JUSTICE ACT

ABA MODEL ACCESS TO JUSTICE ACT 104
AM. BAR ASS'N 2010

* * * *

SECTION 1. LEGISLATIVE FINDINGS

The [hypothetical Legislature of a state adopting the Model Access Act] finds and declares as follows:

A.   There is a substantial, and increasingly dire, need for civil legal services for the poor in this State. Due to insufficient funding from all sources, existing program resources for providing free legal services in civil matters to indigent persons cannot meet the existing need.

B.   A recent report from Legal Services Corporation, *Documenting the Justice Gap in America*, concludes that "only a fraction of the legal problems experienced by low income individuals is addressed with the help of an attorney." It also concludes that, "Nationally, on average, only one legal aid attorney is available to serve 6,415 low income individuals. In comparison, there is one private attorney providing personal legal services for every 429 individuals in the general population." The report further notes that the number of unrepresented litigants is increasing, particularly in family and housing courts.

C.   Fair and equal access to justice is a fundamental right in a democratic society. It is especially critical when an individual who is unable to afford legal representation is at risk of being deprived of certain basic human needs. * * * * Therefore, meaningful access to justice must be available to all persons, including those of limited means, when such basic needs are at stake. * * * *

E.   Many of those living in this State cannot afford to pay for the services of lawyers when needed for those residents to enjoy fair and equal access to justice. In order for them to enjoy this essential right of citizens when their basic human needs are at stake, the State government accepts its responsibility to provide them with lawyers at public expense.

F.   Providing legal representation to low-income persons at public expense will result in greater judicial efficiency by avoiding repeated appearances and delays caused by incomplete paperwork or unprepared litigants, will produce fairer outcomes, and will promote public confidence in the systems of justice.

G.   * * * This Act shall not supersede the local or national priorities of legal service programs in existence on the date that this Act is enacted. * * * *

SECTION 3. RIGHT TO PUBLIC LEGAL SERVICES.

A.   Subject to the exceptions and conditions set forth below, public legal services shall be available at State expense, upon application by a financially-eligible person, in any adversarial proceeding in a state trial or appellate court, a state administrative proceeding, or an arbitration hearing, in which basic human needs * * * are at stake. Depending on the circumstances described in the following Sections, appropriate public legal services may include full legal representation or limited scope representation as necessary for the person to obtain fair and equal access to justice for the particular dispute or problem that person confronts, including, where necessary, translation or other incidental services essential to achieving this goal.

B.   In a State trial or appellate court, administrative tribunal, or arbitration proceeding, whereby law or established practice parties may be represented only by a licensed legal professional, public legal services shall consist of full legal representation as defined herein, provided pursuant to the following conditions and with the following exceptions:

   i.   Full public legal representation services shall be available to a plaintiff or petitioner if a basic human need as defined herein is at stake and that person has a reasonable possibility of achieving a successful outcome. Full public legal representation services shall be available to a financially eligible defendant or respondent if a basic human need as defined herein is at stake, so long as the applicant has a non-frivolous defense.

Initial determinations of eligibility for services may be based on facial review of the application for assistance or the pleadings. However, the applicant shall be informed that any initial finding of eligibility is subject to a further review after a full investigation of the case has been completed. In family matters, the person seeking a change in either the de facto or de jure status quo shall be deemed the plaintiff and the person defending the status quo shall be deemed the defendant for purposes of this Act, regardless of their formal procedural status. However, any order awarding temporary custody pending resolution on the merits shall not alter which party is deemed to be the plaintiff and defendant in the case * * * *

ii.   Eligibility for full public legal representation services in State appellate courts is a new and different determination after the proceedings in a trial court or other forum conclude. If the financially eligible applicant is an appellant or equivalent, full legal representation services shall be available when there is a reasonable probability of success on appeal under existing law or when there is a non-frivolous argument for extending, modifying, or reversing existing law or for establishing new law. If the financially eligible applicant is a respondent or equivalent, however, full legal representation services shall be available unless there is no reasonable possibility the appellate court will affirm the decision of the trial court or other forum that the opposing party is challenging in the appellate court. In determining the likely outcome of the case, the Board shall take into account whether the record was developed without the benefit of counsel for the applicant.

iii. Irrespective of the provisions of Sections 3.B.i and 3B.ii above, full public legal representation services shall not be available to an applicant in the following circumstances:

a.   in proceedings in any forum where parties are not allowed to be represented by licensed legal professionals * * * *

b.   if legal representation is otherwise being provided to the applicant in the particular case, such as through existing civil legal aid programs, the services of a lawyer who provides such representation on a contingent fee basis, as the result of the provisions of an insurance policy, as part of a class action that will reasonably serve the legal interests of the applicant and that he or she is able to join * * * *

d. if under standards established by the Board, and under the circumstances of the particular matter, the Board deems a certain type and level of limited scope representation is sufficient to afford fair and equal access to justice and is sufficient to ensure that the basic human needs at stake in the proceeding are not jeopardized due to the absence of full representation by counsel * * * *

SECTION 4. STATE ACCESS BOARD.

A. There is established within the State judicial system an independent State Access Board ("Board") that shall have responsibility for policy-making and overall administration of the program defined in this Act, consistent with the provisions of this Act. * * * *

E. The Board shall:

i. Ensure that all eligible persons receive appropriate public legal services when needed in matters in which basic human needs * * * are at stake. It is the purpose and intent of this Section that the Board manage these services in a manner that is effective and cost-efficient, and that ensures recipients fair and equal access to justice.

ii. Establish, certify, and retain specific organizations to make eligibility determinations (including both financial eligibility and the applicable standard defined in Section 3.B hereof) and scope of service determinations pursuant to Section 3 hereof.

iii. Establish and administer a system that timely considers and decides appeals by applicants found ineligible for legal representation at public expense, or from decisions to provide only limited scope representation.

iv. Administer the State Access Fund established and defined in Section 5, which provides the funding for all public legal service representation needs required by this Act.

v. Inform the general public, especially population groups and geographic areas with large numbers of financially eligible persons, about their legal rights and responsibilities, and the availability of public legal representation, should they experience a problem involving a basic human need.

* * * *

SECTION 5. STATE ACCESS FUND.

A.   The State Access Fund supplies all the financial support needed for the services guaranteed by the provisions of this Act as well as the costs of administering the program established under this Act.

B.   In conjunction with preparation of the state judicial budget, the Board shall submit an estimate of anticipated costs and revenues for the forthcoming fiscal year and a request for an appropriation adequate to provide sufficient revenues to match the estimated costs. Annually thereafter, the Board shall provide the Governor, the Legislature, and the Judiciary with a status report of revenues and expenditures during the prior year. Within three months after the end of the state's fiscal year the Board shall submit to the Governor, the Legislature, and the Judiciary a request for the funds required from general revenues to make up the difference, if any, between revenues received and appropriated pursuant to the initial budget estimate and the obligations incurred in order to support the right defined in this law.

Notes and Questions

1.   In determining the scope of publicly funded legal services, the ABA Model Access Act provides for "*full legal representation or limited scope representation as necessary for the person to obtain fair and equal access to justice for the particular dispute or problem that person confronts . . .*". Does either the open-ended nature of the representation or the lack of a hard-financial cap concern you as impediments to state legislatures that may want to adopt the ABA Model Access Act? What safeguards against ballooning costs or unlimited representation of indigent clients do you see built into the Act? Would you add any other safeguards, caps, or limitations to entice budget-conscious state legislatures?

2.   In finding for a limited right to legal aid at state expense, Judge Moloto of the South African Land Claims Court reasons that effectuating constitutional and legislative land entitlements is structurally impossible without subsidized legal representation. As noted previously, the U.S. Supreme Court has refused to extend the Sixth Amendment right to state-appointed counsel to *civil* cases. Could other portions of the Constitution (beyond the Sixth Amendment) be used as the basis for recognizing a right to counsel?

3.   To date, no state has adopted the ABA Model Access to Justice Act; however, the Model Access Act has served as impetus for change at the local level. Virtually every state now provides a right to counsel in at least some civil areas, with the most common being child welfare, termination of parental rights and guardianship of adults, civil commitment, civil incarceration (in matters such as civil contempt for

failure to pay child support or court order fees/fines), and eviction. In addition, five cities now recognize a right to counsel. *See* https://perma.cc/7PEH-GLND. Some of these changes have been accomplished via litigation much like the *Nkuzi* decision, and some via legislation. *See* John Pollock, *The Case Against Case-By-Case: Courts Identifying Categorical Rights to Counsel in Basic Human Needs Civil Cases*, 61 DRAKE L.J. 763 (Spring 2013).

4.   States also address the access to civil justice problem through IOLTA programs ("interest on lawyer trust accounts"), established by the state bars or state bar foundations. These programs provide funding for civil legal services to the indigent and disadvantaged. More than 40 states and territories have also established Access to Justice Commissions. Generally created by state supreme court order, these commissions are collaborative entities that bring together courts, the bar, and civil legal aid providers to adopt a range of possible strategies aimed at removing barriers to civil justice for low income people. For a state by state comparison of these commissions (as of 2017/18), see https://perma.cc/QRF3-FDL2. The core function of access to justice commissions is to expand access to civil justice through three primary functions: (1) assessing civil legal needs, (2) developing strategies to meet those needs, and (3) evaluating progress.

5.   The *Nkuzi* decision makes clear that Section 25(6) of the South African Constitution, the Labor Tenants Act, and the ESTA are all part of a larger remedial scheme designed to remedy lingering structural and racial inequalities of the *Apartheid* era. Although the U.S. movement for a civil right to counsel often falls under the larger anti-poverty agenda, *see generally* Robert J. Derocher, *Access to Justice: Is Civil Gideon a Piece of the Puzzle?* 32 BAR LEADER, no. 6, July–Aug. 2008, at 11, might a similar argument be made in the United States that a right to counsel in civil cases is part of a larger imperative to remedy racial inequalities?

6.   As the *Nkuzi* decision recognizes, access to state-sponsored civil legal aid means little to poor and indigent plaintiffs if they remain unaware that they actually have such access. Assuming that a large amount of money is allocated each year in a developing nation for access-to-justice initiatives, how would you balance the percentage of funds that gets spent on lawyers versus, say, the percentage of funds that is used to publicize the availability of those lawyers? What modern methods of advertising civil legal aid should be used to reach indigent defendants? Where should they be deployed (e.g., the courthouse, local big box retail stores, Social Security Administration offices, the internet)?

7.   Paterson states that "there is a remarkable measure of agreement [among legal aid experts] that the ideal way forward for western countries is a model that involves a mixture of judicare and salaried elements." But does this supposed "expert" preference for a hybrid civil legal aid model actually reflect the best possible approaches

for western nations? What about nonlawyer representations? Until recently, the State of Washington had a limited license legal technicians' program, and Utah and Arizona are beginning conversations about one. In other countries, such as China, India, and Uganda, community paralegals and "barefoot lawyers" have long served an important role in social movements and civil justice. *See, e.g.,* https://perma.cc/3832-FHUR.

8. In conflating access to justice with access to lawyers and the courts, are we blinding ourselves to the fact that the legal problems of indigent defendants often start as (and are, in fact, easier to solve as) civil justice and poverty problems? Professor Katherine Wallat argues that such a change of reference is needed among access-to-justice advocates and the legal community more generally ("The conception of a problem as a legal one is a viewpoint that comes not from the people experiencing the problems but from the attorneys seeking to help solve them."). To Wallat, true access to justice can only take place before the matter gets to the courthouse door. Achieving equal access to justice, she argues, must be defined more broadly: achieving just and fair solutions as part of the larger fight against poverty. Katherine S. Wallat, *Reconceptualizing Access to Justice*, 103 MARQ. L. REV. (2019).

9. A more recent and controversial form of litigation financing is third-party funding of legal cases. Legal financing companies provide funding to litigants—usually plaintiffs—in exchange for a percentage of the judgment or settlement. The method started in Australia and the United Kingdom in the mid-1990s and entered the U.S. commercial market in the mid-2000s. Proponents of litigation funding say it levels the litigation playing field, but critics contend that litigation funding disrupts the legal process by bringing in an outside party that can potentially exert control, encouraging the filing of frivolous suits, and giving plaintiffs' attorneys an unfair advantage in settlement talks. Litigation financing companies have also used technology and algorithms to score court dockets to identify suitable clients. Mary Ellen Egan, *Other People's Money: Rise of Litigation Finance Companies Raises Legal and Ethical Concerns*, 104 A.B.A. J. 54 (2018).

Chapter 6

COMPARATIVE PLEADINGS

Every procedural system must decide how easy or difficult to make it for a litigant to get a dispute heard in court. Litigation normally commences with a statement of the dispute filed with the court along with notice to the opposing party. Yet, how detailed this filing must be often turns on a set of policy choices that reflects the role that civil litigation plays in the system and the trust the system places in the various actors within that system. Too lax a standard and the system is flooded with frivolous claims; too strict a standard and meritorious claims might be wrongly filtered out.

Until recently, the United States had one of the most relaxed pleading standards in the world. Most other countries require detailed fact pleading and often demand that the plaintiff produce evidentiary support at the outset. By contrast, Federal Rule of Civil Procedure 8 requires only "a short and plain statement of the claim showing that the pleader is entitled to relief." So long as the complaint gives some "notice" to the opposing party as to what the dispute is about, then under the Federal Rules the complaint is accepted by the court. Subsequent discovery is then used in the U.S. system as the primary mechanism to filter out non-meritorious claims.

China, by contrast, had one of the strictest and arguably most unpredictable filing requirements. Filing often meant an initial review by the court even before a case was accepted.

Interestingly, both countries in recent years have converged somewhat in their standards. Consider the following article:

MARGARET Y.K. WOO, *MANNING THE COURTHOUSE GATES: PLEADINGS, JURISDICTION, AND THE NATION-STATE*

15 NEV. L. J. 1261 (2015)

* * * *

A. Changing U.S. Pleadings Standards

* * * [C]ivil justice reforms in the United States have meant changes in summary judgment standards, discovery rules, and greater case management, all of which have led to a problematic decrease in the trial rate in the United States. Scholars argue that this has resulted in a democratic crisis because, "[s]ince the founding of our country, trials in open court resulting in decisions by either a judge or a jury have been thought to be constitutive of American democracy." The focus of these concerns is the absence of trials and determinations by juries—symbols of participation and democracy. This era of dramatic decreases in trials is what Professors Subrin and Main called "the fourth era of civil procedure."

While this "fourth era" is problematic in its decreased focus on trials, equally problematic is its focus on the process of disposing cases at the early stages of pre-filing and filing of complaints. While the trial event is important in ensuring transparency and publicity and its deprivation is cause for alarm, the deprivation of court access at the complaint stage is similarly—and maybe even more—critical. Closing the courthouse gate decreases democratic participation when litigants' voices are filtered out of the court system from the start.
* * * *

There have been numerous procedural reforms, but none more problematic than narrowing pleading requirements. The reason is that pleading rules distribute power between litigants and judges, individuals and the state. Pleading rules may vary depending upon the role civil litigation serves in a particular system at a particular juncture—be it private conflict resolution, social control, or democratic participation. In the United States, the liberal pleading rules encompassed in the original Federal Rules of Civil Procedure meant access to courts and an opportunity for ordinary citizens to participate in the application of top-down norms. In allowing the control of the lawsuit to rest with private litigants, liberal pleading is one way to balance against concentrated state power, even as the federal courts grew. * * * *

Yet, in recent years, the philosophy of allowing liberal pleadings has changed. Federal district courts have been told by the Supreme Court to become more aggressive gatekeepers, clearing dockets without the opportunity for discovery or trials. While in the past, the gatekeeping function of district judges was limited to an initial determination of "jurisdiction, ripeness, mootness, political questions, immunity, abstention," and a determination of whether the complainant has articulated "any" grounds for relief, the Supreme Court has now turned district judges into gatekeepers, with heightened pleading standards in a variety of settings. The Supreme Court's *Iqbal*, *Twombly*, and *Dukes* decisions have dismissed cases with an early initial assessment of the "plausibility" of the plaintiff's claims and requests for class certification.

This narrowing of the pleading requirement is problematic not only because it can deprive private litigants of their rights of action, but also because as an institutional barrier, it closes off the courthouse gate at such an initial stage that it prevents participation, a component of democracy. While trials ensure greater transparency and publicity, complaints are the entry to the courthouse itself, and denial means the denial of access to the entire court process. Unlike the "notice" pleading standard, which was relatively clear in deeming all complaints sufficient so long as they provided notice to the defendant of the underlying disputes, the present new standard of "plausibility" is highly discretionary and places broader authority and control in the hands of federal judges. The present pleading standard of "plausibility" gives judges greater discretion in deciding what goes in and what goes out, discretion that can be based on judges' personal conceptions of the plausibility of plaintiff's version of the facts and, more problematically, can be tainted by judges' political orientations and agendas. Rather than limiting the power of the judge, the new "plausibility" pleading standard expands the power of judges and takes away from the power of the litigant to have his case heard.

Given the context of broad federal court jurisdiction, empowering judges to assess the complaint under such a discretionary standard could mean greater [governmental] control in deciding what comes in and what stays out of court. * * * *

B.   *Recent Chinese Procedural Reforms*

The Chinese story is slightly different and yet all too similar. While law may be used to promote "socialism with Chinese characteristics," rather than democracy, recent changes to civil procedure in China also narrow entry to the courts and, in so doing, challenge the underlying goal of the system itself, with the most recent goal being to promote social harmony and stability.

In the race to achieve global parity with other developed nations, China has also added to its great internal [economic] inequality.

* * * *. With disparity has come greater unrest, as Chinese citizens have taken to the courts problems ranging from land confiscation to inadequate social security to labor and employment disputes. From 1991 to 2010, the number of civil first instance cases accepted by the Chinese courts increased at an annual rate of more than 10 percent. Faced with rising caseloads and more complex cases, overworked Chinese judges would sometimes avoid cases and fail to docket them at filing. When litigants failed to get satisfaction from the courts, they took to the streets, and the number of protests increased.

To counter the greater discontent in the general population, then-President Hu Jintao and the Chinese Communist Party in 2006 formally endorsed a political doctrine that called for the creation of a "harmonious society" (*héxié shèhuì*). It is a policy that signals a movement away from sole reliance on economic reform to solve worsening social tensions and, to some critics, towards an avenue to maintain stability at all costs. Notably, the call for "socialist harmonious society" comes at a time when China is striving to achieve international prominence and state building. According to some, the call for harmony also reflects a return to traditional Confucian values and a national emphasis on "order over freedom, duties over rights, and group interests over individual ones."

It is within this context of addressing problems of social instability, nation-building, and public dissatisfaction with the work of the courts that * * * [these] civil justice reforms in China must be understood. As mentioned above, with growing social unrest and discontent, China saw an increase in letters of complaint, as well as rising numbers of petitions (a method of seeking review of cases after final appeals). Government officials attributed this rise in petitions to the courts' inability to resolve disputes, as well as increased corruption and graft in the courts. Concerned that the courts were unable to contain social discord and fearing a loss of legitimacy for the party state, the Chinese government equated improved legal work with greater consideration of the social and political context of cases and commenced another round of judicial reforms.

Beginning in the mid-2000s, China initiated the first sets of major amendments to the Chinese civil procedure code since its enactment. [These] * * * amendments simultaneously empower and limit the courts. They empower the courts vis-à-vis the litigants but limit the court vis-à-vis the party state. They provide greater authority to courts to streamline cases but also ensure greater oversight of courts by other judicial institutions.

The resultant procedural amendments retreat from the move toward an adversarial process and return to an emphasis on judicial control of litigation and the encouragement of mediation. Under the call of "harmonious society," the * * * civil procedure amendments retain the judge's discretion to not accept cases, reemphasize mediation over adjudication, and establish a multi-tracked case management system to divert cases.

Under these amendments, Chinese courts continue the rule that the judge must decide whether or not to accept the case within seven days. * * * [A] complaint [must] meet four conditions—a qualified plaintiff; a definite defendant; specific claims, facts, and causes of action; and * * * the complaint [must] fall within the scope of acceptance for civil actions by the people's court and within the jurisdiction of the people's court where the suit is filed. All four conditions, but in particular the condition requiring "specific claims, facts, and causes of action," are left undefined, with interpretation resting in the discretion of the court. Since it is not obligatory for defendants to file a statement of defense, the plaintiffs must satisfy the judge, rather than the defendant, that they have enough evidence to get the case docketed. Significantly, the rules do not provide an opportunity for the plaintiff to respond or argue his case. It is simply when the judge is satisfied with the complaint that the complaint is served on the defendant. Thereafter, the case filing division will also attempt to mediate the case.

Both because of the piling up of cases and limited judicial resources, the case filing division has the incentive to avoid controversial cases that will consume a great deal of judicial time and energy. This discretion has led courts to deny acceptance to cases that they view as troublesome and politically sensitive. * * * * Some courts * * * even issued directives stating that certain categories of cases (land and labor disputes) would not be accepted temporarily. At one point, * * * the Supreme People's Court instructed lower courts not to accept certain civil cases, including those challenging controversial property confiscation and compensation.

Notes and Questions

1.   Procedural reforms within a country's legal system are more than attempts to increase efficiency and reduce the costs of litigation. They also reflect a dialectic between law and political or cultural goals. Notice that, although the United States and China may be pursuing entirely different goals, both utilize procedure as a way to embody political and cultural values. Procedural systems in each country reaffirm a commitment to the underlying goals of nation-building, whether that means the strengthening of democracy, the pursuit of economic efficiency, or the promotion of social harmony. The question, then, is whether procedural reforms in these countries adequately

address their intended ends. Consider how both a country's history *and* its aspirations may work together to influence what procedural reform looks like. In what ways are the paths of the United States and China, in terms of their process of modifying procedure, similar and different? What might explain these similarities and differences?

2.   In both China and the United States, the pleading process remains and/or has become increasingly bent to the subjective will of judges. But is that such a bad thing? After all, whether judges receive training bureaucratically or through practice at the Bar, they have an eye for the law. The German context might suggest a possible middle-ground between China's state-controlled pleading regime and the more party-controlled regime of the U.S. system. In Germany, judges engage in *Richterliche Hinweispflicht*—a process by which judges provide "hints and feedback" to the litigants to narrow the scope of the legal and factual issues involved in the case. This process is described below:

ROBERT W. EMERSON, *JUDGES AS GUARDIAN ANGELS: THE GERMAN PRACTICE OF HINTS AND FEEDBACK*

48 VAND. J. TRANSNAT'L L. 707 (2015)

* * * *

Germany is a civil law system, rather than a common law system such as America. Since a successful reform movement in the late nineteenth century, the German legal system has been dominated by codes and legislation. Because judicial decisions other than those made by the Federal Constitutional Court are not considered a source of law in Germany, judges are not bound by precedent or a body of case law. In theory, German judges are to apply, rather than create, law and are strictly bound to decide cases in deference to codified law. However, because young judges' performances are evaluated by their superiors (more tenured judges), there is a tendency for judges to rely on precedent to avoid having their decisions reversed at a higher level—therefore receiving good "reviews" of their performance. Nonetheless, many cases involve factual circumstances under which straightforward application of the law becomes difficult; consequently, judges must engage in some degree of interpretation and creativity.

The judiciary in Germany is a career wholly separate from that of the attorney. Those entering the judiciary receive special judicial training and education, as is the practice in other civil law nations such as France. German judges, though highly respected, do not enjoy the same level of public veneration as American judges for many reasons: they are more numerous; they start younger; they do some of the "grunt work" that American judges leave to other civil servants; and, most importantly, they are not considered creators of law. In line with the inquisitorial nature of German judicial proceedings, judges conduct most of the witness interrogations in civil litigation. The parties' attorneys may ask follow-up questions of a witness after the judge has finished his or her examination in order to object to the judge's summation of the witness's testimony, comment on the court-appointed expert's report, or offer other experts to challenge the opinion of the court-appointed expert. German judges also create the record of the case by periodically dictating summaries of events into the record. They are able to take on these more labor-intensive tasks because there are more judges per capita than in any other state in the world, and because they have probationary and associate judges to assist them.

In Germany, there are no juries in civil trials, eliminating the need for a concentrated trial. In America, litigation is conducted in stages leading up to a single trial that is concentrated into an uninterrupted period of days or weeks. In theory, the trial needs to be concentrated because it is staged for a jury. All stages of litigation prior to the trial are for the purpose of preparing for the trial. However, as mentioned earlier, the vast majority of cases in the United States settle or are disposed of prior to trial. This means that a jury trial is more of a threat or a bargaining chip than an impending reality. The Seventh Amendment right to a jury trial remains theoretically intact but has been eroded in practice by systems of resolving disputes that steer parties away from expensive jury trials. Because of the high number of cases that settle out of court and the large number of parties that consent to a bench trial, the U.S. system may be closer than initially apparent to the German system of no jury trials for civil disputes.

Interestingly, the German and U.S. systems seem to have switched roles over time. * * * U.S. civil procedure has historically had an inquisitorial component in the courts of equity, while early German civil procedure was much more like the contemporary U.S. party-controlled system. In early German law, parties were left to decide the context of the pleadings and the time of submissions. Thus, like in the United States, parties had a great deal of control over the length of legal proceedings. However, because this practice led to very long proceedings, the principle of party control (Grundsatz der Parteiherrschaft) is "now more generally restricted by a greater responsibility imposed on the court to conduct proceedings."

Until 2007, the parties in American procedure were not required to make specific factual allegations during the pleadings phase, but only had to put each other on notice of the basic claims and defenses they would seek to prove at trial. Then, during the discovery and disclosure phases of the litigation, parties gathered and exchanged documentary and testimonial evidence they would later use to support and prove their claims at trial. The nature of the pleadings stage has recently changed, as evidenced by the 2007 U.S. Supreme Court decision regarding antitrust conspiracy claims in *Bell Atlantic Corp. v. Twombly*, which replaced a liberal pleadings standard (in existence since 1957) with a fact-pleading standard. *Twombly* was followed by the 2009 decision *Ashcroft v. Iqbal*, which extended *Twombly* beyond the realm of antitrust and imposed a "plausibility" standard for fact-based pleading under Federal Rule of Civil Procedure 8(a)(2). With these two decisions, American courts have moved closer to their European counterparts. In fact, these decisions may make it more likely that the United States will accept the ALI/UNIDROIT proposed pleading standard, which reads, "[i]n the pleading phase, the parties must present in reasonable detail the relevant facts, their contentions of law, and the relief requested, and describe with sufficient specification the available evidence to be offered in support of their allegations."

In Germany, cases can be tried in a series of hearings. Intensive pretrial preparation is not necessary. If it becomes clear that additional proof is needed on a particular matter, the parties can simply schedule an additional hearing to adjudicate the sufficiency of the evidence. The parties initiate the case by pleading the facts with specificity and going into detail about the events that gave rise to the legal claims. From there, the case proceeds with a series of hearings and adjournments as more information is needed or requested. Because of the recent U.S. decisions mentioned above, the civil suit in the United States must be pled with specificity or run the risk of a dismissal. In contrast, although the pleading standard is higher and based on fact-pleading in Germany, the judge has more authority to gather the facts necessary to decide the claim because of the more inquisitorial nature of the process. The German judge, as fact-gatherer, may proceed with the facts and issues in a case in a way that disposes of them in a certain order, thus giving the court more power to shape the case and understand the facts before making a decision. * * * *

[The German Code of Civil Procedure] provides as follows:

(1) The court must, to the extent necessary, discuss with the parties the facts and issues in dispute from a factual and legal perspective. It must cause the parties to explain themselves promptly and completely as to all material facts, particularly in order to supplement insufficient data as to relevant facts, to designate means of proof, and to set forth pertinent claims.

(2) The court may base its decision on an aspect that a party has apparently ignored or considered insignificant only if the aspect does not concern an ancillary claim, and the court has given hints and feedback regarding that aspect and given an opportunity to address it. The same applies for an aspect that the court assesses differently than both parties.

(3) The court must call attention to its concerns as to those points which the court takes into account ex officio.

(4) Hints and feedback made according to this rule are to be given and documented on record as early as possible. The fact that hints and feedback were given may be proved only by reference to the content of the record. Only evidence of forgery may contradict the record.

(5) If an immediate response by a party to judicial hints and feedback is not possible, then the court should, upon that party's request, determine a period of time in which the party can respond in a written statement.

As noted in the article excerpted above, the American Law Institute (ALI), in combination with the International Institute for the Unification of Private Law (UNIDROIT), initiated at the turn of the twenty-first century a major effort to harmonize civil procedure rules. This effort resulted in the ALI/UNIDROIT Principles of Transnational Civil Procedure. The Principles, as explained in Principle 1 "are standards for adjudication of transnational commercial disputes. [They] may be equally appropriate for adjudication of other kinds of civil disputes and may be the basis for future initiatives in reforming civil procedure." As you can see from the excerpt below, these principles stopped short of specifying a single standard regarding just how detailed a pleading should be. Rather, the emphasis is on the autonomy of the party. Thus, the proceeding should be initiated through the claims of the plaintiff, not by the initiative of the court. Further, the scope of the proceeding is determined by the parties through their pleadings.

PRINCIPLES OF TRANSNATIONAL
CIVIL PROCEDURE

Am. Law Inst. & UNIDROIT, 2004

10. PARTY INITIATIVE AND SCOPE
OF THE PROCEEDING

10.1 The proceeding should be initiated through the claim or claims of the plaintiff, not by the court acting on its own motion.

10.2 The time of lodging the complaint with the court determines compliance with statutes of limitation, lis pendens, and other requirements of timeliness.

10.3 The scope of the proceeding is determined by the claims and defenses of the parties in the pleadings, including amendments.

10.4 A party, upon showing good cause, has a right to amend its claims or defenses upon notice to other parties, and when doing so does not unreasonably delay the proceeding or otherwise result in injustice.

10.5 The parties should have a right to voluntary termination or modification of the proceeding or any part of it, by withdrawal, admission, or settlement. A party should not be permitted unilaterally to terminate or modify the action when prejudice to another party would result.

Comment:

P–10A   All modern legal systems recognize the principle of party initiative concerning the scope and particulars of the dispute. It is within the framework of party initiative that the court carries out its responsibility for just adjudication. See Principles 10.3 and 28.2. These Principles require the parties to provide details of fact and law in their contentions. See Principle 11.3. This practice contrasts with the more loosely structured system of "notice pleading" in American procedure.

P–10B   All legal systems impose time limits for commencement of litigation, called statutes of limitation in common-law systems and prescription in civil-law systems. Service of process must be completed or attempted within a specified time after commencement of the proceeding, according to forum law. Most systems allow for an objection that service of process was not completed or attempted within a specified time after commencement of the proceeding.

P–10C　The right to amend a pleading is very restricted in some legal systems. However, particularly in transnational disputes, the parties should be accorded some flexibility, particularly when new or unexpected evidence is confronted. Adverse effect on other parties from exercise of the right of amendment may be avoided or moderated by an adjournment or continuance, or adequately compensated by an award of costs.

P–10D　The forum law may permit a claimant to introduce a new claim by amendment even though it is time-barred (statute of limitations or prescription), provided it arises from substantially the same facts as those that underlie the initial claim.

P–10E　Most jurisdictions do not permit a plaintiff to discontinue an action after an initial phase of the proceeding over the objection of the defendant.

Notes and Questions

1.　A strict requirement of "fact pleading" can over-deter plaintiffs. If plaintiffs do not (or in some cases cannot) know some of the facts of their case from the outset, they are unable to plead those facts and could be denied the ability ever to discover or introduce evidence relating to such facts. For example, one scholarly examination of the Scottish pleading system in personal injury cases concludes that overly rigid fact pleading requirements skewed procedural systems in favor of repeat institutional defendants and against individual plaintiffs. Elizabeth Thornburg, *Detailed Fact Pleadings: Lessons from Scottish Civil Procedure*, 36 INT'L LAW. 1185 (2002). The problem is even worse if the claim is for private discrimination or is against the Government, and the evidence needed to prove the case is uniquely in the hands of the defendant. Then, there is very little ability for plaintiffs to plead and prove enough facts at the outset of the case, absent access to discovery. In light of these concerns, what other procedural mechanisms might be warranted if a system adopts a more detailed fact-pleading regime?

2.　A major 1976 study asked individuals in both the United States and Germany to judge 12 models of procedure, to state their preferences regarding the procedures, and to evaluate the characteristics of the models. The results suggest that participants prefer to control the process of evidence presentation themselves, while a third party controls the result. *See* Stephen LaTour et al., *Procedure: Transnational Perspectives and Preferences*, 86 YALE L. J. 258 (1976). If litigants overall prefer controlling the process of the litigation, would undermining party-controlled pleading also undermine the legitimacy of the litigation process?

3.　Comment P–10A of the ALI/UNIDROIT Principles for Transnational Procedure declares that "all modern legal systems recognize the principle of party initiative concerning the scope and particulars of the dispute. It is within the framework of party initiatives that the court carries out the responsibility for just adjudication." Does this comment assume equal access to good legal assistance for civil litigants? What if such legal assistance is unavailable? Should a lawsuit depend on the efforts of the best lawyer money can buy? What is the obligation, if any, of a legal system to step in and assist in the litigation?

4.   It is worth noting that the proposed ALI/UNIDROIT pleading rules have yet to be adopted by any legal system anywhere in the world. Why do you think that is? In general, do you think it would be better to create harmonized international pleading regimes, or do you think it makes sense for different legal systems to maintain different approaches to pleading?

Chapter 7

SERVICE UPON FOREIGN DEFENDANTS

The service of a summons and complaint formally notifies the defendant of the filing of an action. Service is also an exercise of a court's authority, because process demands a response from the defendant. In the United States, Federal Rule of Civil Procedure 4 details the provisions regarding service of process on various types of defendants and service in various locations, and it includes provisions for service on foreign defendants. Under Rule 4 service on domestic defendants may be executed by private process servicer and even by mail, if the parties agree. Most civil law jurisdictions, by contrast, consider process to be a judicial act to be performed by official, public authorities with more formality. This distinction may mean that private means of service or service by mail may in some countries be perceived as an infringement on state sovereignty by the state where service is effectuated.

To ease disputes over service of legal documents in cross-border cases, two international conventions were established to which the United States is a party: Service Abroad of Judicial and Extrajudicial Documents in Civil or Commercial Matters ("Hague Service Convention") and the Inter-American Convention on Letters Rogatory, and Additional Protocol ("Inter-American Service Convention"). Both conventions facilitate ease of international judicial assistance. While the Hague Service Convention provides a uniform framework for serving a summons and complaint in civil or commercial cases upon defendants located in any of the dozens of Contracting States, the Inter-American Service Convention is for the legal service of documents only.

A primary purpose of the Hague Service Convention is to require signatory states to designate a Central Authority that can handle cross-border service requests. In the United States, The Office of International Judicial Assistance (OIJA) of the Department of Justice serves as the U.S. Central Authority. OIJA also serves as the Central Authority pursuant to the Inter-American Service Convention for purposes of legal service of documents. In addition,

OIJA handles service requests received from non-Convention States through diplomatic channels. Since 2003, however, the Department of Justice has delegated its function as the Central Authority with respect to the service of judicial and extrajudicial documents directed at individuals and companies in the United States to a private contractor to effectuate service. Requests for service on the United States Government, which includes its departments, agencies, or instrumentalities, remain with OIJA.

The Hague Service Convention framework is relatively straight-forward, and the Convention is generally considered to have been a success. The Hague Service Convention authorizes, but does not require, use of the Central Authority method, however. The Convention permits several other methods of service, such as via consular agents, and it also permits signatory countries to authorize still other methods via bilateral agreements or international law. For cases that fall within the scope of the Hague Service Convention, service must be completed through one of several delineated methods. These alternative methods help to bridge the different requirements of various systems. Regardless of the method used, it is important to note that service abroad as a general matter is a fraught process, demanding considerable time and resources.

HAGUE CONVENTION ON THE SERVICE ABROAD OF JUDICIAL AND EXTRAJUDICIAL DOCUMENTS IN CIVIL OR COMMERCIAL MATTERS ("HAGUE SERVICE CONVENTION")

Nov. 15, 1965, [1969] 20 U.S.T. 361

Article 1

The present Convention shall apply in all cases, in civil or commercial matters, where there is occasion to transmit a judicial or extrajudicial document for service abroad.

This Convention shall not apply where the address of the person to be served with the document is not known.

Article 2

Each Contracting State shall designate a Central Authority which will undertake to receive requests for service coming from other Contracting States and to proceed in conformity with the provisions of Articles 3 to 6.

Each State shall organise the Central Authority in conformity with its own law.

Article 3

The authority or judicial officer competent under the law of the State in which the documents originate shall forward to the Central Authority of the State addressed a request conforming to the model annexed to the present Convention, without any requirement of legalisation or other equivalent formality.

The document to be served or a copy thereof shall be annexed to the request. The request and the document shall both be furnished in duplicate.

Article 4

If the Central Authority considers that the request does not comply with the provisions of the present Convention it shall promptly inform the applicant and specify its objections to the request.

Article 5

The Central Authority of the State addressed shall itself serve the document or shall arrange to have it served by an appropriate agency, either—

a)   by a method prescribed by its internal law for the service of documents in domestic actions upon persons who are within its territory, or

b)   by a particular method requested by the applicant, unless such a method is incompatible with the law of the State addressed. * * * *

Article 6

The Central Authority of the State addressed or any authority which it may have designated for that purpose, shall complete a certificate in the form of the model annexed to the present Convention.

The certificate shall state that the document has been served and shall include the method, the place and the date of service and the person to whom the document was delivered. If the document has not been served, the certificate shall set out the reasons which have prevented service. * * * *

Article 8

Each Contracting State shall be free to effect service of judicial documents upon persons abroad, without application of any compulsion, directly through its diplomatic or consular agents.

Any State may declare that it is opposed to such service within its territory, unless the document is to be served upon a national of the State in which the documents originate.

Article 9

Each Contracting State shall be free, in addition, to use consular channels to forward documents, for the purpose of service, to those authorities of another Contracting State which are designated by the latter for this purpose.

Each Contracting State may, if exceptional circumstances so require, use diplomatic channels for the same purpose.

Article 10

Provided the State of destination does not object, the present Convention shall not interfere with—

(a) the freedom to send judicial documents, by postal channels, directly to persons abroad,

(b) the freedom of judicial officers, officials or other competent persons of the State of origin to effect service of judicial documents directly through the judicial officers, officials or other competent persons of the State of destination,

(c) the freedom of any person interested in a judicial proceeding to effect service of judicial documents directly through the judicial officers, officials or other competent persons of the State of destination.

Article 11

The present Convention shall not prevent two or more Contracting States from agreeing to permit, for the purpose of service of judicial documents, channels of transmission other than those provided for in the preceding Articles and, in particular, direct communication between their respective authorities. * * * *

Article 13

Where a request for service complies with the terms of the present Convention, the State addressed may refuse to comply therewith only if it deems that compliance would infringe its sovereignty or security.

It may not refuse to comply solely on the ground that, under its internal law, it claims exclusive jurisdiction over the subject-matter of the action or that its internal law would not permit the action upon which the application is based.

The Central Authority shall, in case of refusal, promptly inform the applicant and state the reasons for the refusal. * * * *

Article 19

To the extent that the internal law of a Contracting State permits methods of transmission, other than those provided for in the preceding Articles, of documents coming from abroad, for service within its territory, the present Convention shall not affect such provisions. * * * *

For cases that fall within the scope of the Hague Service Convention, the presumption is that service must be completed through one of the channels delineated in the Convention, unless judges can identify a reason why those channels should not be applicable. However, as can be seen in the following case, there has been some controversy as to when the Convention actually applies:

VOLKSWAGENWERK AKTIENGESELLSCHAFT V. SCHLUNK

Supreme Court of the United States, 1988
486 U.S. 694

O'CONNOR, J.

This case involves an attempt to serve process on a foreign corporation by serving its domestic subsidiary which, under state law, is the foreign corporation's involuntary agent for service of process. We must decide whether such service is compatible with the Convention on Service Abroad of Judicial and Extrajudicial Documents in Civil and Commercial Matters, Nov. 15, 1965 (Hague Service Convention), [1969] 20 U.S.T. 361, T. I. A. S. No. 6638.

I

After his parents were killed in an automobile accident, respondent filed a wrongful death action in an Illinois court, alleging that defects in the automobile designed and sold by Volkswagen of America, Inc. (VWoA), in which the parents were driving, caused or contributed to their deaths. When VWoA's answer denied that it had designed or assembled the vehicle, respondent amended his complaint to add as a defendant petitioner here (VWAG), a German corporation which is the sole owner of VWoA. Respondent attempted to serve the amended complaint on VWAG by serving VWoA as VWAG's agent. Filing a special and limited appearance, VWAG moved to quash the service on the grounds that it could be served only in accordance with the Hague Service Convention and that respondent had not complied with the Convention's requirements. The court denied the motion, reasoning that VWoA and VWAG are so closely related that VWoA is VWAG's agent for service of process as a matter of law, notwithstanding VWAG's failure or refusal to appoint VWoA formally as an agent. The court concluded that, because service was accomplished in this country, the Convention did not apply. The Appellate Court of Illinois affirmed, ruling that the Illinois long-arm statute authorized substituted service on VWoA, and that such service did not violate the Convention.

Article 1 defines the scope of the Convention, which is the subject of controversy in this case. It says: "The present Convention shall apply in all cases, in civil or commercial matters, where there is occasion to transmit a judicial or extrajudicial document for service abroad." 20 U.S. T., at 362. * * * * This language is mandatory, as we acknowledged last Term in *Société Nationale Industrielle Aérospatiale v. United States District Court*, 482 U.S. 522, 534, n. 15 (1987). By virtue of the Supremacy Clause, U.S. Const., Art. VI, the Convention pre-empts inconsistent methods of service prescribed by state law in all cases to which it applies. Schlunk does not purport to have served his complaint on VWAG in accordance with the Convention. Therefore, if service of process in this case falls within Article 1 of the Convention, the trial court should have granted VWAG's motion to quash.

When interpreting a treaty, we "begin 'with the text of the treaty and the context in which the written words are used.'" *Société Nationale, supra*, at 534 (quoting *Air France v. Saks*, 470 U.S. 392, 397 (1985)). Other general rules of construction may be brought to bear on difficult or ambiguous passages. "'Treaties are construed more liberally than private agreements, and to ascertain their meaning we may look beyond the written words to the history of the treaty, the negotiations, and the practical construction adopted by the parties.'" *Air France v. Saks, supra*, at 396 (quoting *Choctaw Nation of Indians v. United States*, 318 U.S. 423, 431–432 (1943)). The Convention does not specify the circumstances in which there is "occasion to transmit" a complaint "for service abroad." But at least the term "service of process" has a well-established technical meaning. Service of process refers to a formal delivery of documents that is legally sufficient to charge the defendant with notice of a pending action. The legal sufficiency of a formal delivery of documents must be measured against some standard. The Convention does not prescribe a standard, so we almost necessarily must refer to the internal law of the forum state. If the internal law of the forum state defines the applicable method of serving process as requiring the transmittal of documents abroad, then the Hague Service Convention applies. * * * *

The negotiating history of the Convention also indicates that whether there is service abroad must be determined by reference to the law of the forum state. The preliminary draft said that the Convention would apply "where there are grounds" to transmit a judicial document to a person staying abroad. The committee that prepared the preliminary draft realized that this implied that the forum's internal law would govern whether service implicated the Convention. The reporter expressed regret about this solution because it would decrease the obligatory force of the Convention. Nevertheless, the delegates did not change the meaning of Article 1 in this respect. * * * *

VWAG correctly maintains that the Convention also aims to ensure that there will be adequate notice in cases in which there is occasion to serve process abroad. Thus, compliance with the Convention is mandatory in all cases to which it applies, and Articles 15 and 16 provide an indirect sanction against those who ignore it. Our interpretation of the Convention does not necessarily advance this particular objective, inasmuch as it makes recourse to the convention's means of service dependent on the forum's internal law. But we do not think that this country, or any other country, will draft its internal laws deliberately so as to circumvent the Convention in cases in which it would be appropriate to transmit judicial documents for service abroad. For example, there has been no question in this country of excepting foreign nationals from the protection of our Due Process Clause. Under that Clause, foreign nationals are assured of either personal service, which typically will require service abroad and trigger the Convention, or substituted service that provides "notice reasonably calculated, under all the circumstances, to apprise interested parties of the pendency of the action and afford them an opportunity to present their objections." *Mullane v. Central Hanover Bank & Trust Co.*, 339 U.S. 306, 314 (1950).

Furthermore, nothing that we say today prevents compliance with the Convention even when the internal law of the forum does not so require. The Convention provides simple and certain means by which to serve process on a foreign national. Those who eschew its procedures risk discovering that the forum's internal law required transmittal of documents for service abroad, and that the Convention therefore provided the exclusive means of valid service. In addition, parties that comply with the Convention ultimately may find it easier to enforce their judgments abroad. For these reasons, we anticipate that parties may resort to the Convention voluntarily, even in cases that fall outside the scope of its mandatory application. * * * *

Where service on a domestic agent is valid and complete under both state law and the Due Process Clause, our inquiry ends, and the Convention has no further implications. Whatever internal, private communications take place between the agent and a foreign principal are beyond the concerns of this case. The only transmittal to which the Convention applies is a transmittal abroad that is required as a necessary part of service. And, contrary to VWAG's assertion, the Due Process Clause does not require an official transmittal of documents abroad every time there is service on a foreign national. Applying this analysis, we conclude that this case does not present an occasion to transmit a judicial document for service abroad within the meaning of Article 1. Therefore the Hague Service Convention does not apply, and service was proper. * * * *

Notes and Questions

1.   Does *Schlunk* faithfully implement the letter and spirit of the Hague Service Convention? Isn't it inconsistent with the purpose of the Convention to interpret it as applicable only when the internal law of the forum requires service abroad?

2.   FRCP 4(f)(1) specifically acknowledges the Hague Service Convention. FRCP 4(f)(2)(C) further provides for personal service and international registered mail as additional methods of service, unless they are prohibited by the laws of the foreign country. If personal service is used, then a foreign lawyer or agency that has effectuated service may execute an affidavit of service at the nearest U.S. embassy or consulate.

3.   FRCP 4(f)(3) states that service in a foreign country may be accomplished "by other means not prohibited by international agreement, as the court orders." This language generated considerable confusion. Does FRCP 4(f)(3) authorize service by mail? Does the Hague Service Convention prohibit this method of service? Is FRCP 4(f)(3) a safety value only available when the Convention, by its own terms, does not apply? The U.S. Supreme Court addressed these questions in the following case.

WATERSPLASH, INC. V. MENON

Supreme Court of the United States, 2017
137 S. Ct. 1504

ALITO, J.

This case concerns the scope of the Convention on the Service Abroad of Judicial and Extrajudicial Documents in Civil and Commercial Matters, Nov. 15, 1965 (Hague Service Convention). The purpose of that multilateral treaty is to simplify, standardize, and generally improve the process of serving documents abroad. To that end, the Hague Service Convention specifies certain approved methods of service and "pre-empts inconsistent methods of service" wherever it applies. Today we address a question that has divided the lower courts: whether the Convention prohibits service by mail. We hold that it does not.

I

A

Petitioner Water Splash is a corporation that produces aquatic playground systems. Respondent Menon is a former employee of Water Splash. In 2013, Water Splash sued Menon in state court in Texas, alleging that she had begun working for a competitor while still employed by Water Splash. Water Splash asserted several causes of action, including unfair competition, conversion, and tortious interference with business relations. Because Menon resided in Canada, Water Splash sought and obtained permission to effect service by mail. After Menon declined to answer or otherwise enter an appearance, the trial court issued a default judgment in favor of Water Splash. Menon moved to set aside the judgment on the ground that she had not been properly served, but the trial court denied the motion. Menon appealed, arguing that service by mail does not "comport with the requirements of the Hague Service Convention." * * * *

B

The "primary innovation" of the Hague Service Convention—set out in Articles 2–7—is that it "requires each state to establish a central authority to receive requests for service of documents from other countries." *Schlunk, supra*, at 698. When a central authority receives an appropriate request, it must serve the documents or arrange for their service, Art. 5, and then provide a certificate of service, Art. 6.

Submitting a request to a central authority is not, however, the only method of service approved by the Convention. For example, Article 8 permits service through diplomatic and consular agents; Article 11 provides that any two states can agree to methods of service not otherwise specified in the Convention; and Article 19 clarifies that the Convention does not preempt any internal laws of its signatories that permit service from abroad via methods not otherwise allowed by the Convention.

At issue in this case is Article 10 of the Convention, the English text of which reads as follows:

"Provided the State of destination does not object, the present Convention shall not interfere with—

"(a) the freedom to send judicial documents, by postal channels, directly to persons abroad,

"(b) the freedom of judicial officers, officials or other competent persons of the State of origin to effect service of judicial documents directly through the judicial officers, officials or other competent persons of the State of destination,

"(c) the freedom of any person interested in a judicial proceeding to effect service of judicial documents directly through the judicial officers, officials or other competent persons of the State of destination." 20 U.S.T., at 363.

Articles 10(b) and 10(c), by their plain terms, address additional methods of service that are permitted by the Convention (unless the receiving state objects). By contrast, Article 10(a) does not expressly refer to "service." The question in this case is whether, despite this textual difference, the Article 10(a) phrase "send judicial documents" encompasses sending documents *for the purposes of service.*

II

A

* * * * For present purposes, the key word in Article 10(a) is "send." This is a broad term,[1] and there is no apparent reason why it would exclude the transmission of documents for a particular purpose (namely, service). Moreover, the structure of the Hague Service Convention strongly counsels against such a reading.

The key structural point is that the scope of the Convention is limited to service of documents. Several elements of the Convention indicate as much. First, the preamble states that the Convention is intended "to ensure that judicial and extrajudicial documents *to be served abroad* shall be brought to the notice of the addressee in sufficient time." (emphasis added.) And Article 1 defines the Convention's scope by stating that the Convention "shall apply in all cases, in civil or commercial matters, where there is occasion to transmit a judicial or extrajudicial document *for service abroad.*" (emphasis added.) Even the Convention's full title reflects that the Convention concerns "Service Abroad."

We have also held as much. *Schlunk*, 486 U.S., at 701 (stating that the Convention "applies only to documents transmitted for

---

[1]   See Black's Law Dictionary 1568 (10th ed. 2014) (defining "send," in part, as "[t]o cause to be moved or conveyed from a present location to another place; esp., to deposit (a writing or notice) in the mail").

service abroad"). As we explained, a preliminary draft of Article 1 was criticized "because it suggested that the Convention could apply to transmissions abroad that do not culminate in service." *Ibid.* The final version of Article 1, however, "eliminates this possibility." *Ibid.* The wording of Article 1 makes clear that the Convention "applies only when there is both transmission of a document from the requesting state to the receiving state, and service upon the person for whom it is intended." *Ibid.*

In short, the text of the Convention reveals, and we have explicitly held, that the scope of the Convention is limited to service of documents. In light of that, it would be quite strange if Article 10(a)—apparently alone among the Convention's provisions—concerned something other than service of documents.

Indeed, under that reading, Article 10(a) would be superfluous. The function of Article 10 is to ensure that, absent objection from the receiving state, the Convention "shall not interfere" with the activities described in 10(a), 10(b) and 10(c). But Article 1 already "eliminates [the] possibility" that the Convention would apply to any communications that "do not culminate in service," *id.*, at 701, so it is hard to imagine how the Convention could interfere with any non-service communications. Accordingly, in order for Article 10(a) to do any work, it *must* pertain to sending documents for the purposes of service.

Menon attempts to avoid this superfluity problem by suggesting that Article 10(a) does refer to serving documents—but only *some* documents. Specifically, she makes a distinction between two categories of service. According to Menon, Article 10(a) does not apply to *service of process* (which we have defined as "a formal delivery of documents that is legally sufficient to charge the defendant with notice of a pending action," *id.*, at 700. But Article 10(a) does apply, Menon suggests, to the service of "post-answer judicial documents" (that is, any additional documents which may have to be served later in the litigation). The problem with this argument is that it lacks any plausible textual footing in Article 10.

If the drafters wished to limit Article 10(a) to a particular subset of documents, they presumably would have said so—as they did, for example, in Article 15, which refers to "a writ of summons or an equivalent document." Instead, Article 10(a) uses the term "judicial documents"—the same term that is featured in 10(b) and 10(c). Accordingly, the notion that Article 10(a) governs a different set of documents than 10(b) or 10(c) is hard to fathom. And it certainly derives no support from the use of the word "send," whose ordinary meaning is broad enough to cover the transmission of *any* judicial documents (including litigation-initiating documents). Nothing about the word "send" suggests that Article 10(a) is *narrower* than 10(b) and 10(c), let alone that Article 10(a) is somehow limited to "post-answer" documents.

Ultimately, Menon wishes to read the phrase "send judicial documents" as "serve a subset of judicial documents." That is an entirely atextual reading, and Menon offers no sustained argument in support of it. Therefore, the only way to escape the conclusion that Article 10(a) includes service of process is to assert that it does not cover service of documents at all—and, as shown above, that reading is structurally implausible and renders Article 10(a) superfluous.

B

The text and structure of the Hague Service Convention, then, strongly suggest that Article 10(a) pertains to service of documents. The only significant counterargument is that, unlike many other provisions in the Convention, Article 10(a) does not include the word "service" or any of its variants. The Article 10(a) phrase "send judicial documents," the argument goes, should mean something different than the phrase "effect service of judicial documents" in the other two subparts of Article 10.

This argument does not win the day for several reasons. First, it must contend with the compelling structural considerations discussed above. Second, the argument fails on its own terms. Assume for a second that the word "send" must mean something other than "serve." That would not imply that Article 10(a) must *exclude* service. Instead, "send[ing]" could be a broader concept that includes service but is not limited to it. That reading of the word "send" is probably *more* plausible than interpreting it to exclude service, and it does not create the same superfluity problem. Third, it must be remembered that the French version of the Convention is "equally authentic" to the English version. *Schlunk,* 486 U.S., at 699. Menon does not seriously engage with the Convention's French text. But the word "adresser"—the French counterpart to the word "send" in Article 10(a)—"has been consistently interpreted as meaning service or notice." Hague Conference on Private Int'l Law, Practical Handbook on the Operation of the Service Convention ¶ 279, p. 91 (4th ed. 2016).

In short, the most that could possibly be said for this argument is that it creates an ambiguity as to Article 10(a)'s meaning. And when a treaty provision is ambiguous, the Court "may look beyond the written words to the history of the treaty, the negotiations, and the practical construction adopted by the parties." *Schlunk, supra,* at 700 (internal quotation marks omitted). As discussed below, these traditional tools of treaty interpretation comfortably resolve any lingering ambiguity in Water Splash's favor. * * * *

To be clear, this does not mean that the Convention affirmatively *authorizes* service by mail. Article 10(a) simply provides that, as long as the receiving state does not object, the Convention does not "interfere with ... the freedom" to serve documents through postal channels.

In other words, in cases governed by the Hague Service Convention, service by mail is permissible if two conditions are met: first, the receiving state has not objected to service by mail; and second, service by mail is authorized under otherwise-applicable law.

Because the Court of Appeals concluded that the Convention prohibited service by mail outright, it had no occasion to consider whether Texas law authorizes the methods of service used by Water Splash. We leave that question, and any other remaining issues, to be considered on remand to the extent they are properly preserved. * * * *

Notes and Questions

1. In *Menon*, the Supreme Court determines that the Hague Service Convention does not "affirmatively authorize" service by mail, but as long as the receiving state does not object and service by mail is authorized under otherwise-applicable law, service by mail is permissible. It is important to note that the mode of service analyzed in *Menon* was postal mail, and the opinion did not directly address the validity of service by other means, such as electronic mail.

2. Of course, not all countries are signatory states to the Hague Service Convention. What happens, then, when service is to be made in a non-signatory state?

PREWITT ENTERPRISES, INC. V. ORGANIZATION OF PETROLEUM EXPORTING COUNTRIES

United States Court of Appeals for the Eleventh Circuit, 2003
353 F.3d 916

BARKETT, CIRCUIT JUDGE.

* * * *

I.   BACKGROUND

Prewitt is a corporation organized and existing under the laws of Alabama with its principal place of business in Birmingham, Alabama. Prewitt purchases substantial quantities of gasoline and other refined petroleum products for resale at its Eastwood Texaco Service Center gasoline station.

OPEC is an intergovernmental organization originally established in 1960 via resolutions promulgated at the Conference of the Representatives of the Governments of Iran, Iraq, Kuwait, Saudi Arabia and Venezuela in Baghdad, Iraq. The principal aim of OPEC is "the co-ordination and unification of the petroleum policies of Member Countries and the determination of the best means for safeguarding their interests, individually and collectively." OPEC Stat. art. 2(A) (2000). Presently, OPEC's membership consists of: Algeria, Indonesia, Iran, Iraq, Kuwait, Libya, Nigeria, Qatar, Saudi Arabia, the United Arab Emirates and Venezuela. Since September 1, 1965, OPEC has been headquartered in Vienna, Austria. Its relationship with the Austrian government is governed by the Agreement Between the Republic of Austria and the Organization of the Petroleum Exporting Countries Regarding the Headquarters of the Organization of the Petroleum Exporting Countries, February 18, 1974, BGBL 1974/382 ("Austrian/OPEC Headquarters Agreement" or "Headquarters Agreement").

Prewitt filed a complaint with the district court against OPEC on behalf of itself and as the representative of all persons or entities who have indirectly purchased petroleum or petroleum products in the United States since March 1999. Prewitt claimed that OPEC has been coordinating an international conspiracy through agreements among its Member States and non-OPEC members to limit the production and export of oil in order to fix world oil prices above competitive levels. Prewitt argued that these agreements constitute violations of United States antitrust laws, specifically the Sherman and Clayton Acts, and have resulted in a substantial and adverse impact on United States trade and commerce. Prewitt claimed that as a result of OPEC's illegal conduct, its own acquisition and inventory costs for gasoline have increased significantly. Consequently, Prewitt requested that the court declare the OPEC-coordinated agreements illegal under United States law, enjoin implementation of the agreements, grant any other appropriate equitable relief, and award costs of the suit against OPEC for injuries sustained by Prewitt.

Prewitt attempted service on OPEC by requesting that the trial court send a copy of the complaint to OPEC by international registered mail, return receipt requested. The court clerk did so, mailing Prewitt's summons and complaint to OPEC at its headquarters in Vienna. The pleadings were signed for, stamped "received" by OPEC's Administration and Human Resources Department, and forwarded to the Director of OPEC's Research Division as well as other departments including the Secretary General's office. Ultimately, the Secretary General decided that the

OPEC Secretariat would not take any action with regard to the summons and complaint.

Without the participation of OPEC, the district court certified a class defined as all persons or entities who purchased refined petroleum products in the United States from March 1999 to the present and entered a default final judgment and order of injunction against OPEC. The court found that there was a conspiracy between OPEC, its Member States, and non-OPEC members, namely Norway, Mexico, the Russian Federation and Oman, to fix and control crude oil prices; that the agreements coordinated and implemented by OPEC were illegal under United States antitrust laws; that OPEC's illegal conduct has resulted in substantial and adverse impact on United States trade and commerce of approximately $80–120 million per day; and that OPEC and those acting in concert with OPEC should be enjoined from entering into, implementing, and enforcing any further oil price-fixing agreements for a period of twelve months. Copies of the court's orders were delivered to each of the United States embassies for the Member States of OPEC.

In response, OPEC made a special appearance and filed a motion to set aside the default judgment and stay its enforcement pursuant to Rule 60(b)(1), (4), (5) and (6) of the Federal Rules of Civil Procedure, which the district court granted, vacating the default judgment and injunction. OPEC then filed a motion to dismiss Prewitt's complaint on various grounds including insufficient service of process pursuant to Fed. R. Civ. P. 12(b)(5). The district court dismissed the case without prejudice, finding that Prewitt had failed to serve OPEC its summons and complaint properly under the Federal Rules. Prewitt then filed a motion to pursue alternative means of effecting service or to amend the judgment. The district court denied the motion finding that, in this case, OPEC cannot be effectively served with process.

II.   DISCUSSION

* * * * The threshold issue in this case is whether OPEC has been effectively served under the Federal Rules of Civil Procedure. If it has not, we must then determine whether extraterritorial service of process on OPEC may be effectuated at all under the circumstances here. * * * *

There are two rules of federal civil procedure that apply to service of process upon an international entity located outside of United States jurisdiction: Fed. R. Civ. P. 4(f) (Service Upon Individuals in a Foreign Country) and Fed. R. Civ. P. 4(h) (Service of Process Upon Corporations and Associations). The latter governs service on unincorporated associations located outside of the United States and provides that:

> Unless otherwise provided by federal law, service upon a[n] . . . unincorporated association that is subject to suit under a common name, and from which a waiver of service has not been obtained and filed, shall be effected: . . .
>
>> (2) in a place not within any judicial district of the United States *in any manner prescribed for individuals by subdivision (f)* except personal delivery. . . .

Fed. R. Civ. P. 4(h)(2) (emphasis added). Thus, an "unincorporated association" headquartered outside of the United States * * * may be served in any manner authorized under Fed. R. Civ. P. 4(f) for individuals in a foreign country except for personal delivery.

Turning to Fed. R. Civ. P. 4(f), the first relevant section provides that:

> Unless otherwise provided by federal law, service upon an individual from whom a waiver has not been obtained and filed, other than an infant or an incompetent person, may be effected in a place not within any judicial district of the United States:
>
>> (1) by any internationally agreed means reasonably calculated to give notice, such as those means authorized by the Hague Convention on the Service Abroad of Judicial and Extrajudicial Documents. . . .

Fed. R. Civ. P. 4(f)(1). In this case, no other means of service has been "otherwise provided by federal law" nor is there an "internationally agreed means reasonably calculated to give notice such as those means authorized by the Hague Convention on the Service Abroad of Judicial and Extrajudicial Documents. . . ." * * * *

Thus, we must look to the remainder of Fed. R. Civ. P. 4(f), which provides for other methods by which an unincorporated association may be served in the absence of relevant federal law or international agreements:

>> (2) if there is no internationally agreed means of service or the applicable international agreement allows other means of service, provided that service is reasonably calculated to give notice:
>>
>>> (A) in the manner prescribed by the law of the foreign country for service in that country in an

action in any of its courts of general jurisdiction; or

(B) as directed by the foreign authority in response to a letter rogatory or letter of request; or

(C) unless prohibited by the law of the foreign country, by

> (i)   delivery to the individual personally of a copy of the summons and the complaint; or

> (ii) any form of mail requiring a signed receipt, to be addressed and dispatched by the clerk of the court to the party to be served; or

(3) by other means not prohibited by international agreement as may be directed by the court.

Fed. R. Civ. P. 4(f)(2) and (3).

Prewitt originally chose to attempt service of process on OPEC under Fed. R. Civ. P. 4(f)(C)(ii). However, the method set forth under that provision applies only if it is not prohibited by the law of the foreign country. Based on the evidence presented, the district court correctly found that service on OPEC was prohibited by the law of Austria. * * * *

Prewitt nonetheless suggests that we should liberally construe the formal requirements for service under the Federal Rules because OPEC received actual notice but simply chose to "ignore the whole thing." Br. of Appellant at 23. However, we find no support for such an argument. Due process under the United States Constitution requires that "before a court may exercise personal jurisdiction over a defendant, there must be *more than* notice to the defendant . . . [t]here also must be a *basis* for the defendant's amenability to service of summons. Absent consent, this means there must be *authorization* for service of summons on the defendant." *Omni Capital Int'l v. Rudolf Wolff & Co.,* 484 U.S. 97, 104 (1987) (emphasis added). In other words, an individual or entity "is not obliged to engage in litigation unless [officially] notified of the action . . . under a court's authority, by formal process." *Murphy Bros., Inc. v. Michetti Pipe Stringing, Inc.,* 526 U.S. 344, 347 (1999). In this case, Fed. R. Civ. P. 4(f)(2)(C)(ii) clearly states that service of process by registered mail is only authorized where it is not prohibited by foreign law. * * * *

Alternatively, Prewitt argues that even if service failed under Fed. R. Civ. P. 4(f)(2)(C)(ii), service by registered mail upon OPEC nonetheless complied with Fed. R. Civ. P. 4(f)(2)(A), which permits service if it is effectuated "in the manner prescribed by the law of the foreign country for service in that country in an action in any of its courts of general jurisdiction." The provisions of Austrian law that Prewitt references from Austria's Civil Procedure Code and regulations for service of process by mail relate to service by Austrian courts on persons resident in Austria and abroad. None of these Austrian law provisions directly pertain to service mailed *from abroad* upon international organizations resident in Austria. Prewitt argues that we should look only to the approved "method" of service within the foreign jurisdiction and not to the substance of Austrian law. However, the substance of the law specifically relating to service of process cannot be divorced from the "method" of service. Indeed, §§ 12(1) and 11(2) of the Austrian Service Act specifically address service from authorities abroad upon residents in Austria and trump the more general provisions cited by Prewitt from the Austrian Code of Civil Procedure and regulations for service of process by Austrian courts on residents in Austria or abroad. Moreover, the Regulation Regarding the Service of Process by Mail upon Persons Abroad in Civil Proceedings that Prewitt argues applies in this case specifically states that it *does not* apply to service on entities specified under § 11(2) of the Austrian Service Act. Section 12(1) (as amended 1990) of the Austrian Service Act requires that:

The service of documents generated by authorities abroad to recipients in Austria shall be carried out in accordance with the existing international conventions, *in the absence of which it has to be done in accordance with this law.* . . . (emphasis added).

Section 11(2) (as amended 1998) of the Austrian Service Act directly addresses service from abroad upon international organizations such as OPEC requiring that:

the mediation of the Federal Ministry for Foreign Affairs shall be enlisted in undertaking service of process on foreigners or international organizations that enjoy privileges and immunities under international law, regardless of their place of residence or headquarters.

There would be no way for Prewitt to serve OPEC under § 11(2) of the Austrian Service Act because we must assume that if it had gone to the Austrian Federal Ministry of Foreign Affairs, the Ministry would have applied the laws of its own country and obeyed the dictates of the Austrian/OPEC Headquarters Agreement prohibiting service without OPEC's consent.

In response, Prewitt again argues that actual notice can cure defective service of process pursuant to Section 7 of the Austrian Service Act, which provides:

> Should defects in service of process occur, service shall be deemed effectuated at the time when the document has actually reached the recipient designated by the authority.

Section 7 (as amended January 1, 1991) of the Austrian Service Act. However, this section has specifically been interpreted in Austria not to apply to defects in service of process that are in breach of the requirements for service under an international agreement * * *.

Finally, Prewitt contends that even if its service by registered mail on OPEC could not be effectuated pursuant to any of the provisions of Fed. R. Civ. P. 4(f)(2), the district court still had the discretion to order service of process pursuant to Fed. R. Civ. P. 4(f)(3), which provides that service may be effected "by *other means* not prohibited by international agreement as may be directed by the court." (emphasis added). We agree with Prewitt that a district court's denial of relief under 4(f)(3) is reviewed under an abuse of discretion standard. However, there is no abuse of discretion here; on the contrary, any circumvention of 4(f)(2)(C)(ii) by the district court in directing service again by registered mail would constitute such an abuse. On these facts, we cannot read 4(f)(3) as permitting that which has already been specifically prohibited under 4(f)(2).

Prewitt then argues that, even if service by registered mail is prohibited by 4(f)(2), other means of giving actual notice, such as fax or e-mail, that are not mentioned in the rule or prohibited by international agreement could be employed to serve OPEC under Fed. R. Civ. P. 4(f)(3), even if the service is contrary to the laws of Austria. However, the 1993 Advisory Committee Notes to Fed. R. Civ. P. 4(f)(3) instruct that:

> Paragraph (3) authorizes the court to approve other methods of service not prohibited by international agreements. . . . Inasmuch as our Constitution requires that reasonable notice be given, *an earnest effort* should be made to devise a method of communication that is *consistent with due process* and *minimizes offense to foreign law.*

(emphasis added). Rather than minimizing offense to Austrian law, the failure to obtain OPEC's consent would constitute a substantial affront to Austrian law. We can find no support permitting such a consequence in the face of Austria's direct prohibition of service on OPEC without its consent. The case relied upon as persuasive by

Prewitt, *Rio Properties, Inc. v. Rio Int'l Interlink,* 284 F.3d 1007, 1014 (9th Cir. 2002), is not at all applicable to the circumstances here. In *Rio,* * * * the court determined that the defendant, an international internet company doing business in the United States, had a viable presence in the United States; that physical personal service had been legally attempted by actually serving a legitimate agent of the defendant in the United States; and that the defendant had evaded the attempted service. The most important distinction, however, is that in Rio, there was no discussion of Costa Rican law at all, much less of any prohibitions relating to service of process and thus, no need to take into account the advisory note to Fed. R. Civ. P. 4(f)(3) directing that alternative service of process should minimize offense to foreign law.[21]

Austrian law clearly provides protection to OPEC as an international organization from all methods of service of process without its consent and also requires that any service of process from abroad be effected through Austrian authorities. In this case, OPEC has made clear that it refuses to consent expressly to service of process by Prewitt; thus, the district court did not abuse its discretion in denying Prewitt's motion to authorize alternative means of service. * * * *

Notes and Questions

1.   In many countries, service of process is an official act. As a result, improper service not only creates needless international friction, it can also be a violation of national law. Most importantly, for the international litigant improper service also reduces the likelihood that any judgment obtained in the action will be enforceable.

2.   Can private actors choose to contract around the Hague Service Convention? State courts addressing this question have held that they can. *See Rockefeller Technology Investments (Asia) VII v. Changzhou SinoType Technology Company, Ltd.,* 460 P.3d 764 (Cal. Sup. Ct. 2020); *Alfred E. Mann Living Trust v. ETIRC Aviation S.A.R.L.* 78 A.D.3d 137, 141 (N.Y. App. Div. 2010).

3.   It is generally understood that Rule 4(f)(3) is not a rule of last resort, meaning the party seeking court approval in using an alternative method of service does not need to show other methods of service have been attempted. *See Patrick's Rest., LLC v. Singh,* 2018 U.S. Dist. LEXIS 183966, *3–4 (D. Minn. 2018). However, there is some authority holding that Rule 4(f)(3) cannot be the *first* option plaintiffs use. *See Graphic*

---

[21] We do not say that a district court *never* has discretion to direct service of process under Fed. R. Civ. P. 4(f)(3) that is in contravention of a foreign law. Rather, we are satisfied that under the facts and circumstances of this case, directing service of process would constitute a clear abuse of discretion.

Styles/Styles Int'l LLC v. Men's Wear Creations, 99 F. Supp. 3d 519, 524–25 (E.D. Pa. 2015) (denying alternative method of service under Rule 4(f)(3) because "Graphic Styles has not made any such showing of the need to resort to alternative means of service at this time"); *see also* Maggie Gardner, *Parochial Procedure,* 69 STAN. L. REV. 941, 999–1000 (2017). ("The Advisory Committee's notes to Rule 4(f) make clear that Rule 4(f)(3) was intended as a safety valve available only when the Convention, by its own terms, does not apply.").

Chapter 8

FORUM NON CONVENIENS

Forum non conveniens is a controversial judge-made doctrine, originating in the United Kingdom, that common law courts deploy to dismiss cases despite having proper jurisdiction to hear the case (significantly, civil law jurisdictions do not have any similar doctrine). In the landmark decision of *Piper v. Reyno*, 454 U.S. 235 (1981), the U.S. Supreme Court dismissed a suit brought on behalf of Scottish people who died in an airplane crash in Scotland. The Court ruled that dismissal was appropriate even though the defendants were U.S.-based corporations. In the aftermath of *Piper*, *forum non conveniens* poses a significant barrier to non-U.S. citizens attempting to bring suit against U.S. defendants in federal courts when the injury occurred abroad.

The *Piper* plaintiffs wished to sue in the United States rather than in Scotland in large part because Scottish law would have been less favorable to them. The U.S. Supreme Court, however, rejected the idea that an unfavorable difference in law was a sufficient reason, in and of itself, to block a *forum non conveniens* dismissal. Nevertheless, the Court offered the following caveat:

> We do not hold that the possibility of an unfavorable change in law should *never* be a relevant consideration in a *forum non conveniens* inquiry. Of course, if the remedy provided by the alternative forum is so clearly inadequate or unsatisfactory that it is no remedy at all, the unfavorable change in law may be given substantial weight; the district court may conclude that dismissal would not be in the interests of justice.

Id. at 254. Not surprisingly, this passage has sparked considerable litigation, as plaintiffs have tried to argue that a particular legal regime or procedure of a foreign forum "is so clearly inadequate or unsatisfactory that it is no remedy at all." In *Piper* itself, the Supreme Court held that the absence of a strict liability theory of recovery did not make Scotland sufficiently inadequate. But what about other differences? For example, what if the foreign system does not allow broad U.S.-style discovery? Or it doesn't recognize a jury-trial right? Or it doesn't allow class actions? Or it caps wrongful death damages? And so on.

These differences often are the key to the entire litigation. Indeed, significant differences between the local and foreign forum often mean that, *as a practical matter*, the litigation will be highly unlikely ever to proceed in the foreign forum. Despite the practical unavailability of a foreign forum, however, U.S. courts have largely been unwilling to use this ground as a reason not to dismiss for *forum non conveniens*, so long as the foreign forum is technically available and not deemed to be a completely non-functioning legal system.

In response, some countries have attempted to enact statutes formally blocking jurisdiction in their courts over any cases previously dismissed on *forum non conveniens* grounds. By doing so, the legislatures of these countries are attempting to artificially make their own courts unavailable, thereby potentially rendering a *forum non conveniens* dismissal less likely. How should U.S. courts respond to such statutes? Consider the following case.

DEL ISTMO ASSUR. CORP. V. PLATON

United States District Court for the Southern District of Florida, 2011
No. 11–61599–CIV, 2011 WL 5508641

COHN, DISTRICT JUDGE.

* * * *

Plaintiff Del Istmo Assurance Corp. ("Plaintiff") filed the instant suit against Defendants Italkitchen International, Inc. ("Italkitchen") and Meletios P. Platon a/k/a Ted Platon ("Platon") (collectively "Defendants") on July 19, 2011. Plaintiff is a corporation organized under the laws of the Republic of Panama and the successor in interest to American Assurance Corp. Platon is a resident of Miami-Dade County, Florida. Italkitchen is a Florida corporation with its principal place of business in Miami-Dade County, Florida. According to the Complaint, Platon, through his companies Italkitchen and Eurogroup International Panama, Inc. ("Eurogroup"), specializes in custom kitchens, cabinets, doors, and other wood-based fixtures. In or around December 2008, Platon, through Eurogroup, entered four contracts with Opcorp-Arsesa International, Inc., a Panamanian corporation, to install kitchens, doors, carpentry, and other fixtures at the Trump Ocean Club International Hotel & Tower development (the "Opcorp contracts"). The Opcorp contracts provided that Opcorp-Arsesa International, Inc. would make advance payments to Eurogroup. In exchange, Eurogroup was required to place these payments in trust and obtain prepayment bonds to ensure the funds.

In early 2009, Platon met with Plaintiff's representatives to obtain the necessary prepayment bonds. Based on representations made by Mr. Platon at a March 4, 2009 meeting and his execution of an indemnity agreement/personal guaranty in Plaintiff's favor, Plaintiff agreed to underwrite the bonds. Thereafter, on March 6, 2009, Eurogroup executed a trust instrument to comply with the Opcorp contracts which named Plaintiff as the beneficiary. Additionally, on August 30, 2009, Platon, on behalf of Italkitchen, executed an indemnity agreement in Plaintiff's favor which required Italkitchen to indemnify Plaintiff for the bonds.

Plaintiff alleges that sometime starting in or around March 2009, Platon began to systematically withdraw money from the trust which he used to pay other debts rather than third-party suppliers under the Opcorp contracts. Because Platon did not pay the third-party suppliers, Plaintiff was required, pursuant to the bonds it underwrote, to pay the third-party suppliers and cover all expenses related to shipping and importation of the materials needed to complete the Trump Ocean Club International Hotel & Tower development. Eurogroup later delayed its performance at the development, necessitating that Plaintiff pay $900,000 to complete Eurogroup's work. Plaintiff filed the instant suit against Platon and Italkitchen when they failed to reimburse Plaintiff under the personal guaranty and indemnity agreements. The Complaint raises separate breach of contract claims against Platon and Italkitchen related to breach of the indemnity agreements and a fraud claim against Platon for misrepresentations he allegedly made to induce Plaintiff to underwrite the bonds.

Defendants separately filed motions to dismiss. Both Motions to Dismiss allege that the Complaint should be dismissed under the doctrine of *forum non conveniens* because the suit should be resolved in Panama. * * * *

Under the doctrine of *forum non conveniens*, a federal district court may dismiss an action if a foreign court is a more appropriate and convenient forum for adjudicating the matter. *Sinochem Int'l Co. Ltd. v. Malay. Int'l Shipping Corp.*, 549 U.S. 422, 425 (2007). To obtain dismissal under the doctrine of *forum non conveniens*, the moving party must demonstrate (1) an adequate alternate forum is available; (2) the public and private factors weigh in favor of dismissal; and (3) the plaintiff can reinstate its suit in the alternative forum without undue inconvenience or prejudice. Although ordinarily there is a strong presumption in favor of a plaintiff's choice of forum, where, as here, a plaintiff chooses a forum that is not its home forum, this presumption "applies with less force." *Piper Aircraft Co. v. Reyno*, 454 U.S. 235, 255, 102 S. Ct. 252, 70 L. Ed. 2d

419 (1981). After reviewing the relevant law and submissions of all parties, the Court concludes that dismissal for *forum non conveniens* is warranted.

Before granting a motion to dismiss for *forum non conveniens*, the Court must consider both whether an alternate forum is adequate and available. An alternative forum is available when the foreign court can assert jurisdiction over the litigation. Generally, an alternative forum is available when the defendant is amenable to process in the other jurisdiction. *Aldana v. Del Monte Fresh Produce N.A., Inc.*, 578 F.3d 1283, 1290 (11th Cir. 2009) "[A]n adequate forum need not be a perfect forum." *Id.* (internal citations and quotations omitted). A remedy is inadequate when it amounts to "no remedy at all." *Piper Aircraft Co.,* 454 U.S. at 254. The Eleventh Circuit has elaborated that it is "only in rare circumstances where the remedy offered by the other forum is clearly unsatisfactory" that an alternative forum will be considered inadequate. *Aldana,* 578 F. 3d at 1290.

Defendant Platon contends that "Panama is a civil law jurisdiction with an impartial court system and the civil code of Panama recognizes all of the causes of action alleged in Plaintiff's Complaint." In support, Platon cites the affidavit of Panamanian lawyer Rolando Villalobos who avers that Panamanian courts have jurisdiction over this matter. Defendant Italkitchen similarly argues that Panama provides an available and adequate forum.

In opposition, Plaintiff contends that Panama is not an adequate forum because if the case is dismissed on *forum non conveniens* grounds, Panama law precludes Plaintiff from reinstating its suit against the Defendants in Panama. According to Plaintiff's legal expert Octavio Del Real, Article 1421–J of the Panama Rules of Civil Procedure provides that:

> For any legal proceeding under this Chapter [Panamanian] judges are not competent [to hear the case] if the complaint or the action being commenced in [Panama] has been previously dismissed or denied by a foreign judge under the application of forum non conveniens. In these cases, judges should dismiss or not recognize the complaint or demand on grounds of constitutional or preemptive jurisdiction.

Based on this provision, Del Real concludes that "if the Action were to be dismissed by the United States Federal Court on *forum non conveniens* grounds, the courts [in] Panama would not be an available forum for Plaintiff to reinstate this action as a matter of Panama law."

In his Reply, Platon contends that this Court need not be bound by Article 1421–J because "Panama law does not trump United States law." Article 1421–J is a "blocking statute," enacted "to permit foreign plaintiffs, sanctioned by their national governments, to take advantage of the U.S. judicial system without regard to the burden placed on its courts or taxpayers." Jena A. Sold, *Inappropriate Forum or Inappropriate Law? A Choice-of-Law Solution to the Jurisdictional Standoff Between the United States and Latin America*, 60 EMORY L.J. 1437, 1466 (2011). The Florida District Court of Appeal has addressed the effect of Article 1421–J on dismissal of actions for *forum non conveniens*. In *The Scotts Company v. Hacienda Loma Linda*, 942 So. 2d. 900 (Fla. Dist. Ct. App. 2006), the Third District Court of Appeal reversed the lower court's denial of a defendant's motion to dismiss for *forum non conveniens*, holding that Panama was an adequate, alternate forum available to resolve the parties' dispute.[3] As in this case, a Panamanian plaintiff sued an American defendant in the United States for injuries that allegedly occurred in Panama. *The Scotts Co.*, 942 So. 2d at 902. Although the court concluded that Panama was an available forum, it retained "jurisdiction in the event the Panama court does not entertain the case based on preemption." *Id.* at 903.

After the case was dismissed, the Panamanian plaintiff reinstated its suit in Florida circuit court on the basis that the Panamanian court had declined jurisdiction pursuant to Article 1421–J. After the defendant appealed, the Third District Court of Appeal ordered that the circuit court dismiss the case. The court held that "the case plainly belongs in Panama" and United States' "courts cannot be compelled by other countries' courts and lawmakers to resolve cases that should be determined in those countries." Thus, "[i]f the foreign country chooses to turn away its citizen's lawsuit for damages suffered in that very country," there was no reason for United States' resources to be devoted to hearing the matter.

Other courts, both state and federal, have refused to recognize foreign laws that purport to make the home forum unavailable because of a prior U.S. filing. *See Morales v. Ford Motor Co.*, 313 F. Supp. 2d 672, 676 (S.D. Tex. 2004) (finding Venezuela an adequate, alternate forum because defendant consented to jurisdiction there); *Aguinda v. Texaco, Inc.*, 142 F. Supp. 2d 534, 546 (S.D.N.Y. 2001) (finding argument that Ecuador courts would deny plaintiff jurisdiction doubtful, but conditioning dismissal as a safeguard); *Paulownia Plantations De Pan. Corp. v. Rajamannan*, 793 N.W. 2d

---

[3] The *forum non conveniens* analysis the Florida court applied is identical to the analysis that federal courts apply. *Aldana*, 578 F.3d at 1289.

128, 134–35 (Minn. 2009) (affirming Panama as an adequate and available public forum despite the passage of Article 1421–J).

* * * *

Plaintiff also argues that even if a court in Panama would hear its case, Panama is still an inadequate forum because Plaintiff would be deprived of full remedies in Panama such as punitive damages or piercing the corporate veil to hold Platon personally liable for Italkitchen's breach of its indemnity contract. However, * * * a forum is adequate when "the parties will not be deprived of all remedies or treated unfairly . . . *even though they may not enjoy the same benefits as they might receive in an American court.*" *Raytheon Eng'rs & Constructors, Inc. v. HLH & Assocs. Inc.*, No. 97–20187, 1998 U.S. App. LEXIS 38882, 1998 WL 224531, at *2 (5th Cir. Apr. 17, 1998). (emphasis added). Thus, Panama cannot be considered an inadequate forum merely because Plaintiff would be unable to seek punitive damages or pierce the corporate veil.

* * * *

When considering a motion to dismiss for *forum non conveniens,* the Court must weigh the advantages and disadvantages of each prospective forum. The public factors the Court must consider are: " 'the relative ease of access to sources of proof; availability of compulsory process for attendance of willing, witnesses; possibility of view of premises, if view would be appropriate to the action; and all other practical problems that make trial of a case easy, expeditious, and inexpensive.' " *Piper Aircraft Co.,* 454 U.S. at 241 n.6 (quoting *Gulf Oil Corp. v. Gilbert,* 330 U.S. 501, 508, 67 S. Ct. 839, 91 L. Ed. 1055 (1947)). The public factors include "the administrative difficulties flowing from court congestion; the 'local interest in having localized controversies decided at home'; the interest in having the trial of a diversity case in a forum that is at home with the law that must govern the action; the avoidance of unnecessary problems in conflict of laws, or in the application of foreign law; and the unfairness of burdening citizens in an unrelated form with jury duty." *Piper Aircraft Co.,* 454 U.S. at 241 n.6 (citing *Gilbert,* 330 U.S. at 509). A trial court "look[s] at the private interests first, and then if the balance of the private interests are found to be in equipoise or near equipoise, it will determine whether or not factors of public interest tip the balance in favor of a trial in a foreign forum." *Wilson v. Island Seas Invs., Ltd.,* 590 F.3d 1264, 1271 (11th Cir. 2009). Here, application of both the private and public factors strongly favors dismissal.

The first private interest factor, relative ease to sources of proof, supports trial of this case in Panama. Defendants contend that

Panama offers superior access to sources of proof. After considering the arguments of the parties, the Court agrees. The events giving rise to this action occurred in Panama. The majority of the witnesses are located in Panama. Except for Defendants themselves, all the sources of proof are in Panama and have no relationship with the United States or Florida. * * * Platon submitted an affidavit which identifies 12 Panamanian-based witnesses Defendants would depose or call at trial. Additionally, this affidavit identifies various correspondence and documents, all located in Panama, that are essential to litigation of this case. Thus, the Court finds that Defendants have established that Panama offers superior access to sources of proof.

The second private interest factor, availability of compulsory process for attendance of witnesses, also supports trial of this case in Panama. Defendants contend that the vast majority of witnesses in this case are located in Panama, outside the subpoena power of this Court. Defendants' Rule 26(a) Initial Disclosures list 17 individuals who may support Defendants' defenses, 16 of whom are located in Panama. Defendants have also represented that they may seek to implead Opcorp-Arsesa International, Inc., a Panamanian corporation, to this case.

The Court agrees with Defendants that witnesses crucial to this case are located in Panama, a fact supported by Plaintiff's very own Complaint. In its Complaint, Plaintiff alleges that Alberto Villageliu, Gilberto Vega, Anayansy Diaz, Ikaru Uno, Raul Gutierrez, and Carlos Stagg were present at the March 4, 2009 meeting where Defendant Platon allegedly made misrepresentations to induce Plaintiff to underwrite the bonds. Because these individuals, and others Defendants have identified as potential witnesses, are outside the subpoena power of this Court, the Court could not compel their attendance at trial. Even if witnesses consented to appear before this Court, their travel arrangements would be costly. By contrast, these witnesses are within the subpoena power of Panamanian courts and costly travel arrangements would be unnecessary. The Court also does not have jurisdiction over the potential Panamanian third-party defendant, Opcorp-Arsesa International, Inc. Thus, this factor also supports trying this case in Panama.

The third private interest factor, possibility of a view of the premises, also favors Panama. If the need for a view of the Trump Ocean Club International Hotel & Tower development became necessary, not outside the realm of possibility given that this litigation involves a development project, such view would necessarily take place in Panama. Thus, this factor also favors resolution of this case in Panama.

The fourth and final private interest factor, which requires the Court to consider all other practical problems that make trial of a case easy, expeditious, and inexpensive, supports trial of this case in Panama. Potential language barriers for Spanish-speaking witnesses and the need to translate documents from Spanish to English make it more efficient to resolve this suit in Panamanian courts where Spanish is the official language. Given these language-related impediments, this case is most easily, expeditiously, and inexpensively tried in Panama.[9]

The public interest factors also strongly support resolving this case in Panama.[10] Given the vast number of cases pending in the Southern District of Florida, the administrative difficulties flowing from court congestion favor trying this case in Panama. * * * * The Court rejects Plaintiff's argument that "there is evidence that the court system in Panama is massively backlogged" because this contention is unsupported with specific facts about the length of delay.

Second, Panama clearly has a superior interest in resolving this dispute than the United States. The Eleventh Circuit has held that "it is clear that a sovereign has a very strong interest when its citizens are allegedly victims and the injury occurs on home soil." *Tazoe*, 631 F.3d at 1334; see also *Piper Aircraft Co.*, 454 U.S. at 260 (finding that America's interest in a foreign airplane accident "is simply not sufficient to justify the enormous commitment of judicial time and resources that would inevitably be required if the case were to be tried" in the United States); *The Scotts Co.*, 942 So. 2d at 903 (finding that "Florida has no interest in adjudicating the dispute of a Panama corporation whose property was injured in Panama by events taking place" in Panama). Here, the Plaintiff is a Panamanian corporation which suffered an injury related to business transactions which occurred largely in Panama. Additionally, there is already

---

[9]   Some courts have described the fourth public interest factor as "enforceability of a judgment." This public interest factor also supports trial of this case in Panama. * * * [T]here is a Florida statute which permits plaintiffs to domesticate and execute foreign judgments. Uniform Foreign Money-Judgments Recognition Act, Fla. Stat. §§ 55.601–55.607. Thus, enforceability of a judgment also weighs in favor of Panama because Florida law explicitly provides a mechanism to enforce a Panamanian judgment against Florida residents.

[10]   Although the Court finds that the private interest factors overwhelming favor dismissal, the Court has nonetheless also analyzed each of the public interest factors even though it is not required to do so. See *Aldana*, 578 F.3d at 1298 (finding that because the district court had concluded that the private interest factors overwhelmingly favored dismissal, it was not necessary to analyze the public interest factors).

related litigation pending in Panama. Panama's interest in resolving this dispute, therefore, is greater than the United States' interest.

The third and fourth public interest factors require the Court to assess which jurisdiction's law will apply. Because the Court concludes that Panamanian law will likely govern all counts of Plaintiff's complaint, both the third and fourth public interest factors favor trial of this case in Panama. * * * *

As to the fifth and final public interest factor, the Court finds that it is unfair to burden jurors from South Florida with jury duty to resolve a dispute centered in Panama. As discussed above, this case involves a Panamanian plaintiff injured in Panama. It is unfair for Florida citizens to devote their valuable time to resolve a dispute which properly belongs in Panama.

The final part of the *forum non conveniens* analysis requires the Court to assess whether Plaintiff can reinstate its suit in Panama without undue inconvenience or prejudice. In their reply memoranda, both Defendants argue that Plaintiff can reinstate its suit in Panama. Additionally, both Defendants have consented to jurisdiction in Panama to resolve this case. * * * * Numerous state and federal courts have conditioned dismissal on the ability of a party to reinstate its suit in a foreign jurisdiction. *See Gschwind v. Cessna Aircraft Co.*, 161 F.3d 602, 607 (10th Cir. 1998) (conditioning dismissal on consent to reinstatement if jurisdiction in France was declined); *Aguinda*, 142 F. Supp. 2d at 546 (finding argument that Ecuador courts would deny plaintiff jurisdiction doubtful, but conditioning dismissal as a safeguard); *Rajamannan*, 793 N.W. 2d at 134 (holding that the district court may dismiss on forum non conveniens grounds even though the adequacy of the forum is not absolutely certain, if the dismissal is conditional).

In fact, the Eleventh Circuit has held that the uncertainty of whether a foreign forum may hear a case is not a barrier to a *forum non conveniens* dismissal: "Nor is the alleged uncertainty over Law No. 55 an obstacle to dismissal; the District Court would presumably reassert jurisdiction over the case in the event that jurisdiction in the Ecuadorian courts is declined." *Leon*, 251 F.3d at 1313. In *Leon*, the Eleventh Circuit modified the district court's order of dismissal to provide that jurisdiction could be reinstated in the United States if the Ecuadorian court refused to hear the case. *Id.* at 1316. Thus, because Defendants have consented to jurisdiction in Panama and the Court will allow Plaintiff to reinstate its case in this Court if a Panama court refuses jurisdiction, the Court hereby dismisses Plaintiff's Complaint based on *forum non conveniens*.

Notes and Questions

1.   As you consider *forum non conveniens* in a transnational context, ask yourself first whether you think the doctrine is truly necessary. After all, if a court has proper jurisdiction over all parties to a dispute as a statutory or constitutional matter, why should a judge be able to refuse to hear the case? And if, for some reason, some of these cases are deemed inappropriate for adjudication, might it make more sense simply to change the jurisdictional rules rather than adding a new doctrinal inquiry?

On the other hand, perhaps *forum non conveniens* addresses concerns that are distinct from jurisdiction. Consider this discussion, from a judge in the United Kingdom:

> In my opinion, the burden resting on the defendant is not just
> to show that England is not the natural or appropriate forum
> for the trial, but to establish that there is another available
> forum which is clearly or distinctly more appropriate than the
> English forum. In this way, proper regard is paid to the fact
> that jurisdiction has been founded in England as of right; and
> there is the further advantage that, on a subject where comity
> is of importance, it appears that there will be a broad
> consensus among major common law jurisdictions. I may add
> that if, in any case, the connection of the defendant with the
> English forum is a fragile one (for example, if he is served with
> proceedings during a short visit to this country), it should be
> all the easier for him to prove that there is another clearly
> more appropriate forum for the trial overseas.

Spiliada Maritime Corporation Appellants v Cansulex Ltd Respondents, [1986] 3 W.L.R. 972, [1987] A.C. 460. Thus, given that multiple communities might plausibly assert jurisdiction over a single dispute, perhaps it makes sense to have an additional doctrine focused on where a dispute is *best* resolved rather than where it jurisdictionally *can be* resolved.

2.   Even assuming *forum non conveniens* is a useful doctrine, how broadly should it be applied? In particular, plaintiffs often choose their initial forum for a strategic reason. Is that choice entitled to any deference? Usually, it is assumed that plaintiffs may bring suits in their desired forum (assuming proper jurisdiction over the case), but is there any justification for allowing plaintiffs to do so? After all, every strategic reason a plaintiff might have for bringing a case in a forum is, reciprocally, also a reason for the defendant *not* to have the case heard in that forum. Is one interest necessarily entitled to more weight than another?

3.   With regard to the reality of transnational suits, *forum non conveniens* dismissals tend to disadvantage foreign plaintiffs who sue

U.S. corporations in U.S. courts. Is this the appropriate result? One might think that U.S. courts have an interest in regulating U.S. corporations, and it is difficult to see why these courts should allow impunity to these U.S. corporations when their actions cause harm, even if that harm occurs abroad. In addition, it may seem cruel to deny an effective remedy to people who have been harmed. On the other hand, should foreign plaintiffs be permitted to take advantage of U.S. substantive or procedural laws? Such laws presumably were enacted to benefit U.S. plaintiffs, and if foreign plaintiffs prefer U.S. law, perhaps they should have worked politically within their own countries to ensure a more plaintiff-friendly litigation system. It is even possible that some products cost less in other countries because tort liability is less likely. If so, then allowing those who have benefitted from the lower prices to sue in the United States would create a sort of windfall.

4.   With regard to a blocking statute such as Panama's, do you think the court in *Del Istmo* was right to ignore its effect? After all, the plaintiff may now be literally unable to bring suit anywhere, which seems unfair. On the other hand, perhaps such unfairness is not the fault of the U.S. court, but the Panamanian legislature for enacting the blocking statute in the first place. And, of course, the U.S. court reserved the power to reinstate the suit if Panamanian courts actually deny jurisdiction.

5.   Panama (and other countries) have enacted these blocking statutes to try to prevent *forum non conveniens* dismissals, thereby allowing their nationals to sue in the United States. But if such countries really want to help their plaintiffs, they could instead change their own legal systems to make them more plaintiff-friendly. Why do you think they have chosen not to do so?

Chapter 9

SUING FOREIGN NATIONALS IN UNITED STATES COURTS

A. THE FOREIGN SOVEREIGN IMMUNITIES ACT

Foreign *individuals and corporations* can, in general, be sued in U.S. courts, so long as the court has proper personal jurisdiction over the defendant and the court chooses not to dismiss on *forum non conveniens* grounds (see Chapter Eight).

However, *foreign states* traditionally were afforded absolute immunity from suit. For example, according to the Restatement (Fourth) of Foreign Relations Law § 451, "International law requires a state to provide other states with immunity from the jurisdiction of its domestic courts, subject to exceptions." This immunity is known as the "sovereign immunity" doctrine.

In 1952 the U.S. Department of State adopted a "restrictive" theory of sovereign immunity that only extended to the *official* acts of those governments. In contrast, to the extent disputes arise over *commercial* activities of those governments, foreign sovereign immunity would not apply.* In 1976 Congress passed the Foreign Sovereign Immunities Act (FSIA), which codified the State Department's approach.

The FSIA is now "the sole basis for obtaining jurisdiction over a foreign state in [United States federal and state] courts." *Argentine Republic v. Amerada Hess Shipping Corp.*, 488 U.S. 428, 424 (1989). Accordingly, foreign states and governments, including their political subdivisions, agencies, and instrumentalities, are presumptively immune from suit unless their activity falls under one of the

---

* *See* Letter from Jack B. Tate, Acting Legal Adviser, U.S. Dep't of State, to Acting U.S. Att'y Gen. Philip B. Perlman (May 19, 1952), *reprinted in* U.S. Dep'. St. Bull. 984–985 (1952) ("[T]he immunity of the sovereign is recognized with regard to sovereign or public acts (*jure imperii*) of a state, but not with respect to private acts (*jure gestionis*).").

statutory exceptions enumerated in the FSIA. 28 U.S.C. §§ 1603, 1604.

The FSIA creates nine statutory exceptions, of which the three most significant are discussed below.

The Commercial Activity Exception

The most frequently invoked and important exception to the FSIA is the commercial activity exception, § 1605(a)(2). The U.S. Supreme Court addressed this provision in 1992:

REPUBLIC OF ARGENTINA V. WELTOVER, INC.

Supreme Court of the United States, 1992
504 U.S. 607

SCALIA, J.

Since Argentina's currency is not one of the mediums of exchange accepted on the international market, Argentine businesses engaging in foreign transactions must pay in United States dollars or some other internationally accepted currency. In the recent past, it was difficult for Argentine borrowers to obtain such funds, principally because of the instability of the Argentine currency. To address these problems, petitioners, the Republic of Argentina and its central bank, Banco Central (collectively Argentina), in 1981 instituted a foreign exchange insurance contract program (FEIC), under which Argentina effectively agreed to assume the risk of currency depreciation in cross-border transactions involving Argentine borrowers. This was accomplished by Argentina's agreeing to sell to domestic borrowers, in exchange for a contractually predetermined amount of local currency, the necessary United States dollars to repay their foreign debts when they matured, irrespective of intervening devaluations.

Unfortunately, Argentina did not possess sufficient reserves of United States dollars to cover the FEIC contracts as they became due in 1982. The Argentine Government thereupon adopted certain emergency measures, including refinancing of the FEIC-backed debts by issuing to the creditors government bonds. These bonds, called "Bonods," provide for payment of interest and principal in United States dollars; payment may be made through transfer on the London, Frankfurt, Zurich, or New York market, at the election of the creditor. Under this refinancing program, the foreign creditor had the option of either accepting the Bonods in satisfaction of the initial debt, thereby substituting the Argentine Government for the private debtor, or maintaining the debtor/creditor relationship with the private borrower and accepting the Argentine Government as guarantor.

When the Bonods began to mature in May 1986, Argentina concluded that it lacked sufficient foreign exchange to retire them. Pursuant to a Presidential Decree, Argentina unilaterally extended the time for payment and offered bondholders substitute instruments as a means of rescheduling the debts. Respondents, two Panamanian corporations and a Swiss bank who hold, collectively, $1.3 million of Bonods, refused to accept the rescheduling and insisted on full payment, specifying New York as the place where payment should be made. Argentina did not pay, and respondents then brought this breach-of-contract action in the United States District Court for the Southern District of New York, relying on the Foreign Sovereign Immunities Act of 1976 as the basis for jurisdiction. * * * *

The Foreign Sovereign Immunities Act of 1976 (FSIA), 28 U.S.C. § 1602 *et seq.*, establishes a comprehensive framework for determining whether a court in this country, state or federal, may exercise jurisdiction over a foreign state. Under the Act, a "foreign state *shall* be immune from the jurisdiction of the courts of the United States and of the States" unless one of several statutorily defined exceptions applies. § 1604 (emphasis added). The FSIA thus provides the "sole basis" for obtaining jurisdiction over a foreign sovereign in the United States. The most significant of the FSIA's exceptions—and the one at issue in this case—is the "commercial" exception of § 1605(a)(2), which provides that a foreign state is not immune from suit in any case

> "in which the action is based upon a commercial activity carried on in the United States by the foreign state; or upon an act performed in the United States in connection with a commercial activity of the foreign state elsewhere; or upon an act outside the territory of the United States in connection with a commercial activity of the foreign state elsewhere and that act causes a direct effect in the United States." § 1605(a)(2).

* * * * [It is uncontested] that the cause of action [in this case] is * * * "based upon an act outside the territory of the United States" (presumably Argentina's unilateral extension) * * *. The dispute pertains to whether the unilateral refinancing of the Bonods was taken "in connection with a commercial activity" of Argentina, and whether it had a "direct effect in the United States." We address these issues in turn.

Respondents * * * contend that Argentina's issuance of, and continued liability under, the Bonods constitute a "commercial activity" and that the extension of the payment schedules was taken "in connection with" that activity. The latter point is obvious enough, and Argentina does not contest it; the key question is whether the activity is "commercial" under the FSIA.

The FSIA defines "commercial activity" to mean:

> "[E]ither a regular course of commercial conduct or a particular commercial transaction or act. The commercial character of an activity shall be determined by reference to the nature of the course of conduct or particular transaction or act, rather than by reference to its purpose." 28 U.S.C. § 1603(d).

This definition, however, leaves the critical term "commercial" largely undefined: The first sentence simply establishes that the commercial nature of an activity does *not* depend upon whether it is a single act or a regular course of conduct; and the second sentence merely specifies what element of the conduct determines commerciality (*i.e.*, nature rather than purpose), but still without saying what "commercial" means. Fortunately, however, the FSIA was not written on a clean slate. * * * [T]he Act (and the commercial exception in particular) largely codifies the so-called "restrictive" theory of foreign sovereign immunity first endorsed by the State Department in 1952. The meaning of "commercial" is the meaning generally attached to that term under the restrictive theory at the time the statute was enacted. * * * *

[W]e conclude that when a foreign government acts, not as regulator of a market, but in the manner of a private player within it, the foreign sovereign's actions are "commercial" within the meaning of the FSIA. Moreover, because the Act provides that the commercial character of an act is to be determined by reference to its "nature" rather than its "purpose," 28 U.S.C. § 1603(d), the question is not whether the foreign government is acting with a profit motive or instead with the aim of fulfilling uniquely sovereign objectives. Rather, the issue is whether the particular actions that the foreign state performs (whatever the motive behind them) are the *type* of actions by which a private party engages in "trade and traffic or commerce," Black's Law Dictionary 270 (6th ed. 1990). Thus, a foreign government's issuance of regulations limiting foreign currency exchange is a sovereign activity, because such authoritative control of commerce cannot be exercised by a private party; whereas a contract to buy army boots or even bullets is a "commercial" activity, because private companies can similarly use sales contracts to acquire goods.

The commercial character of the Bonods is confirmed by the fact that they are in almost all respects garden-variety debt instruments: They may be held by private parties; they are negotiable and may be traded on the international market (except in Argentina); and they promise a future stream of cash income. * * * *

* * * * Argentina argues that the Bonods differ from ordinary debt instruments in that they "were created by the Argentine Government to fulfill its obligations under a foreign exchange program designed to address a domestic credit crisis, and as a component of a program designed to control that nation's critical shortage of foreign exchange." * * * * We think this line of argument is squarely foreclosed by the language of the FSIA. However difficult it may be in some cases to separate "purpose" (*i.e.*, the *reason* why the foreign state engages in the activity) from "nature" (*i.e.*, the outward form of the conduct that the foreign state performs or agrees to perform), the statute unmistakably commands that to be done, 28 U.S.C. § 1603(d). * * * [I]t is irrelevant *why* Argentina participated in the bond market in the manner of a private actor; it matters only that it did so. We conclude that Argentina's issuance of the Bonods was a "commercial activity" under the FSIA.

The remaining question is whether Argentina's unilateral rescheduling of the Bonods had a "direct effect" in the United States, 28 U.S.C. § 1605(a)(2). * * * *

We * * * have little difficulty concluding that Argentina's unilateral rescheduling of the maturity dates on the Bonods had a "direct effect" in the United States. Respondents had designated their accounts in New York as the place of payment, and Argentina made some interest payments into those accounts before announcing that it was rescheduling the payments. Because New York was thus the place of performance for Argentina's ultimate contractual obligations, the rescheduling of those obligations necessarily had a "direct effect" in the United States: Money that was supposed to have been delivered to a New York bank for deposit was not forthcoming. We reject Argentina's suggestion that the "direct effect" requirement cannot be satisfied where the plaintiffs are all foreign corporations with no other connections to the United States. * * * [T]he FSIA permits "a foreign plaintiff to sue a foreign sovereign in the courts of the United States, provided the substantive requirements of the Act are satisfied," 461 U.S., at 489, 103 S.Ct., at 1969.

Finally, Argentina argues that a finding of jurisdiction in this case would violate the Due Process Clause of the Fifth Amendment, and that, in order to avoid this difficulty, we must construe the "direct effect" requirement as embodying the "minimum contacts" test of *International Shoe Co. v. Washington,* 326 U.S. 310 (1945). Assuming, without deciding, that a foreign state is a "person" for purposes of the Due Process Clause, we find that Argentina possessed "minimum contacts" that would satisfy the constitutional test. By issuing negotiable debt instruments denominated in United States dollars and payable in New York and by appointing a financial agent in that city, Argentina " 'purposefully avail[ed] itself of the privilege of conducting activities within the [United States].' " *Burger King Corp. v. Rudzewicz,* 471 U.S. 462, 475 (1985), quoting *Hanson v. Denckla,* 357 U.S. 235, 253 (1958). * * * *

The 2008 Amendment for State-Sponsored Terrorism

In 2008 Congress amended the FSIA to create a new cause of action for U.S. citizens, employees, and armed forces members to sue foreign states for "personal injury or death * * * caused by an act of torture, extrajudicial killing, aircraft sabotage, hostage taking, or the provision of material support or resources for such an act * * * if engaged in by an official, employee, or agent of such foreign state while acting within the scope of his * * * employment." 28 U.S.C. § 1605A. Although this exception to sovereign immunity seems broad, it is only available if the foreign state being sued has been designated a state sponsor of terrorism by the U.S. Department of State. As of December 2020, only three states have this designation: Democratic People's Republic of Korea, Iran, and Syria.

In the case of *Opati v. Republic of Sudan*, the plaintiffs were a group of victims and family members who sued Sudan (which was at that time on the list of state sponsors of terrorism) in federal court in response to a 1998 attack on U.S. Embassies in Kenya and Tanzania by the terrorist group al Qaeda. The District Court found evidence of "material support"* by Sudan to al Qaeda based on the fact that Sudan had provided to al Qaeda Sudanese passports, places to train for the attacks, border passage without restriction, and passage of weapons and money to the Kenyan al Qaeda cell. *Owens v. Republic of Sudan*, 826 F.Supp. 2d 128, 139–46 (D.D.C. 2011). On appeal, the D.C. Circuit ruled that as long as the injury to the plaintiffs was reasonably foreseeable and the support was a substantial factor to the injury, there is proximate causation, and the suit can proceed. The foreign state need not specifically intend the injury for the FSIA exception to apply. *Owens v. Republic of Sudan*, 864 F.3d 751, 798–99

---

*   18 U.S.C.A. § 2339A(b)(1) (West 2010) (defining "material support" as "any property * * * or service, including * * * financial services, lodging, training * * * safehouses * * * facilities * * * and transportation, except medicine or religious materials.").

(D.C. Cir. 2017), *rev'd on other grounds sub nom. Opati v. Republic of Sudan*, 140 S. Ct. 1601 (2020).

The Justice Against Sponsors of Terrorism Act

The most recent notable amendment to the FSIA is the Justice Against Sponsors of Terrorism Act (JASTA), Pub. L. No. 114–222 § 3(a), 130 Stat. 852 (codified at 28 U.S.C. § 1605B). It was passed in 2016 in response to the terrorist attacks of September 11, 2001 (the "9/11 Attacks"). Under JASTA, sovereign immunity is waived

> in any case in which money damages are sought * * * for physical injury to person or property or death occurring in the United States and caused by—
>
> (1)   an act of international terrorism in the United States; and
>
> (2)   a tortious act or acts of the foreign state, or of any official, employee, or agent of that foreign state while acting within the scope of his or her office, employment, or agency, regardless [of] where the tortious act or acts of the foreign state occurred.

Unlike § 1605A, which requires a foreign nation to be designated a state sponsor of terrorism, JASTA allows plaintiffs to bring suits against any foreign state, or its official, employee, or agent, for a tortious act that occurs anywhere in the world, as long as the physical injury to person or property occurs in the United States. However, the Act does contain several restrictions. Most importantly, it excludes suits based on omissions or merely negligent acts, and it allows the Attorney General to request a stay if the suit would "significantly interfere with a criminal investigation or prosecution, or a national security operation." 28 U.S.C. § 1605(g)(1) (1976). As this is a fairly recent amendment specifically targeted to suits arising from acts of terrorism, there is not yet much litigation invoking this exception. One of the few notable cases to date is *Ashton v. Al Qaeda Islamic Army (In re Terrorist Attacks on September 11, 2001)*, 298 F. Supp. 3d 631 (S.D.N.Y. 2018), a multidistrict litigation against several defendants, including Saudi Arabia, for providing support in the 9/11 Attacks. In that case, the court found that Saudi Arabia could potentially be held vicariously liable for several of its instrumentalities' and agents' actions and therefore ordered further discovery to be conducted so that plaintiffs could gather evidence to support their claims.

Notes and Questions

1.   What do you think is the justification for granting sovereign immunity to foreign governments? Is sovereign immunity *ever* justified?

2.   If you think sovereign immunity serves important purposes, then why should there be any exceptions at all? After all, aren't those same important purposes implicated in all the situations discussed above? Do you think the exceptions are appropriate? Why or why not?

3.   Would you create *further* exceptions to sovereign immunity? What about foreign states that are involved in cyber-intrusions upon U.S. citizens or corporations? Should such violations be actionable in civil suits? Certainly, victims of cybercrime and other forms of malicious cyber activity want and deserve justice for the attacks perpetrated against them. On the other hand, are civil suits the appropriate way to handle such concerns? Are there any consequences to carving out so many exceptions to the sovereign immunity doctrine?

4.   One important issue in many FSIA cases is how a court can properly assert personal jurisdiction over a foreign state. In *Weltover*, the Supreme Court articulated the inquiry as whether the sovereign defendant purposefully availed itself of the privilege of conducting activities within the United States as a whole, rather than any particular state. This is a broader standard than the one the Court has articulated for a foreign corporation, which must direct conduct to a particular state. *See McIntyre v. Nicastro*, 564 U.S. 873 (2011). Is this difference justifiable?

5.   Finally, litigation involving the FSIA sometimes turns on whether the defendant is appropriately considered a "state" for sovereign immunity purposes. An agency or instrumentality is treated as a state under the FSIA if it is (1) a separate legal entity, (2) an organ or political subdivision of a foreign state, or an entity that is majority owned by a foreign state or political division, and (3) not a citizen of the United States. § 1603(b). Even if it meets this definition, however, an agent or instrumentality of a state is treated somewhat differently under the statute from an actual foreign state or its political subdivision. §§ 1605(a)–(b) (enumerating the scope of property subject to attachment and other exceptions concerning expropriations for agencies and instrumentalities).

In practice, it is difficult to satisfy these criteria and sue a private party as an instrumentality of a state. The U.S. Supreme Court has held that instrumentalities should be presumed to be independent and not entitled to immunity unless the instrumentality can be characterized as the "alter ego" of the state. *First Nat'l City Bank v. Banco Para El Comercio Exterior de Cuba*, 406 U.S. 759 (1972); *see also Rubin v. Sialmic Republic of Iran*, 138 S. Ct. 816, 822 (2018) (determining that 28 U.S.C. § 1610(g) incorporated nearly verbatim the *Banco* factors). When asking whether a state can be responsible for a separate entity's behavior, courts have noted that a foreign state's separate juridical status can only be overcome if the state is routinely involved in the daily affairs of the other entity, or when it would perpetuate a fraud or injustice. David P. Stewart, *The Foreign Sovereign Immunities Act: A Guide for Judges*, 2018 FED. JUD. CTR., at 39. *See Sachs v. Republic of Austria*, 695 F.3d 1021 (9th Cir. 2012), *rev'd on other grounds, OBB Personenverkehr AG v. Sachs*, 577 U.S. 27 (2015).

6.   The U.S. Supreme Court has made clear, however, that individual governmental officials can be sued, even if they were acting in their official capacities at the time. In *Samantar v. Yousouf*, 560 U.S. 305 (2010), the Court ruled that the FSIA does *not* immunize individual governmental officials. According to the Court, an individual governmental official is not within the scope of § 1603(b). Do you think that is the right result? If sovereign immunity is meant to protect foreign states from litigation for official acts, why should that protection not extend to governmental officials of that state, at least when carrying out official duties? Can you think of reasons for differentiating between suits against states and suits against individual governmental officials? Should it matter whether those officials are still part of the government when the suit is filed?

B. THE ALIEN TORT STATUTE

As noted above, although the Foreign Sovereign Immunities Act involves claims against governments or their agents and instrumentalities, it does not apply to suits against foreign individuals (even governmental officials) or to corporations. Therefore, U.S. plaintiffs are free to sue such defendants, assuming the court has personal jurisdiction. But what if *foreign* nationals wish to sue other foreign nationals in U.S. courts? The Alien Tort Statute, 28 U.S.C. § 1350, was enacted as part of the Judiciary Act of 1789 and grants jurisdiction to federal district courts over "all causes where an alien sues for a tort only in violation of the law of nations or of a treaty of the United States." The "law of nations" is what today we refer to as international law. Therefore, the statute seems to grant broad subject matter jurisdiction for foreign nationals to sue other foreign nationals in U.S. federal courts for international law violations, again assuming they can also get personal jurisdiction over the defendants (for example, if the defendant were visiting the United States and were served in person).

The Alien Tort Statute was rarely, if ever, invoked until the 1980s, when human rights lawyers began to use the statute to sue individuals—and later corporations—accused of committing gross human rights violations. In response to this litigation, the U.S.

Supreme Court, in three cases decided between 2004 and 2018, sought to limit the scope of the statute.

KIOBEL V. ROYAL DUTCH PETROLEUM CO.

Supreme Court of the United States, 2013
569 U.S. 108

ROBERTS, J.

Petitioners, a group of Nigerian nationals residing in the United States, filed suit in federal court against certain Dutch, British, and Nigerian corporations. Petitioners sued under the Alien Tort Statute, 28 U.S.C. § 1350, alleging that the corporations aided and abetted the Nigerian Government in committing violations of the law of nations in Nigeria. The question presented is whether and under what circumstances courts may recognize a cause of action under the Alien Tort Statute for violations of the law of nations occurring within the territory of a sovereign other than the United States.

I

Petitioners were residents of Ogoniland, an area of 250 square miles located in the Niger delta area of Nigeria and populated by roughly half a million people. When the complaint was filed, respondents Royal Dutch Petroleum Company and Shell Transport and Trading Company, p. l. c., were holding companies incorporated in the Netherlands and England, respectively. Their joint subsidiary, respondent Shell Petroleum Development Company of Nigeria, Ltd. (SPDC), was incorporated in Nigeria, and engaged in oil exploration and production in Ogoniland. According to the complaint, after concerned residents of Ogoniland began protesting the environmental effects of SPDC's practices, respondents enlisted the Nigerian Government to violently suppress the burgeoning demonstrations. Throughout the early 1990's, the complaint alleges, Nigerian military and police forces attacked Ogoni villages, beating, raping, killing, and arresting residents and destroying or looting property. Petitioners further allege that respondents aided and abetted these atrocities by, among other things, providing the Nigerian forces with food, transportation, and compensation, as well as by allowing the Nigerian military to use respondents' property as a staging ground for attacks.

Following the alleged atrocities, petitioners moved to the United States where they have been granted political asylum and now reside as legal residents. They filed suit in the United States District Court for the Southern District of New York, alleging jurisdiction under the Alien Tort Statute and requesting relief under customary international law. The ATS provides, in full, that "[t]he district courts shall have original jurisdiction of any civil action by an alien for a tort only, committed in violation of the law of nations or a treaty of the United States." 28 U.S.C. § 1350. According to petitioners, respondents violated the law of nations by aiding and abetting the Nigerian Government in committing (1) extrajudicial killings; (2) crimes against humanity; (3) torture and cruel treatment; (4) arbitrary arrest and detention; (5) violations of the rights to life, liberty, security, and association; (6) forced exile; and (7) property destruction. The District Court dismissed the first, fifth, sixth, and seventh claims, reasoning that the facts alleged to support those claims did not give rise to a violation of the law of nations. The court denied respondents' motion to dismiss with respect to the remaining claims, but certified its order for interlocutory appeal pursuant to § 1292(b). * * * *

II

Passed as part of the Judiciary Act of 1789, the ATS was invoked twice in the late 18th century, but then only once more over the next 167 years. The statute provides district courts with jurisdiction to hear certain claims, but does not expressly provide any causes of action. We held in *Sosa v. Alvarez-Machain*, 542 U.S. 692, 714 (2004), however, that the First Congress did not intend the provision to be "stillborn." The grant of jurisdiction is instead "best read as having been enacted on the understanding that the common law would provide a cause of action for [a] modest number of international law violations." *Id.*, at 724. We thus held that federal courts may "recognize private claims [for such violations] under federal common law." *Id.*, at 732. The Court in *Sosa* rejected the plaintiff's claim in that case for "arbitrary arrest and detention," on the ground that it failed to state a violation of the law of nations with the requisite "definite content and acceptance among civilized nations." *Id.*, at 699, 732 (internal quotation marks omitted).

The question here is not whether petitioners have stated a proper claim under the ATS, but whether a claim may reach conduct occurring in the territory of a foreign sovereign. Respondents contend that claims under the ATS do not, relying primarily on a canon of statutory interpretation known as the presumption against extraterritorial application. That canon provides that "[w]hen a statute gives no clear indication of an extraterritorial application, it has none," *Morrison v. National Australia Bank Ltd.*, 561 U.S. 247, 255 (2010), and reflects the "presumption that United States law governs domestically but does not rule the world," *Microsoft Corp. v. AT&T Corp.*, 550 U.S. 437, 454 (2007).

This presumption "serves to protect against unintended clashes between our laws and those of other nations which could result in international discord." *EEOC v. Arabian American Oil Co.*, 499 U.S. 244, 248, 111 S. Ct. 1227 (1991) (*Aramco*). As this Court has explained:

> "For us to run interference in ... a delicate field of international relations there must be present the affirmative intention of the Congress clearly expressed. It alone has the facilities necessary to make fairly such an important policy decision where the possibilities of international discord are so evident and retaliative action so certain." *Benz v. Compania Naviera Hidalgo, S. A.*, 353 U.S. 138, 147 (1957).

The presumption against extraterritorial application helps ensure that the Judiciary does not erroneously adopt an interpretation of U.S. law that carries foreign policy consequences not clearly intended by the political branches.

We typically apply the presumption to discern whether an Act of Congress regulating conduct applies abroad. The ATS, on the other hand, is "strictly jurisdictional." *Sosa*, 542 U.S., at 713. It does not directly regulate conduct or afford relief. It instead allows federal courts to recognize certain causes of action based on sufficiently definite norms of international law. But we think the principles underlying the canon of interpretation similarly constrain courts considering causes of action that may be brought under the ATS.

Indeed, the danger of unwarranted judicial interference in the conduct of foreign policy is magnified in the context of the ATS, because the question is not what Congress has done but instead what courts may do. This Court in *Sosa* repeatedly stressed the need for judicial caution in considering which claims could be brought under the ATS, in light of foreign policy concerns. As the Court explained, "the potential [foreign policy] implications . . . of recognizing . . . . causes [under the ATS] should make courts particularly wary of impinging on the discretion of the Legislative and Executive Branches in managing foreign affairs." *Id.*, at 727. These concerns, which are implicated in any case arising under the ATS, are all the more pressing when the question is whether a cause of action under the ATS reaches conduct within the territory of another sovereign.

These concerns are not diminished by the fact that *Sosa* limited federal courts to recognizing causes of action only for alleged violations of international law norms that are " 'specific, universal, and obligatory.' " *Id.*, at 732. * * * *. The principles underlying the presumption against extraterritoriality thus constrain courts exercising their power under the ATS.

III

Petitioners contend that even if the presumption applies, the text, history, and purposes of the ATS rebut it for causes of action brought under that statute. It is true that Congress, even in a jurisdictional provision, can indicate that it intends federal law to apply to conduct occurring abroad. But to rebut the presumption, the ATS would need to evince a "clear indication of extraterritoriality." *Morrison*, 561 U.S., at 265. It does not.

To begin, nothing in the text of the statute suggests that Congress intended causes of action recognized under it to have extraterritorial reach. The ATS covers actions by aliens for violations of the law of nations, but that does not imply extraterritorial reach— such violations affecting aliens can occur either within or outside the United States. Nor does the fact that the text reaches "*any* civil action" suggest application to torts committed abroad; it is well established that generic terms like "any" or "every" do not rebut the presumption against extraterritoriality. * * * *

Nor does the historical background against which the ATS was enacted overcome the presumption against application to conduct in the territory of another sovereign. We explained in *Sosa* that when Congress passed the ATS, "three principal offenses against the law of nations" had been identified by Blackstone: violation of safe conducts, infringement of the rights of ambassadors, and piracy. 542 U.S., at 723. Indeed, Blackstone—in describing them—did so in terms of conduct occurring within the forum nation.

Two notorious episodes involving violations of the law of nations occurred in the United States shortly before passage of the ATS. Each concerned the rights of ambassadors, and each involved conduct within the Union. * * * * The two cases in which the ATS was invoked shortly after its passage also concerned conduct within the territory of the United States. These prominent contemporary examples— immediately before and after passage of the ATS—provide no support for the proposition that Congress expected causes of action to be brought under the statute for violations of the law of nations occurring abroad.

The third example of a violation of the law of nations familiar to the Congress that enacted the ATS was piracy. Piracy typically occurs on the high seas, beyond the territorial jurisdiction of the United States or any other country. This Court has generally treated the high seas the same as foreign soil for purposes of the presumption against extraterritorial application. Petitioners contend that because Congress surely intended the ATS to provide jurisdiction for actions against pirates, it necessarily anticipated the statute would apply to conduct occurring abroad.

Applying U.S. law to pirates, however, does not typically impose the sovereign will of the United States onto conduct occurring within the territorial jurisdiction of another sovereign, and therefore carries less direct foreign policy consequences. Pirates were fair game wherever found, by any nation, because they generally did not operate within any jurisdiction. We do not think that the existence of a cause of action against them is a sufficient basis for concluding that other causes of action under the ATS reach conduct that does occur within the territory of another sovereign; pirates may well be a category unto themselves. * * * *

Finally, there is no indication that the ATS was passed to make the United States a uniquely hospitable forum for the enforcement of international norms. As Justice Story put it, "No nation has ever yet pretended to be the custos morum of the whole world . . . ." *United States v. La Jeune Eugenie*, 26 F. Cas. 832, 847 (No. 15,551) (CC. Mass. 1822). It is implausible to suppose that the First Congress wanted their fledgling Republic—struggling to receive international recognition—to be the first. Indeed, the parties offer no evidence that any nation, meek or mighty, presumed to do such a thing.

The United States was, however, embarrassed by its potential inability to provide judicial relief to foreign officials injured in the United States. Such offenses against ambassadors violated the law of nations, "and if not adequately redressed could rise to an issue of war." *Sosa*, 542 U.S., at 715. The ATS ensured that the United States could provide a forum for adjudicating such incidents. Nothing about this historical context suggests that Congress also intended federal common law under the ATS to provide a cause of action for conduct occurring in the territory of another sovereign.

Indeed, far from avoiding diplomatic strife, providing such a cause of action could have generated it. Recent experience bears this out. *See Doe v. Exxon Mobil Corp.*, 654 F.3d 11, 77–78, 397 U.S. App. D.C. 371 (CADC 2011) (Kavanaugh, J., dissenting in part) (listing recent objections to extraterritorial applications of the ATS by Canada, Germany, Indonesia, Papua New Guinea, South Africa, Switzerland, and the United Kingdom). Moreover, accepting petitioners' view would imply that other nations, also applying the law of nations, could hale our citizens into their courts for alleged violations of the law of nations occurring in the United States, or anywhere else in the world. The presumption against extraterritoriality guards against our courts triggering such serious foreign policy consequences, and instead defers such decisions, quite appropriately, to the political branches.

We therefore conclude that the presumption against extraterritoriality applies to claims under the ATS, and that nothing in the statute rebuts that presumption. "[T]here is no clear indication of extraterritoriality here," *Morrison,* 561 U.S., at 265, and petitioners' case seeking relief for violations of the law of nations occurring outside the United States is barred.

IV

On these facts, all the relevant conduct took place outside the United States. And even where the claims touch and concern the territory of the United States, they must do so with sufficient force to displace the presumption against extraterritorial application. Corporations are often present in many countries, and it would reach too far to say that mere corporate presence suffices. If Congress were to determine otherwise, a statute more specific than the ATS would be required. * * * *

KENNEDY, J., concurring.

The opinion for the Court is careful to leave open a number of significant questions regarding the reach and interpretation of the Alien Tort Statute. In my view that is a proper disposition. Many serious concerns with respect to human rights abuses committed abroad have been addressed by Congress in statutes such as the Torture Victim Protection Act of 1991 (TVPA), 106 Stat. 73, note following 28 U.S.C. § 1350, and that class of cases will be determined in the future according to the detailed statutory scheme Congress has enacted. Other cases may arise with allegations of serious violations of international law principles protecting persons, cases covered neither by the TVPA nor by the reasoning and holding of today's case; and in those disputes the proper implementation of the presumption against extraterritorial application may require some further elaboration and explanation.

ALITO, J. with whom JUSTICE THOMAS joins, concurring.

I concur in the judgment and join the opinion of the Court as far as it goes. Specifically, I agree that when Alien Tort Statute (ATS) "claims touch and concern the territory of the United States, they must do so with sufficient force to displace the presumption against extraterritorial application." This formulation obviously leaves much unanswered, and perhaps there is wisdom in the Court's preference for this narrow approach. I write separately to set out the broader standard that leads me to the conclusion that this case falls within the scope of the presumption.

In *Morrison v. Nat'l Austl. Bank Ltd.*, 561 U.S. 247 (2010), we explained that "the presumption against extraterritorial application would be a craven watchdog indeed if it retreated to its kennel whenever *some* domestic activity is involved in the case." *Id.*, at 266. We also reiterated that a cause of action falls outside the scope of the presumption—and thus is not barred by the presumption—only if the event or relationship that was "the 'focus' of congressional concern" under the relevant statute takes place within the United States. For example, because "the focus of the [Securities] Exchange Act [of 1934] is not upon the place where the deception originated, but upon purchases and sales of securities in the United States," we held in *Morrison* that § 10(b) of the Exchange Act applies "only" to "transactions in securities listed on domestic exchanges, and domestic transactions in other securities." 561 U.S., at 266, 267.

The Court's decision in *Sosa v. Alvarez-Machain,* 542 U.S. 692 (2004), makes clear that when the ATS was enacted, "congressional concern" was " 'focus[ed],' " on the "three principal offenses against the law of nations" that had been identified by Blackstone: violation of safe conducts, infringement of the rights of ambassadors, and piracy, *Sosa,* 542 U.S., at 723–724. The Court therefore held that "federal courts should not recognize private claims under federal common law for violations of any international law norm with less definite content and acceptance among civilized nations than the historical paradigms familiar when [the ATS] was enacted." *Id.,* at 732. In other words, only conduct that satisfies *Sosa*'s requirements of definiteness and acceptance among civilized nations can be said to have been "the 'focus' of congressional concern," *Morrison, supra*, at 266, when Congress enacted the ATS. As a result, a putative ATS cause of action will fall within the scope of the presumption against extraterritoriality—and will therefore be barred—unless the domestic conduct is sufficient to violate an international law norm that satisfies *Sosa*'s requirements of definiteness and acceptance among civilized nations.

BREYER, J. with whom JUSTICE GINSBURG, JUSTICE SOTOMAYOR, and JUSTICE KAGAN join, concurring in the judgment.

I agree with the Court's conclusion but not with its reasoning. * * * *

Unlike the Court, I would not invoke the presumption against extraterritoriality. Rather, guided in part by principles and practices of foreign relations law, I would find jurisdiction under this statute where (1) the alleged tort occurs on American soil, (2) the defendant is an American national, or (3) the defendant's conduct substantially and adversely affects an important American national interest, and that includes a distinct interest in preventing the United States from becoming a safe harbor (free of civil as well as criminal liability) for a torturer or other common enemy of mankind. In this case, however, the parties and relevant conduct lack sufficient ties to the United States for the ATS to provide jurisdiction.

I

A

* * * *

Recognizing that Congress enacted the ATS to permit recovery of damages from pirates and others who violated basic international law norms as understood in 1789, *Sosa* essentially leads today's judges to ask: Who are today's pirates? We provided a framework for answering that question by setting down principles drawn from international norms and designed to limit ATS claims to those that are similar in character and specificity to piracy.

In this case we must decide the extent to which this jurisdictional statute opens a federal court's doors to those harmed by activities belonging to the limited class that *Sosa* set forth *when those activities take place abroad.* To help answer this question here, I would refer both to *Sosa* and, as in *Sosa,* to norms of international law.

B

In my view the majority's effort to answer the question by referring to the "presumption against extraterritoriality" does not work well. That presumption "rests on the perception that Congress ordinarily legislates with respect to domestic, not foreign matters." *Morrison v. National Australia Bank Ltd.,* 561 U.S. 247, 255 (2010). The ATS, however, was enacted with "foreign matters" in mind. The statute's text refers explicitly to "alien[s]," "treat[ies]," and "the law of nations." 28 U.S.C. § 1350. The statute's purpose was to address "violations of the law of nations, admitting of a judicial remedy and at the same time threatening serious consequences in international affairs." *Sosa,* 542 U.S., at 715. And at least one of the three kinds of activities that we found to fall within the statute's scope, namely piracy, normally takes place abroad.

The majority cannot wish this piracy example away by emphasizing that piracy takes place on the high seas. That is because the robbery and murder that make up piracy do not normally take place in the water; they take place on a ship. And a ship is like land,

in that it falls within the jurisdiction of the nation whose flag it flies.
Indeed, in the early 19th century Chief Justice Marshall described
piracy as an "offenc[e] against the nation under whose flag the vessel
sails, and within whose particular jurisdiction all on board the vessel
are." *United States v. Palmer,* 16 U.S. 610 (1818).

The majority nonetheless tries to find a distinction between
piracy at sea and similar cases on land. It writes, "Applying U.S. law
to pirates ... does not typically impose the sovereign will of the
United States onto conduct occurring within the *territorial*
jurisdiction of another sovereign and therefore carries less direct
foreign policy consequences." But, as I have just pointed out,
"[a]pplying U.S. law to pirates" *does* typically involve applying our
law to acts taking place within the jurisdiction of another sovereign.
* * * *

The majority also writes, "Pirates were fair game wherever
found, by any nation, because they generally did not operate within
any jurisdiction." I very much agree that pirates were fair game
"wherever found." Indeed, that is the point. That is why we asked, in
Sosa, who are today's pirates? Certainly, today's pirates include
torturers and perpetrators of genocide. And today, like the pirates of
old, they are "fair game" where they are found. Like those pirates,
they are "common enemies of all mankind and all nations have an
equal interest in their apprehension and punishment." 1
Restatement § 404 Reporters' Note 1, p. 256 (quoting *In re
Demjanjuk,* 612 F. Supp. 544, 556 (ND Ohio 1985) (internal quotation
marks omitted)). And just as a nation that harbored pirates provoked
the concern of other nations in past centuries, so harboring "common
enemies of all mankind" provokes similar concerns today.

Thus the Court's reasoning, as applied to the narrow class of
cases that *Sosa* described, fails to provide significant support for the
use of any presumption against extraterritoriality; rather, it suggests
the contrary.

In any event, as the Court uses its "presumption against
extraterritorial application," it offers only limited help in deciding
the question presented, namely " 'under what circumstances the
Alien Tort Statute ... allows courts to recognize a cause of action for
violations of the law of nations occurring within the territory of a
sovereign other than the United States.' " The majority * * * makes
clear that a statutory claim might sometimes "touch and concern the
territory of the United States ... with sufficient force to displace the
presumption." It leaves for another day the determination of just
when the presumption against extraterritoriality might be
"overcome."

II

In applying the ATS to acts "occurring within the territory of a[nother] sovereign," I would assume that Congress intended the statute's jurisdictional reach to match the statute's underlying substantive grasp. That grasp, defined by the statute's purposes set forth in *Sosa,* includes compensation for those injured by piracy and its modern-day equivalents, at least where allowing such compensation avoids "serious" negative international "consequences" for the United States. And just as we have looked to established international substantive norms to help determine the statute's substantive reach, so we should look to international jurisdictional norms to help determine the statute's jurisdictional scope.

The Restatement is helpful. Section 402 recognizes that, subject to § 403's "reasonableness" requirement, a nation may apply its law (for example, federal common law), not only (1) to "conduct" that "takes place [or to persons or things] within its territory" but also (2) to the "activities, interests, status, or relations of its nationals outside as well as within its territory," (3) to "conduct outside its territory that has or is intended to have substantial effect within its territory," and (4) to certain foreign "conduct outside its territory . . . that is directed against the security of the state or against a limited class of other state interests." In addition, § 404 of the Restatement explains that a "state has jurisdiction to define and prescribe punishment for certain offenses recognized by the community of nations as of universal concern, such as piracy, slave trade," and analogous behavior.

Considering these jurisdictional norms in light of both the ATS' basic purpose (to provide compensation for those injured by today's pirates) and *Sosa*'s basic caution (to avoid international friction), I believe that the statute provides jurisdiction where (1) the alleged tort occurs on American soil, (2) the defendant is an American national, or (3) the defendant's conduct substantially and adversely affects an important American national interest, and that includes a distinct interest in preventing the United States from becoming a safe harbor (free of civil as well as criminal liability) for a torturer or other common enemy of mankind.

I would interpret the statute as providing jurisdiction only where distinct American interests are at issue. * * * * That restriction * * * should help to minimize international friction. Further limiting principles such as exhaustion, *forum non conveniens,* and comity would do the same. So would a practice of courts giving weight to the views of the Executive Branch.

As I have indicated, we should treat this Nation's interest in not becoming a safe harbor for violators of the most fundamental international norms as an important jurisdiction-related interest justifying application of the ATS in light of the statute's basic purposes—in particular that of compensating those who have suffered harm at the hands of, *e.g.,* torturers or other modern pirates. * * * * [T] the statute's language, history, and purposes suggest that the statute was to be a weapon in the "war" against those modern pirates who, by their conduct, have "declar[ed] war against all mankind." 4 Blackstone 71.

International norms have long included a duty not to permit a nation to become a safe harbor for pirates (or their equivalent). More recently two lower American courts have, in effect, rested jurisdiction primarily upon that kind of concern. In *Filartiga,* 630 F. 2d 876, an alien plaintiff brought a lawsuit against an alien defendant for damages suffered through acts of torture that the defendant allegedly inflicted in a foreign nation, Paraguay. Neither plaintiff nor defendant was an American national, and the actions underlying the lawsuit took place abroad. The defendant, however, "had . . . resided in the United States for more than ninth months" before being sued, having overstayed his visitor's visa. *Id.,* at 878–879. Jurisdiction was deemed proper because the defendant's alleged conduct violated a well-established international law norm, and the suit vindicated our Nation's interest in not providing a safe harbor, free of damages claims, for those defendants who commit such conduct.

In *Marcos,* the plaintiffs were nationals of the Philippines, the defendant was a Philippine national, and the alleged wrongful act, death by torture, took place abroad. A month before being sued, the defendant, "his family, . . . and others loyal to [him] fled to Hawaii," where the ATS case was heard. As in *Filartiga,* the court found ATS jurisdiction.

And in *Sosa,* we referred to both cases with approval, suggesting that the ATS allowed a claim for relief in such circumstances. Not surprisingly, both before and after *Sosa,* courts have consistently rejected the notion that the ATS is categorically barred from extraterritorial application.

Application of the statute in the way I have suggested is consistent with international law and foreign practice. Nations have long been obliged not to provide safe harbors for their own nationals who commit such serious crimes abroad. Many countries permit foreign plaintiffs to bring suits against their own nationals based on unlawful conduct that took place abroad. Other countries permit some form of lawsuit brought by a foreign national against a foreign national, based upon conduct taking place abroad and seeking damages. Certain countries, which find "universal" criminal "jurisdiction" to try perpetrators of particularly heinous crimes such as piracy and genocide, see Restatement § 404, also permit private persons injured by that conduct to pursue *"actions civiles,"* seeking civil damages in the criminal proceeding. * * * *

At the same time the Senate has consented to treaties obliging the United States to find and punish foreign perpetrators of serious crimes committed against foreign persons abroad. And Congress has sometimes authorized civil damages in such cases.

Congress, while aware of the award of civil damages under the ATS—including cases such as *Filartiga* with foreign plaintiffs, defendants, and conduct—has not sought to limit the statute's jurisdictional or substantive reach. Rather, Congress has enacted other statutes, and not only criminal statutes, that allow the United States to prosecute (or allow victims to obtain damages from) foreign persons who injure foreign victims by committing abroad torture, genocide, and other heinous acts.

Thus, the jurisdictional approach that I would use is analogous to, and consistent with, the approaches of a number of other nations. It is consistent with the approaches set forth in the Restatement. Its insistence upon the presence of some distinct American interest, its reliance upon courts also invoking other related doctrines such as comity, exhaustion, and *forum non conveniens*, along with its dependence (for its workability) upon courts obtaining, and paying particular attention to, the views of the Executive Branch, all should obviate the majority's concern that our jurisdictional example would lead "other nations, also applying the law of nations," to "hale our citizens into their courts for alleged violations of the law of nations occurring in the United States, or anywhere else in the world."

Most importantly, this jurisdictional view is consistent with the substantive view of the statute that we took in *Sosa*. This approach would avoid placing the statute's jurisdictional scope at odds with its substantive objectives, holding out "the word of promise" of compensation for victims of the torturer, while "break[ing] it to the hope."

III

Applying these jurisdictional principles to this case, however, I agree with the Court that jurisdiction does not lie. The defendants are two foreign corporations. Their shares, like those of many foreign corporations, are traded on the New York Stock Exchange. Their only presence in the United States consists of an office in New York City (actually owned by a separate but affiliated company) that helps to explain their business to potential investors. The plaintiffs are not United States nationals but nationals of other nations. The conduct at issue took place abroad. And the plaintiffs allege, not that the defendants directly engaged in acts of torture, genocide, or the equivalent, but that they helped others (who are not American nationals) to do so.

Under these circumstances, even if the New York office were a sufficient basis for asserting general jurisdiction, it would be farfetched to believe, based solely upon the defendants' minimal and indirect American presence, that this legal action helps to vindicate a distinct American interest, such as in not providing a safe harbor for an "enemy of all mankind." * * * *

I consequently join the Court's judgment but not its opinion.

Notes and Questions

1.   Do you agree with the majority that the presumption against extraterritorial application of statutes resolves this case? What about Justice Breyer's argument that the whole point of this statute was to allow foreign citizens to sue for violations of international law?

2.   Do you agree with Justice Breyer that human rights abusers are modern-day pirates who should be able to be sued wherever they are found? Or do human rights suits such as the one contemplated here raise sovereignty and diplomacy concerns not found in suits against pirates?

3.   In 2018 the U.S. Supreme Court further restricted the scope of the Alien Tort Statute, ruling in *Jesner v. Arab Bank, PLC*, 138 S. Ct. 1386, 1403 (2018), that ATS claims can only be brought against individuals, not corporations. The 5–4 majority was fractured, leaving no single majority opinion. However, all five justices in the majority focused in part on potential separation-of-powers concerns, noting that allowing ATS suits against corporations might interfere with international relations and that a cause of action against corporations should not be inferred from the language of the ATS without more explicit congressional action.

Justice Sotomayor, joined by Justices Ginsburg, Breyer, and Kagan, dissented, arguing that the proper analysis, under *Sosa v. Alvarez-Machain*, 542 U.S. 692 (2004), was to ask whether the Complaint alleges that a specific, universal, and obligatory norm of international law had been violated. According to the dissenters, the focus should be on the norm, not the type of defendant claimed to have violated that norm. As to the majority's separation-of-powers concerns, the dissenting justices stated that "[n]othing about the corporate form in itself raises foreign-policy concerns that require the Court, as a matter of common-law discretion, to immunize all foreign corporations from liability under the ATS." *Id.* at 1419.

4.   After *Sosa*, *Kiobel*, and *Jesner*, what is left of the ATS? Are any suits still possible? If you were in Congress, would you amend the ATS? If so, how? Or would you repeal it altogether?

Chapter 10

GATHERING EVIDENCE

The materials in this chapter focus on the task of gathering evidence for trial—what common law systems label "discovery." This stage is central to the judicial process of any system because it provides litigants with the means to obtain evidence that may be necessary to prove their case. Justice, or at least the ascertainment of truth, would seem to require the consideration of all non-cumulative evidence that may be relevant to the case.

Rules that are designed to facilitate discovery of all of that evidence, however, may sacrifice other important values. Indeed, the American system of discovery, while credited for leaving no stone unturned, is also notorious throughout the world for its inefficiency and intrusiveness. In addition, the nature of a single continuous trial in the U.S. system means that all relevant evidence to the claim must be gathered at once. Even in the common law world the discovery practice of the U.S. system is an outlier, often leading to clashes in transnational or cross-border litigation.

Cross-border disputes in U.S. courts can result in discovery requests seeking information located in foreign jurisdictions. Similarly, foreign lawsuits may involve information located within U.S. borders. In many legal systems, fact-finding is very much the responsibility of judges, while in the United States, it is the parties who are granted broad "discovery powers." Today's converging systems may have blurred the distinctions somewhat, as the practice of "managerial judging" in the federal courts have moved the United States closer to the civil law model, while lawyers in the civil law world increasingly are tasked with more responsibility for gathering evidence.

Nevertheless, the kinds of "fishing expeditions" allowed by the broad "relevancy" standard and the pre-trial nature of U.S. discovery continue to trigger conflicts when the discovery request is directed outside the U.S. system. If the scope of these requests exceeds what would have been allowed in the receiving states, tensions flare that go beyond the litigation attempts by U.S. litigants to gather evidence abroad. In such instances, U.S. litigation may be viewed as usurping foreign sovereignty. In response, some countries have enacted what are known as blocking statutes in an effort to protect their sovereignty and the interests of persons under their jurisdiction.

This chapter begins with comparative materials outlining key differences in the conduct of discovery in different legal systems in the world, then turns to transnational materials revealing conflicts at the intersection of different systems, and concludes with international materials documenting efforts at multinational cooperation.

A. NATIONAL PRACTICES

National approaches to gathering evidence can vary widely, even among neighboring countries that derive from the same legal tradition. Explanations for these variations include politics and culture, perceptions about the purposes of litigation, and other rules and doctrines. Systems vary in their approach to: (i) the available mechanisms; (ii) the scope of inquiry permitted; (iii) the timing; (iv) the extent of judicial involvement; and (v) the participation of experts.

Gathering Evidence Mechanisms. American litigators have at their disposal a number of formal discovery techniques, including document requests, interrogatories, depositions, requests for admissions, and physical examinations. This set is unusually broad. Other common law systems, including Australia, the United Kingdom, Hong Kong, India, the Philippines and Singapore, offer only a subset of this list. In particular, no common law countries other than the United States and (parts of) Canada liberally allow pre-trial depositions for the purpose of gathering evidence.

Civil law countries tend to maintain a still narrower set of pre-trial mechanisms for gathering evidence. In many countries, such as Argentina, Germany and France, pretrial discovery of documents as understood in common law countries is not generally available. A party would have to request a judge to order the production of evidence during the course of the proceeding. In other countries, such as Japan, some limited discovery, including documents (and perhaps interrogatories) are exchanged in advance of trial. In Belgium, the most that a party can do to elicit detail from the opposing party— other than receiving documents—is to use the opponent's written submissions to the court to ask questions challenging the other party openly to respond. Many civil and common law countries have other discovery mechanisms (including depositions) available, but these techniques are for the limited use of preserving testimony that might be impossible to obtain at trial.

Among the tools of almost all systems are automatic disclosure requirements. Parties typically are obliged to disclose documents, either with the pleadings or at some later point. Some systems require the disclosure only of documents that support the disclosing party's position; many others require the disclosure of all relevant documents.

Scope of Inquiry. A system's philosophy toward the gathering of evidence is also reflected in what it considers permissible scope. At one end of the spectrum, the U.S. Federal Rules of Civil Procedure permit the discovery of any non-privileged matter that is relevant to the claim or defense of any party (provided the request is not unreasonably cumulative or burdensome and is proportional to the needs of the case). Under this regime, litigants tend to make broad requests, seeking unspecified information for the purpose of turning up anything that might be (or become) relevant to the case, so long as the information "appears reasonably calculated to lead to the discovery of admissible evidence." These are the sort of "fishing expeditions" that are frequently derided by other systems. In other systems—whether of the common law or the civil law tradition— requests for access to evidence must be more narrowly tailored and directly relevant to the allegations and theories in the pleadings. These constraints are especially significant because in many systems the pleadings are both fixed and more precise. Generally speaking, then, whether a particular request is sufficiently specific depends upon the circumstances leading to the request and the system's tolerance for discovery.

Timing. The timing and sequence of gathering evidence are fundamentally different in the common law and civil law traditions. In common law courts, the discovery stage occurs in preparation for trial, where the evidence is then presented in full. In civil law systems, certain documents and evidence may be disclosed early in the action, but otherwise the evidence is simultaneously gathered and evaluated by the judge in a series of hearings. In Italy, for example, the gathering of evidence occurs over the course of a number of separate hearings spanning months or years. The purpose of the earlier hearings is to determine which mechanisms of evidence will be used; the later hearings involve the "taking" of evidence.

Judicial Involvement. In most common law systems, certain initial disclosures may be required by procedural rule, but discovery otherwise is largely party-controlled. Federal Rules 26(f) and 16(b) require parties and their counsel to meet with the judge to establish the parameters of discovery at the outset. Nevertheless, because discovery requests and responses ordinarily are not filed with the court, the judge is unlikely even to know how discovery is progressing, unless some dispute arises between the parties that requires judicial intervention.

In most civil law systems, by contrast, the parties may not ask one another to produce evidence without the participation of the court. Civil law systems generally view evidence-gathering as a judicial function. Although the parties may offer the names of witnesses and will suggest questions to be put to the witnesses, the civil law judge typically decides which witnesses to summon, conducts the questioning, and records the evidence. The gathering and evaluation of the evidence are intertwined, and both tasks are undertaken as an exercise of the judicial function.

Expert Evidence. Under the Federal Rules, the selection of experts and their deployment are largely within the control of the parties. It is not uncommon, then, that so-called "hired guns" engage in a "battle of the experts." Not all common law systems, however, follow this model. In England, the new Civil Practice Rules restrict the use of expert witnesses "to that which is reasonably required to resolve the proceedings."* In particular, no expert witness can be used in any civil proceeding without the court's permission.

The civil law countries tend to be even more restrictive. Parties ordinarily cannot bring their own expert witnesses or present reports from their own experts. Instead, the court, upon acknowledging the need for expert testimony, appoints a neutral expert who submits a report answering the parties' questions and appears for questioning at trial. In Belgium, for example, the judge determines both the need for, and the tasks of, any expert. At a meeting with the expert, the parties give an overview of their respective positions and the evidence necessary for the expert to offer her opinion. The expert prepares a preliminary report upon which the parties are permitted to comment. The expert then prepares a final report that incorporates and responds to the parties' comments. The court is not bound by the conclusions of the expert, although in practice most courts follow the findings.

STEPHEN N. SUBRIN, *DISCOVERY IN GLOBAL PERSPECTIVE: ARE WE NUTS?*
52 DEPAUL L. REV. 299 (2002)

* * * * Our discovery mechanisms are not so irrational when seen in context. Let me sketch out some examples. Consider our historic distrust of concentrated power. Our doctrines of federalism and separation of powers, the right to a jury trial, and the adversary

---

* UK Civil Procedure Rule 35.1.

system, including party control, reflect our historic distrust of residing power in one person or limited groups. We do not think that judges would ferret out negative aspects of our opponent's case and positive information to prove our own claims or defenses with the same motivation and intensity that self-interest propels. Perhaps if we had more experience with career judges, elevated as the result of performance based on objective criteria, as opposed to politically-appointed or elected judges, we would have more confidence in turning over discovery to the judiciary. * * * *

In the United States, civil litigation plays a more substantial role in the governmental and societal structure than in most other countries. Alexis de Tocqueville noted in the 1830s how many hotly contested political issues end up in the United States courts. These issues are frequently, if not usually, raised by private litigants in civil litigation, as opposed to law enforcement by the state itself. A recent article about the Japanese legal system emphasizes how unusual the United States is in utilizing civil litigation, often through the tort system, to enforce social norms.[53] In this article, the author notes that in Japan, after private individuals sought to enforce environmental and anti-discrimination laws through civil litigation, the government, particularly "the entrenched bureaucracy," sought to curtail private enforcement so that the state could retain its power "as the appropriate enforcer of legal norms." Perhaps a truer comparison of the utilization of discovery in the United States would be between our civil discovery and the methods used in other countries to gain information, through force or otherwise, by the police, prosecutors, and administrative agencies in their attempt to enforce laws. It may well be that other countries permit so little discovery because the bulk of their civil cases are like the routine cases in the United States that engender modest discovery.

Broad discovery seems critical in many situations in which private individuals in the United States use civil litigation to enforce rights. This is particularly true in such cases as civil rights, products liability, securities, and antitrust, in which evidence to make a prima facie case frequently resides in the files and minds of the defendants. In these lawsuits, it would often be very difficult, if not impossible, for the plaintiff to plead her facts or evidence with particularity in the complaint, as is required in the pleading rules of other countries. The lack of precise pleading means that the defendant also frequently needs extensive discovery. The United States Supreme Court has repeatedly drawn the connection between notice pleading

---

[53] Carl F. Goodman, *The Somewhat Less Reluctant Litigant: Japan's Changing View Towards Civil Litigation*, 32 L. & POL'Y INT'L BUS. 769 (2001).

and liberal discovery. * * * * In short, it would be difficult to eliminate extensive discovery in United States civil litigation without also changing the relative places of civil litigation, lawyers, judges, and juries in our culture and the relative roles of pleading, discovery, summary judgment, and other elements of procedure. The rules and the culture are interrelated in complex ways that would be very difficult to disentangle, even if such rearrangements were deemed desirable.

B. TRANSNATIONAL DISCOVERY CONFLICTS

National differences in discovery practice lend themselves to comparative study, but they also create many opportunities for transnational conflict. Indeed, as one scholar has observed, "no aspect of international litigation has caused as much friction as the issue of discovery." ANDREAS LOWENFELD, INTERNATIONAL LITIGATION AND THE QUEST FOR REASONABLENESS 137 (1996). Most of these conflicts tend to develop when documents or other evidence is located in a foreign country that has a more restrictive approach to discovery. Further, a number of objections that are unique to the cross-border context may be asserted in response to a discovery request. These include matters relating to data protection laws and blocking statutes, competing sovereignty interests, and foreign privileges or immunities.

Imagine, for example, that you are defending a French corporation in an action that is pending in a United States District Court. You receive a document request from the plaintiffs seeking unspecified documents that are only tangentially relevant to the underlying cause of action. Given the French system's attitude toward discovery, your client may be outraged by this overly broad request. Yet, you would be required to produce the document. Indeed, if the documents (no matter their location) were within the control and possession of your client, the refusal to produce them would be sanctionable under Federal Rule of Civil Procedure 37.

Many countries were uncomfortable with—even incensed by—this sort of unilateral export of American-style discovery. From their perspective American courts were acting outside their territorial boundaries and flouting the rights and protections granted by foreign law. Moreover, American discovery had essentially privatized the gathering of evidence, which in the civil law tradition is an act of the judicial sovereign.

To protect their citizens and information within their territories, if not also to defend the integrity of their court system, many countries prohibited the disclosure of such information. For example, in 1980 France added to its Penal Code the following offense:

> [I]t is prohibited for any party to request, seek or disclose, in writing, orally or otherwise, economic, commercial, industrial, financial or technical documents or information leading to the constitution of evidence with a view to foreign judicial or administrative proceedings or in connection therewith.

French Penal Code Law No. 80–538. These "blocking statutes" took various forms, including the constructive "seizure" by the (foreign) government of documents otherwise subject to discovery. By invoking such statutes, foreign litigants in American courts could thus argue that it would be a crime for them to cooperate with the discovery requests or point to the fact that the documents were no longer within their custody or control but were controlled by their government.

Other laws, such as the German Federal Data Protection Act or the Swiss Bank Secrecy Act or the Chinese State Secrets Law, perform a similar function. These laws subject the foreign party to the unenviable choice of either answering to the U.S. discovery request and facing sanctions in their home countries or refusing to answer the request, thereby subjecting themselves to U.S. sanctions. Through the wonder of globalization, then, a discovery dispute becomes a question of international relations and diplomacy: which country's laws and values should prevail? Judges tasked with deciding an objection on this basis will often refer to the multifactor test contained in the Restatement (Third) of Foreign Relations Law § 442(1)(c):

> In deciding whether to issue an order directing production of information located abroad, and in framing such an order, a court or agency in the United States should take into account:
>
> > [1]   the importance to the investigation or litigation of the documents or other information requested;
> >
> > [2]   the degree of specificity of the request;
> >
> > [3]   whether the information originated in the United States;
> >
> > [4]   the availability of alternative means of securing the information; and
> >
> > [5]   the extent to which noncompliance with the request would undermine important interests of the

United States, or compliance with the request would undermine important interests of the state where the information is located.

C. INTERNATIONAL SOLUTIONS

The Hague Convention on the Taking of Evidence Abroad in Civil or Commercial Matters (the Hague Evidence Convention) is a multilateral treaty designed to facilitate the taking of evidence in transnational disputes. The Hague Evidence Convention was intended to establish a system that would be tolerable to the state executing the request, yet useful to the requesting state. The United States ratified the Hague Evidence Convention by a unanimous vote of the Senate in 1972. To date, the Hague Evidence Convention is in effect in more than 50 countries. The United States is also a signator of the Inter-American Convention on Letters Rogatory and Additional Protocol ("IACAP"), another convention that facilitates obtaining foreign discovery from signatory countries.

The scope of the Hague Evidence Convention is limited to the discovery of evidence "intended for use in judicial proceedings, commenced or contemplated" in "civil or commercial matters." The Convention requires signatory states to set up a central authority to handle cross-border discovery requests. In the United States, this central authority is the Office of International Judicial Assistance within the Department of Justice. The Convention streamlines procedures for seeking evidence abroad by allowing U.S. courts to request evidence directly from the designated central authority of a foreign state and bypass diplomatic channels. It is the preferred method in the United States to obtain discovery from foreign nonparties, largely because the mechanism provided incorporates the express terms of the responding jurisdiction.

There are two alternative methods for obtaining evidence abroad under the Hague Evidence Convention:

(1) A litigant may request the court where the action is pending to transmit a "Letter of Request" to the Central Authority in the country where the evidence is to be obtained. The Central Authority then transmits the request to the appropriate foreign court, which conducts an evidentiary proceeding under the procedures of the foreign country.

(2) A litigant may request that the evidence be taken before a diplomatic or consular agent or commissioner in the country where the action is pending. The Hague Evidence Convention provides that a contracting state may

reserve the right not to allow the taking of evidence before a diplomatic or consular officer.

Of the two procedures, the Letter of Request is the most useful. It is the only method that applies to compulsory evidentiary proceedings. The latter method is subject to limitations in the Convention, and many countries have taken a variety of exceptions regarding the use of these procedures. Some of the key provisions of the Hague Evidence Convention regarding the procedure for Letters of Request are provided below.

HAGUE CONVENTION ON THE TAKING OF EVIDENCE ABROAD IN CIVIL OR COMMERCIAL MATTERS ("HAGUE EVIDENCE CONVENTION")
Mar. 18, 1970, [1972] 23 U.S.T. 2555

The States signatory to the present Convention,

Desiring to facilitate the transmission and execution of Letters of Request and to further the accommodation of the different methods which they use for this purpose,

Desiring to improve mutual judicial co-operation in civil or commercial matters,

Have resolved to conclude a Convention to this effect and have agreed upon the following provisions:

Article 1

In civil or commercial matters a judicial authority of a Contracting State may, in accordance with the provisions of the law of that State, request the competent authority of another Contracting State, by means of a Letter of Request, to obtain evidence, or to perform some other judicial act.

A Letter shall not be used to obtain evidence which is not intended for use in judicial proceedings, commenced or contemplated.
* * * *

Article 2

A Contracting State shall designate a Central Authority which will undertake to receive Letters of Request coming from a judicial authority of another Contracting State and to transmit them to the authority competent to execute them. Each State shall organize the Central Authority in accordance with its own law.

Letters shall be sent to the Central Authority of the State of execution without being transmitted through any other authority of that State.

Article 3

A Letter of Request shall specify—

    a) the authority requesting its execution and the authority requested to execute it, if known to the requesting authority;

    b) the names and addresses of the parties to the proceedings and their representatives, if any;

    c) the nature of the proceedings for which the evidence is required, giving all necessary information in regard thereto;

    d) the evidence to be obtained or other judicial act to be performed.

Where appropriate, the Letter shall specify, inter alia—

    e) the names and addresses of the persons to be examined;

    f) the questions to be put to the persons to be examined or a statement of the subject-matter about which they are to be examined;

    g) the documents or other property, real or personal, to be inspected;

    h) any requirement that the evidence is to be given on oath or affirmation, and any special form to be used;

    i) any special method or procedure to be followed under Article 9. * * * *

Article 4

A Letter of Request shall be in the language of the authority requested to execute it or be accompanied by a translation into that language. * * * *

Any translation accompanying a Letter shall be certified as correct, either by a diplomatic officer or consular agent or by a sworn translator or by any other person so authorized in either State. * * * *

Article 9

The judicial authority which executes a Letter of Request shall apply its own law as to the methods and procedures to be followed.

However, it will follow a request of the requesting authority that a special method or procedure be followed, unless this is incompatible with the internal law of the State of execution or is impossible of performance by reason of its internal practice and procedure or by reason of practical difficulties. * * * *

Article 11

In the execution of a Letter of Request the person concerned may refuse to give evidence in so far as he has a privilege or duty to refuse to give the evidence—

a)   under the law of the State of execution; or

b)   under the law of the State of origin, and the privilege or duty has been specified in the Letter, or, at the instance of the requested authority, has been otherwise confirmed to that authority by the requesting authority.

A Contracting State may declare that, in addition, it will respect privileges and duties existing under the law of States other than the State of origin and the State of execution, to the extent specified in that declaration.

Article 12

The execution of a Letter of Request may be refused only to the extent that—

a)   in the State of execution the execution of the Letter does not fall within the functions of the judiciary; or

b)   the State addressed considers that its sovereignty or security would be prejudiced thereby.

Execution may not be refused solely on the ground that under its internal law the State of execution claims exclusive jurisdiction over the subject-matter of the action or that its internal law would not admit a right of action on it. . . .

Article 14

The execution of the Letter of Request shall not give rise to any reimbursement of taxes or costs of any nature.

Nevertheless, the State of execution has the right to require the State of origin to reimburse the fees paid to experts and interpreters and the costs occasioned by the use of a special procedure requested by the State of origin under Article 9, paragraph 2. * * * *

Article 23

A Contracting State may at the time of signature, ratification or accession, declare that it will not execute Letters of Request issued for the purpose of obtaining pre-trial discovery of documents as known in Common Law countries.

Article 27

The provisions of the present Convention shall not prevent a Contracting State from—

a) declaring that Letters of Request may be transmitted to its judicial authorities through channels other than those provided for in Article 2;

b) permitting, by internal law or practice, any act provided for in this Convention to be performed upon less restrictive conditions;

c) permitting, by internal law or practice, methods of taking evidence other than those provided for in this Convention.

———————

The Hague Evidence Convention outlined a procedure for foreign discovery that, although narrower in scope and administratively cumbersome in comparison with the Federal Rules, identified important common ground. But this common ground constrained American litigators familiar with American discovery, who argued that they needed discovery broader than simply information "intended for use in a judicial proceeding" in order to meet their burdens of proof. Those litigators tested the limits and durability of the Convention. In particular, they argued that the Hague Convention created only one possible way of obtaining discovery abroad, but did not prevent parties from seeking discovery under the Federal Rules. The U.S. Supreme Court addressed that argument in the following case.

SOCIÉTÉ NATIONALE INDUSTRIELLE AÉROSPATIALE V. UNITED STATES DISTRICT COURT

Supreme Court of the United States, 1987
482 U.S. 522

STEVENS, J.

[Petitioners to the Court (SNIA) were corporations owned by the Republic of France engaged in the business of designing, manufacturing and marketing aircraft. One of their planes, the "Rallye," was allegedly advertised in American aviation publications as "the World's safest and most economical STOL plane." STOL was an acronym for "short takeoff and landing," and it referred to a fixed-wing aircraft that either takes off or lands with only a short horizontal run of the aircraft. On August 19, 1980, a Rallye crashed in Iowa, injuring the pilot and a passenger.

The plaintiffs (later the respondents in the Supreme Court action) brought separate suits based upon this accident in the United States District Court for the Southern District of Iowa, alleging that petitioners had manufactured and sold a defective plane and were thus liable under theories of negligence and breach of warranty. Plaintiffs sought discovery under the Federal Rules, and SNIA filed a motion for a protective order. SNIA argued that, because it was a French corporation, the Hague Evidence Convention was the only means through which the plaintiffs could conduct discovery. The plaintiffs, in turn, argued that compliance with the Convention was not mandatory.]

In arguing their entitlement to a protective order, petitioners correctly assert that both the discovery rules set forth in the Federal Rules of Civil Procedure and the Hague Convention are the law of the United States. This observation, however, does not dispose of the question before us; we must analyze the interaction between these two bodies of federal law. Initially, we note that at least four different interpretations of the relationship between the federal discovery rules and the Hague Convention are possible. Two of these interpretations assume that the Hague Convention by its terms dictates the extent to which it supplants normal discovery rules. First, the Hague Convention might be read as requiring its use to the exclusion of any other discovery procedures whenever evidence located abroad is sought for use in an American court. Second, the Hague Convention might be interpreted to require first, but not exclusive, use of its procedures. Two other interpretations assume that international comity, rather than the obligations created by the treaty, should guide judicial resort to the Hague Convention. Third, then, the Convention might be viewed as establishing a supplemental set of discovery procedures, strictly optional under treaty law, to which concerns of comity nevertheless require first resort by American courts in all cases. Fourth, the treaty may be viewed as an undertaking among sovereigns to facilitate discovery to which an American court should resort when it deems that course of action appropriate, after considering the situations of the parties before it as well as the interests of the concerned foreign state. * * * *

We reject the first two of the possible interpretations as inconsistent with the language and negotiating history of the Hague Convention. The preamble of the Convention specifies its purpose "to facilitate the transmission and execution of Letters of Request" and to "improve mutual judicial co-operation in civil or commercial matters." 23 U.S.T., at 2557, T.I.A.S. No. 7444. The preamble does not speak in mandatory terms which would purport to describe the procedures for all permissible transnational discovery and exclude all other existing practices.[15] The text of the Evidence Convention itself does not modify the law of any contracting state, require any contracting state to use the Convention procedures, either in requesting evidence or in responding to such requests, or compel any contracting state to change its own evidence-gathering procedures.

The Convention contains three chapters. Chapter I, entitled "Letters of Requests," and chapter II, entitled "Taking of Evidence by Diplomatic Officers, Consular Agents and Commissioners," both use permissive rather than mandatory language. Thus, Article 1 provides that a judicial authority in one contracting state "may" forward a letter of request to the competent authority in another contracting state for the purpose of obtaining evidence. Similarly, Articles 15, 16, and 17 provide that diplomatic officers, consular agents, and commissioners "may ... without compulsion," take evidence under certain conditions. The absence of any command that a contracting state must use Convention procedures when they are not needed is conspicuous.

Two of the Articles in chapter III, entitled "General Clauses," buttress our conclusion that the Convention was intended as a permissive supplement, not a pre-emptive replacement, for other means of obtaining evidence located abroad. Article 23 expressly authorizes a contracting state to declare that it will not execute any letter of request in aid of pretrial discovery of documents in a common-law country. Surely, if the Convention had been intended to replace completely the broad discovery powers that the common-law courts in the United States previously exercised over foreign litigants subject to their jurisdiction, it would have been most anomalous for the common-law contracting parties to agree to Article 23, which enables a contracting party to revoke its consent to the treaty's procedures for pretrial discovery.[22] In the absence of explicit textual support, we are unable to accept the hypothesis that the common-law contracting states abjured recourse to all preexisting discovery

---

[15] The Hague Conference on Private International Law's omission of mandatory language in the preamble is particularly significant in light of the same body's use of mandatory language in the preamble to the Hague Service Convention, 20 U.S.T. 361, T.I.A.S. No. 6638. Article 1 of the Service Convention provides: "The present Convention shall apply in all cases, in civil or commercial matters, where there is occasion to transmit a judicial or extrajudicial document for service abroad." * * * [T]he Service Convention was drafted before the Evidence Convention, and its language provided a model exclusivity provision that the drafters of the Evidence Convention could easily have followed had they been so inclined. Given this background, the drafters' election to use permissive language instead is strong evidence of their intent.

[22] Thirteen of the seventeen signatory states have made declarations under Article 23 of the Convention that restrict pretrial discovery of documents.

procedures at the same time that they accepted the possibility that a contracting party could unilaterally abrogate even the Convention's procedures. Moreover, Article 27 plainly states that the Convention does not prevent a contracting state from using more liberal methods of rendering evidence than those authorized by the Convention. Thus, the text of the Evidence Convention, as well as the history of its proposal and ratification by the United States, unambiguously supports the conclusion that it was intended to establish optional procedures that would facilitate the taking of evidence abroad.

An interpretation of the Hague Convention as the exclusive means for obtaining evidence located abroad would effectively subject every American court hearing a case involving a national of a contracting state to the internal laws of that state. Interrogatories and document requests are staples of international commercial litigation, no less than of other suits, yet a rule of exclusivity would subordinate the court's supervision of even the most routine of these pretrial proceedings to the actions or, equally, to the inactions of foreign judicial authorities. * * * * We conclude accordingly that the Hague Convention did not deprive the District Court of the jurisdiction it otherwise possessed to order a foreign national party before it to produce evidence physically located within a signatory nation.[25] * * * *

Petitioners contend that even if the Hague Convention's procedures are not mandatory, this Court should adopt a rule requiring that American litigants first resort to those procedures before initiating any discovery pursuant to the normal methods of

---

[25] The opposite conclusion of exclusivity would create three unacceptable asymmetries. First, within any lawsuit between a national of the United States and a national of another contracting party, the foreign party could obtain discovery under the Federal Rules of Civil Procedure, while the domestic party would be required to resort first to the procedures of the Hague Convention. This imbalance would run counter to the fundamental maxim of discovery that "[m]utual knowledge of all the relevant facts gathered by both parties is essential to proper litigation." *Hickman v. Taylor*, 329 U.S. 495, 507 (1947). Second, a rule of exclusivity would enable a company which is a citizen of another contracting state to compete with a domestic company on uneven terms, since the foreign company would be subject to less extensive discovery procedures in the event that both companies were sued in an American court. Petitioners made a voluntary decision to market their products in the United States. They are entitled to compete on equal terms with other companies operating in this market. But since the District Court unquestionably has personal jurisdiction over petitioners, they are subject to the same legal constraints, including the burdens associated with American judicial procedures, as their American competitors. A general rule according foreign nationals a preferred position in pretrial proceedings in our courts would conflict with the principle of equal opportunity that governs the market they elected to enter. Third, since a rule of first use of the Hague Convention would apply to cases in which a foreign party is a national of a contracting state, but not to cases in which a foreign party is a national of any other foreign state, the rule would confer an unwarranted advantage on some domestic litigants over others similarly situated.

the Federal Rules of Civil Procedure. The Court of Appeals rejected this argument because it was convinced that an American court's order ultimately requiring discovery that a foreign court had refused under Convention procedures would constitute "the greatest insult" to the sovereignty of that tribunal. We disagree with the Court of Appeals' view. It is well known that the scope of American discovery is often significantly broader than is permitted in other jurisdictions, and we are satisfied that foreign tribunals will recognize that the final decision on the evidence to be used in litigation conducted in American courts must be made by those courts. We therefore do not believe that an American court should refuse to make use of Convention procedures because of a concern that it may ultimately find it necessary to order the production of evidence that a foreign tribunal permitted a party to withhold.

Nevertheless, we cannot accept petitioners' invitation to announce a new rule of law that would require first resort to Convention procedures whenever discovery is sought from a foreign litigant. Assuming, without deciding, that we have the lawmaking power to do so, we are convinced that such a general rule would be unwise. In many situations the Letter of Request procedure authorized by the Convention would be unduly time consuming and expensive, as well as less certain to produce needed evidence than direct use of the Federal Rules. A rule of first resort in all cases would therefore be inconsistent with the overriding interest in the "just, speedy, and inexpensive determination" of litigation in our courts. See Fed. R. Civ. P. 1.

Petitioners argue that a rule of first resort is necessary to accord respect to the sovereignty of states in which evidence is located. It is true that the process of obtaining evidence in a civil law jurisdiction is normally conducted by a judicial officer rather than by private attorneys. Petitioners contend that if performed on French soil, for example, by an unauthorized person, such evidence-gathering might violate the "judicial sovereignty" of the host nation. Because it is only through the Convention that civil-law nations have given their consent to evidence-gathering activities within their borders, petitioners argue, we have a duty to employ those procedures whenever they are available. We find that argument unpersuasive. If such a duty were to be inferred from the adoption of the Convention itself, we believe it would have been described in the text of that document. Moreover, the concept of international comity[27] requires in this context a more particularized analysis of the respective

---

[27] Comity refers to the spirit of cooperation in which a domestic tribunal approaches the resolution of cases touching the laws and interests of sovereign states.
* * * *

interests of the foreign nation and the requesting nation than petitioners' proposed general rule would generate. We therefore decline to hold as a blanket matter that comity requires resort to Hague Evidence Convention procedures without prior scrutiny in each case of the particular facts, sovereign interests, and likelihood that resort to those procedures will prove effective.[29]

Some discovery procedures are much more "intrusive" than others. In this case, for example, an interrogatory asking petitioners to identify the pilots who flew flight tests in the Rallye before it was certified for flight by the Federal Aviation Administration, or a request to admit that petitioners authorized certain advertising in a particular magazine, is certainly less intrusive than a request to produce all of the "design specifications, line drawings and engineering plans and all engineering change orders and plans and all drawings concerning the leading edge slats for the Rallye type aircraft manufactured by the Defendants." Even if a court might be persuaded that a particular document request was too burdensome or too "intrusive" to be granted in full, with or without an appropriate protective order, it might well refuse to insist upon the use of Convention procedures before requiring responses to simple interrogatories or requests for admissions. The exact line between reasonableness and unreasonableness in each case must be drawn by the trial court, based on its knowledge of the case and of the claims and interests of the parties and the governments whose statutes and policies they invoke.

---

[29] The French "blocking statute" * * * does not alter our conclusion. It is well settled that such statutes do not deprive an American court of the power to order a party subject to its jurisdiction to produce evidence even though the act of production may violate that statute. *See Société Internationale Pour Participations Industrielles et Commerciales, S.A. v. Rogers*, 357 U.S. 197, 204–06 (1958). Nor can the enactment of such a statute by a foreign nation require American courts to engraft a rule of first resort onto the Hague Convention, or otherwise to provide the nationals of such a country with a preferred status in our courts. It is clear that American courts are not required to adhere blindly to the directives of such a statute. Indeed, the language of the statute, if taken literally, would appear to represent an extraordinary exercise of legislative jurisdiction by the Republic of France over a United States district judge, forbidding him or her to order any discovery from a party of French nationality, even simple requests for admissions or interrogatories that the party could respond to on the basis of personal knowledge. It would be particularly incongruous to recognize such a preference for corporations that are wholly owned by the enacting nation. Extraterritorial assertions of jurisdiction are not one-sided. While the District Court's discovery orders arguably have some impact in France, the French blocking statute asserts similar authority over acts to take place in this country. The lesson of comity is that neither the discovery order nor the blocking statute can have the same omnipresent effect that it would have in a world of only one sovereign. The blocking statute thus is relevant to the court's particularized comity analysis only to the extent that its terms and its enforcement identify the nature of the sovereign interests in nondisclosure of specific kinds of material. * * * *

American courts, in supervising pretrial proceedings, should exercise special vigilance to protect foreign litigants from the danger that unnecessary, or unduly burdensome, discovery may place them in a disadvantageous position. Judicial supervision of discovery should always seek to minimize its costs and inconvenience and to prevent improper uses of discovery requests. When it is necessary to seek evidence abroad, however, the district court must supervise pretrial proceedings particularly closely to prevent discovery abuses. For example, the additional cost of transportation of documents or witnesses to or from foreign locations may increase the danger that discovery may be sought for the improper purpose of motivating settlement, rather than finding relevant and probative evidence. Objections to "abusive" discovery that foreign litigants advance should therefore receive the most careful consideration. In addition, we have long recognized the demands of comity in suits involving foreign states, either as parties or as sovereigns with a coordinate interest in the litigation. American courts should therefore take care to demonstrate due respect for any special problem confronted by the foreign litigant on account of its nationality or the location of its operations, and for any sovereign interest expressed by a foreign state. We do not articulate specific rules to guide this delicate task of adjudication.

BLACKMAN, J., with whom JUSTICE BRENNAN, JUSTICE MARSHALL, and JUSTICE O'CONNOR join, concurring in part and dissenting in part.

Some might well regard the Court's decision in this case as an affront to the nations that have joined the United States in ratifying the Hague Convention. The Court ignores the importance of the Convention by relegating it to an "optional" status, without acknowledging the significant achievement in accommodating divergent interests that the Convention represents. Experience to date indicates that there is a large risk that the case-by-case comity analysis now to be permitted by the Court will be performed inadequately and that the somewhat unfamiliar procedures of the Convention will be invoked infrequently. I fear the Court's decision means that courts will resort unnecessarily to issuing discovery orders under the Federal Rules of Civil Procedure in a raw exercise of their jurisdictional power to the detriment of the United States' national and international interests. The Court's view of this country's international obligations is particularly unfortunate in a world in which regular commercial and legal channels loom ever more crucial.

I do agree with the Court's repudiation of the positions at both extremes of the spectrum with regard to the use of the Convention.

Its rejection of the view that the Convention is not "applicable" at all to this case is surely correct: the Convention clearly applies to litigants as well as to third parties, and to requests for evidence located abroad, no matter where that evidence is actually "produced." The Court also correctly rejects the far opposite position that the Convention provides the exclusive means for discovery involving signatory countries. I dissent, however, because I cannot endorse the Court's case-by-case inquiry for determining whether to use Convention procedures and its failure to provide lower courts with any meaningful guidance for carrying out that inquiry. In my view, the Convention provides effective discovery procedures that largely eliminate the conflicts between United States and foreign law on evidence gathering. I therefore would apply a general presumption that, in most cases, courts should resort first to the Convention procedures. An individualized analysis of the circumstances of a particular case is appropriate only when it appears that it would be futile to employ the Convention or when its procedures prove to be unhelpful.

I

Even though the Convention does not expressly require discovery of materials in foreign countries to proceed exclusively according to its procedures, it cannot be viewed as merely advisory. The Convention was drafted at the request and with the enthusiastic participation of the United States, which sought to broaden the techniques available for the taking of evidence abroad. The differences between discovery practices in the United States and those in other countries are significant, and "[n]o aspect of the extension of the American legal system beyond the territorial frontier of the United States has given rise to so much friction as the request for documents associated with investigation and litigation in the United States." Restatement of Foreign Relations Law of the United States (Revised) § 437, Reporters' Note 1, p. 35 (Tent. Draft No. 7, Apr. 10, 1986). Of particular import is the fact that discovery conducted by the parties, as is common in the United States, is alien to the legal systems of civil-law nations, which typically regard evidence gathering as a judicial function.

The Convention furthers important United States interests by providing channels for discovery abroad that would not be available otherwise. In general, it establishes "methods to reconcile the differing legal philosophies of the Civil Law, Common Law and other systems with respect to the taking of evidence." Rapport de la Commission spéciale, 4 Conférence de La Haye de droit international privé: Actes et documents de la Onzième session 55 (1970) (Actes et documents). It serves the interests of both requesting and receiving countries by advancing the following goals:

> "[T]he techniques for the taking of evidence must be 'utilizable' in the eyes of the State where the lawsuit is pending and must also be 'tolerable' in the eyes of the State where the evidence is to be taken." *Id.,* at 56.

The Convention also serves the long-term interests of the United States in helping to further and to maintain the climate of cooperation and goodwill necessary to the functioning of the international legal and commercial systems.

It is not at all satisfactory to view the Convention as nothing more than an optional supplement to the Federal Rules of Civil Procedure, useful as a means to "facilitate discovery" when a court "deems that course of action appropriate." *Ante,* at 2550. Unless they had expected the Convention to provide the normal channels for discovery, other parties to the Convention would have had no incentive to agree to its terms. The civil-law nations committed themselves to employ more effective procedures for gathering evidence within their borders, even to the extent of requiring some common-law practices alien to their systems. At the time of the Convention's enactment, the liberal American policy, which allowed foreigners to collect evidence with ease in the United States, was in place and, because it was not conditioned on reciprocity, there was little likelihood that the policy would change as a result of treaty negotiations. As a result, the primary benefit the other signatory nations would have expected in return for their concessions was that the United States would respect their territorial sovereignty by using the Convention procedures.[2]

II

By viewing the Convention as merely optional and leaving the decision whether to apply it to the court in each individual case, the majority ignores the policies established by the political branches when they negotiated and ratified the treaty. The result will be a duplicative analysis for which courts are not well designed. The

---

[2] Article 27 of the Convention, see *ante,* at 2552–2553, n. 24, is not to the contrary. The only logical interpretation of this Article is that a state receiving a discovery request may permit less restrictive procedures than those designated in the Convention. The majority finds plausible a reading that authorizes both a requesting and a receiving state to use methods outside the Convention. *Ibid.* If this were the case, Article 27(c), which allows a state to permit methods of taking evidence that are not provided in the Convention, would make the rest of the Convention wholly superfluous. If a requesting state could dictate the methods for taking evidence in another state, there would be no need for the detailed procedures provided by the Convention. * * * *

discovery process usually concerns discrete interests that a court is well equipped to accommodate—the interests of the parties before the court coupled with the interest of the judicial system in resolving the conflict on the basis of the best available information. When a lawsuit requires discovery of materials located in a foreign nation, however, foreign legal systems and foreign interests are implicated as well. The presence of these interests creates a tension between the broad discretion our courts normally exercise in managing pretrial discovery and the discretion usually allotted to the Executive in foreign matters.

It is the Executive that normally decides when a course of action is important enough to risk affronting a foreign nation or placing a strain on foreign commerce. It is the Executive, as well, that is best equipped to determine how to accommodate foreign interests along with our own. * * * * The Convention embodies the result of the best efforts of the Executive Branch, in negotiating the treaty, and the Legislative Branch, in ratifying it, to balance competing national interests. As such, the Convention represents a political determination—one that, consistent with the principle of separation of powers, courts should not attempt to second-guess. * * * *

III

The principle of comity leads to more definite rules than the ad hoc approach endorsed by the majority. The Court asserts that the concept of comity requires an individualized analysis of the interests present in each particular case before a court decides whether to apply the Convention. There is, however, nothing inherent in the comity principle that requires case-by-case analysis. * * * * Comity is not just a vague political concern favoring international cooperation when it is in our interest to do so. Rather it is a principle under which judicial decisions reflect the systemic value of reciprocal tolerance and goodwill. * * * [T]he threshold question in a comity analysis is whether there is in fact a true conflict between domestic and foreign law. When there is a conflict, a court should seek a reasonable accommodation that reconciles the central concerns of both sets of laws. In doing so, it should perform a tripartite analysis that considers the foreign interests, the interests of the United States, and the mutual interests of all nations in a smoothly functioning international legal regime.

In most cases in which a discovery request concerns a nation that has ratified the Convention there is no need to resort to comity principles; the conflicts they are designed to resolve already have been eliminated by the agreements expressed in the treaty. * * * * The Court, however, adds an additional layer of so-called comity analysis by holding that courts should determine on a case-by-case basis whether resort to the Convention is desirable. Although this analysis is unnecessary in the absence of any conflicts, it should lead courts to the use of the Convention if they recognize that the Convention already has largely accommodated all three categories of interests relevant to a comity analysis—foreign interests, domestic interests, and the interest in a well-functioning international order. * * * *

In most instances, use of the Convention will serve to advance United States interests, particularly when those interests are viewed in a context larger than the immediate interest of the litigants' discovery. The approach I propose is not a rigid *per se* rule that would require first use of the Convention without regard to strong indications that no evidence would be forthcoming. All too often, however, courts have simply *assumed* that resort to the Convention would be unproductive and have embarked on speculation about foreign procedures and interpretations. When resort to the Convention would be futile, a court has no choice but to resort to a traditional comity analysis. But even then, an attempt to use the Convention will often be the best way to discover if it will be successful, particularly in the present state of general inexperience with the implementation of its procedures by the various contracting states. An attempt to use the Convention will open a dialogue with the authorities in the foreign state and in that way a United States court can obtain an authoritative answer as to the limits on what it can achieve with a discovery request in a particular contracting state. * * * * [A] comity analysis * * * consider[s] if there is a course that furthers, rather than impedes, the development of an ordered international system. A functioning system for solving disputes across borders serves many values, among them predictability, fairness, ease of commercial interactions, and stability through satisfaction of mutual expectations. These interests are common to all nations, including the United States.

Use of the Convention would help develop methods for transnational litigation by placing officials in a position to communicate directly about conflicts that arise during discovery, thus enabling them to promote a reduction in those conflicts. In a broader framework, courts that use the Convention will avoid foreign perceptions of unfairness that result when United States courts show insensitivity to the interests safeguarded by foreign legal regimes. Because of the position of the United States, economically, politically, and militarily, many countries may be reluctant to oppose discovery orders of United States courts. Foreign acquiescence to orders that ignore the Convention, however, is likely to carry a price tag of accumulating resentment, with the predictable long-term political cost that cooperation will be withheld in other matters. Use of the Convention is a simple step to take toward avoiding that unnecessary and undesirable consequence.

I can only hope that courts faced with discovery requests for materials in foreign countries will avoid the parochial views that too often have characterized the decisions to date. Many of the considerations that lead me to the conclusion that there should be a general presumption favoring use of the Convention should also carry force when courts analyze particular cases. The majority fails to offer guidance in this endeavor, and thus it has missed its opportunity to provide predictable and effective procedures for international litigants in United States courts. It now falls to the lower courts to recognize the needs of the international commercial system and the accommodation of those needs already endorsed by the political branches and embodied in the Convention. To the extent indicated, I respectfully dissent.

Notes and Questions

1. On remand, the French manufacturer in *Aérospatiale* agreed to provide the requested information so the "delicate task" requiring "special vigilance" was not ultimately needed in this case.

2. Under *Aérospatiale*, if foreign discovery is sought in a U.S. proceeding, a requesting party *may* seek evidence under the Hague Evidence Convention but is not required to do so and can use alternative discovery mechanisms. Does that defeat part of the core purpose of the Hague Convention itself? Or, to put it another way, does the Hague Convention now have any impact at all on U.S. discovery practice in transnational disputes?

3. Does the enactment of a "blocking statute" disrespect the laws and institutions of other nations?

4. Consider the doctrine of comity. How do the majority and dissenting opinions conceptualize the doctrine? Are they different from each other, and if so, how? If you were a judge, how would you factor comity into any particular discovery decision?

5. After *Aérospatiale*, district courts must balance the need for discovery against the policies reflected in the treaty. Although there have been some cases where litigants have been forced to use Hague Convention procedures, in the majority of cases the Hague Convention is held not to apply. *See* Patrick J. Borchers, *The Incredible Shrinking Hague Evidence Convention*, 38 TEX. INT'L L.J. 73, 82 (2003). Justice Blackmun's dissent in *Aérospatiale* noted that "it is the Executive that normally decides when a course of action is important enough to risk

affronting a foreign nation or placing a strain on foreign commerce. It is the Executive, as well, that is best equipped to determine how to accommodate foreign interests along with our own." Is the question of foreign discovery more appropriately considered by the Executive and by Congress? On the other hand, isn't the reasonableness of a particular discovery request more appropriately considered by a judge? How should these competing concerns be reconciled?

6.　　Even if the Hague Convention mechanisms are not explicitly used, courts since *Aérospatiale* have applied a balancing test that weighs the "particular facts, sovereign interest and likelihood that resort to those procedures will prove effective." Consider the following effort to perform such balancing.

WULTZ V. BANK OF CHINA LLD

United States District Court for the Southern District of New York, 2012
910 F. Supp. 2d 548

SCHEINDLIN, DISTRICT JUDGE:

This suit arises out of the death of Daniel Wultz and the injuries of Yekutiel Wultz, suffered in a 2006 suicide bombing in Tel Aviv, Israel. Four members of the Wultz family brought suit against Bank of China ("BOC" or "the Bank"), alleging acts of international terrorism and aiding and abetting international terrorism under the Antiterrorism Act ("ATA"), as well as negligence, breach of statutory duty, and vicarious liability. * * * *

Before the Court is plaintiffs' motion to compel BOC to produce documents under its control. Some of these documents are the subject of an outstanding Letter of Request from this Court to the Ministry of Justice of China under the Hague Convention on the Taking of Evidence Abroad in Civil or Commercial Matters (the "Hague Convention"). BOC's opposition to plaintiff's motion encourages this Court to wait for a response to the Letter of Request, and argues that plaintiffs' discovery requests should be narrowed and made more specific. For the reasons stated below, plaintiffs' motion is granted with certain limitations. * * * *

III. Applicable Law

In *Société Nationale Industrielle Aérospatiale,* the Supreme Court established that the use of the Hague Convention process is optional, not mandatory, and does not deprive a District Court of the jurisdiction it would otherwise possess "to order a foreign national party before it to produce evidence physically located within a signatory nation." At the same time, the Supreme Court emphasized that "international comity" ("the spirit of cooperation in which a domestic tribunal approaches the resolution of cases touching the laws and interests of other sovereign states") "requires in this context a . . . particularized analysis of the respective interests of the foreign nation and the requesting nation."

When evaluating the propriety of an order directing the production of information or documents in contravention of foreign law, courts in the Second Circuit consider the following five factors, drawn from *Aérospatiale:*

(1) the importance to the investigation or litigation of the documents or other information requested;

(2) the degree of specificity of the request;

(3) whether the information originated in the United States;

(4) the availability of alternative means of securing the information; and

(5) the extent to which noncompliance with the request would undermine important interests of the United States, or compliance with the request would undermine the important interests of the state where the information is located.

Courts in the Second Circuit also consider:

(6) the hardship of compliance on the party or witness from whom discovery is sought; and

(7) the good faith of the party resisting discovery.

This is not the first case in which a party has sought the production of documents by BOC, BOC has objected that production would threaten it with civil and criminal liability under China's bank secrecy laws, and a court has responded by applying the Second Circuit's multi-factor comity test. In the two most recent cases, the court compelled BOC to produce discovery materials in contravention of Chinese law even though BOC was a non-party. The fact that in the instant case BOC is a party doing business in the United States, and that some of the requested discovery may be physically present in the United States at BOC's New York branches, makes the case for compelling production even stronger.

Two other aspects of the earlier cases are relevant to this Court's application of the comity test in the instant case. *First,* despite BOC's concerns, BOC has apparently never been sanctioned by the Chinese government for complying with American court orders to produce documents in contravention of China's bank secrecy laws. On at least two occasions BOC has now been ordered to produce discovery materials. In both cases, BOC expressed concerns beforehand that doing so could result in sanctions. BOC's brief in opposition to plaintiffs' current motion to compel continues to express concerns regarding the "clear potential for PRC sanctions on BOC for a production unauthorized by the PRC government." But BOC's brief fails to indicate any sanctions that BOC has in fact received as a result of its compliance with the two prior orders, other than a "severe warning" from Chinese banking regulators. To date, the evidence remains strong for the conclusion * * * that meaningful sanctions by the Chinese government against BOC are highly doubtful, especially given the Chinese government's majority interest in BOC.

Second, the Ministry of Justice of China has now responded to at least one Letter of Request for the production of documents by BOC in contravention of China's bank secrecy laws. The Ministry's response to the Letter of Request, dated August 7, 2012, only executed the requests in part. The Ministry's sole reason for its partial refusal was the Chinese government's declaration at its accession to the Hague Convention that it would only execute discovery requests for "documents clearly enumerated in the Letters of Request and of direct and close connection with the subject matter of the litigation." The Ministry concluded that some of the evidence requested by the court's Letter of Request "lacks direct and close connections with the litigation." In contrast to the U.S. Supreme Court's hopes in *Aérospatiale,* the Ministry of Justice appears to have chosen not to defer to the relatively broad scope of American discovery in its treatment of the Hague Convention request. * * * *

1–2. Importance of Documents and Specificity of Request

On the one hand, plaintiffs persuasively argue that each of the general categories of their requested discovery contains documents that are important to their case. BOC does not meaningfully contest this conclusion. On the other hand, BOC persuasively argues that the scope of some of plaintiffs' requests is overbroad. BOC contests the scope of requests 7–9 and 1–5, but not requests 6 or 10. I find that requests 7–9 require substantial narrowing.

Significantly, plaintiffs do not meaningfully contest BOC's conclusion that requests 7–9 are overbroad. In addition, plaintiffs appear to agree with BOC's argument that BOC "is legally barred from producing certain regulatory communications and filings" by U.S. banking laws and regulations.

Based on the above, there may be room for the parties to resolve at least some of their numerous disputes over the scope of discovery without this Court's intervention. As BOC's opposition brief notes, and plaintiffs' reply brief confirms, the parties did not meet and confer regarding the narrowing of plaintiffs' requests prior to the submission of plaintiffs' motion to compel.

The parties are now directed to attempt to negotiate a narrowing of plaintiffs' requests in accord with the Federal Rules of Civil Procedure and relevant U.S. banking laws and regulations. Plaintiffs are entitled to obtain materials relevant to the claims and defenses raised in this case and "reasonably calculated to lead to the discovery of admissible evidence," as limited by consideration of the factors set forth in Rule 26(b)(2)(C). With regard to foreign discovery materials, I recognize that ordinarily it may be "reasonable to limit foreign discovery to information [that is] necessary to the action . . . and directly relevant and material," rather than "information that could lead to admissible evidence." But in light of the significant U.S. interest in eliminating sources of funding for international terrorism, and the other factors discussed below, the law governing discovery disputes in this case must ultimately be the broad discovery rules of the Federal Rules of Civil Procedure.

However, to the extent that plaintiffs' narrowed discovery requests call for the production of confidential regulatory documents *created by the Chinese government* whose production is clearly prohibited under Chinese law, I decline to order production of such regulatory documents. While the issue of whether to order BOC to produce discovery materials in contravention of Chinese bank secrecy laws has now been thoroughly aired in several decisions from this district, the issue of whether to order BOC to produce confidential Chinese governmental regulatory documents in violation of other Chinese laws prohibiting such production has not been sufficiently analyzed or briefed. Ordering the production of the non-public regulatory documents of a foreign government may infringe the sovereignty of the foreign state and violate principles of international comity to a far greater extent than the ordered production of private account information in contravention of foreign bank secrecy laws, and consequently deserves close and distinct attention. If plaintiffs' narrowed discovery requests encompass the production of confidential regulatory documents created by the Chinese government, the parties may submit supplemental letters on this sensitive issue.

Returning to the comity analysis in light of the above, I conclude that the importance of the documents requested by plaintiffs in its First Requests weighs in favor of granting plaintiffs' motion to compel. At present, the lack of specificity of some of plaintiffs' discovery requests weighs against granting plaintiffs' motion. But once plaintiffs' discovery requests have been narrowed in accordance with the principles articulated above, the specificity factor will weigh in plaintiffs' favor as well.

3.   Whether Information Originated in United States

* * * [T]here is no genuine dispute that at least some of the documents to which the present comity analysis applies originated in China. This factor weighs against plaintiffs' discovery request.

4.   Availability of Alternative Means

In earlier cases involving attempts to obtain materials from BOC in contravention of Chinese bank secrecy laws, BOC argued that the Hague Convention would provide "a perfectly adequate means of securing the information . . . requested without forcing the Bank to violate Chinese law," while earlier plaintiffs argued that a request through the Hague Convention would not represent a reasonable alternative means of obtaining the requested discovery.

In the instant case, BOC emphasizes the significance of the pending Hague request, "to which the PRC Supreme Court reportedly has devoted substantial time and resources." BOC argues that the PRC Supreme Court ruling "would inform, and narrow if not obviate, this Court's comity analysis."

BOC also draws this Court's attention to a November 3, 2011 letter from PBOC and the China Banking Regulatory Commission ("CBRC") to four judges of the Southern District of New York. The letter urges "U.S. courts to employ the Hague Convention in order to avoid a conflict between PRC law and U.S. law" * * *. The letter also suggests that through a yearly Strategic and Economic Dialogue established in 2009, the U.S. and PRC governments have reached "an important consensus that bilateral mechanisms [such as the Hague Convention] should be preferred to unilateral actions in cross-border legal enforcement." The letter notes that "a U.S. court . . . enforcing a subpoena to compel production of bank account information in China or ordering a Chinese bank to freeze or turn over client assets in China [would] violate the above-mentioned important consensus," which would have "an unnecessary adverse impact on further discussions and cooperation."

While I recognize and respect the sovereign interest expressed by the PBOC-CRBC letter, and strongly agree that bilateral mechanisms are preferable to unilateral actions in cross-border legal enforcement, I nevertheless conclude that subsequent events have validated the concern in an earlier BOC discovery case "that Hague Convention requests in circumstances similar to those presented here are not a viable alternative method of securing the information Plaintiffs seek."

First, as noted above, the Chinese Ministry of Justice's response to the Hague request in [an earlier case] denied some of the valid discovery requested by the court's Letter of Request. Specifically, the Ministry denied requests that were not "clearly enumerated" and "of direct and close connection with the subject matter of the litigation," echoing the language in China's declaration at its accession to the Hague Convention. * * * * If the Ministry applies a similar standard in the instant case, it is likely that documents relevant to plaintiffs' claims—in particular, documents that may not themselves be admissible at trial, but are "reasonably calculated to lead to the discovery of admissible evidence"—will be denied. In such a scenario, the Hague Convention would definitively not represent a reasonable alternative means for plaintiffs to obtain discovery.

Second, the time that has already passed since this Court's submission of the Letter of Request on August 31, 2011 by itself calls into question whether the Hague Convention process can be viewed as a *reasonable* alternative means of discovery. The U.S. Supreme Court has recognized that where the Hague Convention process "would be unduly time consuming and expensive," requiring the parties to submit to the process is inconsistent with the "overriding interest in the 'just, speedy, and inexpensive determination' of litigation in our courts." In other words, the ease of obtaining documents through the Hague Convention process is relevant to this Court's analysis of the "alternative means" factor. "If the information sought can easily be obtained elsewhere, there is little or no reason to require a party to violate foreign law." "Conversely, if the information cannot be *easily obtained* through alternative means, this factor is said to counterbalance the previous factor—the location of the documents and information—and weighs in favor of disclosure." Here, the elapsed time since the submission of this Court's Letter of Request has already sufficiently demonstrated that plaintiffs' requested discovery materials cannot be *"easily obtained"* through the Hague Convention process.

In light of the preceding considerations, plaintiffs lack sufficient alternative means for obtaining their requested materials. This factor weighs in favor of granting plaintiffs' motion to compel.

5. Weighing of U.S. and Chinese Interests

This factor—the balancing of national interests—"is the most important, as it directly addresses the relations between sovereign nations." The United States has a "profound and compelling interest in combating terrorism at every level, including disrupting the financial underpinnings of terrorist networks." When the U.S. interest "in fully and fairly adjudicating matters before its courts" is combined with its interest in combating terrorism, the U.S. interest "is elevated to nearly its highest point and diminishes any competing interests of the foreign state." The interest of the United States in depriving international terrorist organizations of funding that could be used to kill American citizens strongly outweighs the interest of a foreign nation in bank secrecy laws and the abstract or general assertion of sovereignty.

I have given serious consideration to the countervailing Chinese interest, expressed in the PBOC-CBRC letter, in "the development of China's banking industry" through the enforcement of its bank secrecy laws. More generally, I take seriously the mutual interest of China and the United States in the bilateral resolution of cross-border legal enforcement issues. But the Chinese interest in building confidence in its banking industry does not encompass an interest in protecting the confidentiality of those who participate in the funding of international terrorism. * * * * For these reasons, the balancing of U.S. and Chinese interests weighs heavily in favor of plaintiffs' discovery.

6.   Hardship of Compliance

As earlier cases have noted, BOC's New York branches are not subsidiaries of a foreign parent company, but rather are branches of the same corporate entities as their counterparts in China. There is a presumption that a corporation is in the possession and control of its own books and records, and clear proof of lack of possession and control is necessary to rebut the presumption. BOC has now conceded that its New York branch is not legally separate from BOC and appears no longer to dispute that the documents at issue in this case are in the control of BOC's New York branches. In addition, as noted above, BOC has produced no evidence that it has been meaningfully sanctioned by the Chinese government for complying with the two previous U.S. court orders to produce documents in contravention of China's bank secrecy laws.

Because BOC has produced no evidence that producing the requested foreign documents would entail significant hardship, this factor weighs in favor of plaintiffs' discovery request.

7.   Good Faith of Party Resisting Discovery

Plaintiffs argue that BOC may not be acting in good faith, based on two considerations. *First,* BOC continues to promote the use of the Hague Convention process, despite evidence from past cases that the results of such requests are uncertain, and despite the lack of a response to date to the Letter of Request in this case. *Second,* plaintiffs allege that BOC "has apparently failed to undertake a comprehensive review of even documents located in New York." BOC states in response that it is unable to "undertake a meaningful search for electronic records responsive to plaintiffs' overbroad Requests 7–9 until those requests are narrowed and made more specific."

BOC's response, accompanied by no legal support, is unacceptable. As plaintiffs rightly note, Federal Rule of Civil Procedure 34(b)(2)(C) clearly states: "An objection to part of a request must specify the part and permit inspection of the rest." Plaintiffs' discovery requests 7–9 are clearly overbroad, as noted earlier. But those requests also contained documents that are relevant to plaintiffs' claims. BOC was obligated under the Federal Rules to permit inspection of such documents.

Nevertheless, I lack sufficient evidence at the present time to ascribe bad faith to BOC. On balance, this factor does not weigh for or against plaintiffs' discovery request.

8.　　Weighing the Factors

Considering the totality of the circumstances, I find that the comity test weighs strongly in favor of granting plaintiffs' motion to compel, with the limitations noted above regarding the scope of the requests.

In light of this finding, as stated above, the parties are ordered to meet and confer without further delay concerning the narrowing of plaintiffs' discovery requests. The parties are then to submit a revised and swift discovery schedule, including the immediate production of documents that should already have been produced. If the parties remain unable to resolve specific discovery disputes, they may submit letters regarding those disputes, as prescribed in this Court's Individual Rules.

Notes and Questions

1.　　Review the court's ruling as well as its balancing of interests. Is it significantly different from how a court might have balanced interests in an ordinary domestic discovery dispute? If so, how?

2.　　Is the court's analysis different from how it would have resolved a transnational discovery dispute even if there were no Hague Convention in effect? If so, how?

3.　　A final method for seeking to compel discovery abroad is to use diplomatic channels and apply for a letter rogatory from a U.S. judge. 28 U.S.C. § 1781; Fed. R. Civ. P. 28(b). The letter rogatory must be signed by a U.S. judge and, if required by the foreign state from which assistance is sought, authenticated. It is then typically conveyed through the Department of State to the U.S. Embassy, and forwarded to the

Ministry of Foreign Affairs and to the Ministry of Justice in the receiving jurisdiction before finally arriving in a foreign court that can execute the letter. Once executed, it is transmitted back through the same diplomatic channels and ultimately to the requesting counsel. It is a long and slow process that is not always successful.

4.   Indeed, in the absence of a treaty or an agreement requiring cooperation, the foreign state has no obligation to provide the assistance sought. Foreign courts have rejected assistance on grounds that provision of the evidence would violate foreign blocking or secrecy laws or be duplicative of evidence available in the United States, or even on the grounds that such pretrial discovery is simply too broad.

5.   Aside from a letter rogatory, a federal court may also issue a subpoena if the testimony or documents are sought from a national or resident of the United States who is in a foreign country and if the evidence is "necessary in the interest of justice" and is "not possible to obtain . . . in any other manner." The Walsh Act, 28 U.S.C. § 1783, and Fed. R. Civ. P. 45(b)(3). This provision is seldom used in the context of civil actions.

Because the decision in *Aérospatiale* diluted the significance of the Hague Convention on the Taking of Evidence Abroad, the search for international common ground resumed. The ALI/UNIDROIT Transnational Rules have proposed a set of model discovery rules that reflect a compromise: they are based on a generalized version of a common law system outside the United States. If adopted, they would apply to transnational commercial disputes.

RULES OF TRANSNATIONAL CIVIL PROCEDURE
AM. LAW INST. & UNIDROIT, 2005

21. Disclosure

21.1 In accordance with the court's scheduling order, a party must identify to the court and other parties the evidence on which the party intends to rely, in addition to that provided in the pleading, including:

21.1.1   Copies of documents or other records, such as contracts and correspondence; and

21.1.2   Summaries of expected testimony of witnesses, including parties, witnesses, and experts, then known to the party. Witnesses must be identified, so far as practicable, by name, address, and telephone number. * * * *

22. Exchange of Evidence

22.1 A party who has complied with disclosure duties prescribed in Rule 21, on notice to the other parties, may request the court to order production by any person of any evidentiary matter, not protected by confidentiality or privilege, that is relevant to the case and that may be admissible, including:

> 22.1.1 Documents and other records of information that are specifically identified or identified within specifically defined categories;

> 22.1.2 Identifying information, such as name and address, about specified persons having knowledge of a matter in issue; and

> 22.1.3 A copy of the report of any expert that another party intends to present.

22.2 The court must determine the request and order production accordingly. The court may order production of other evidence as necessary in the interest of justice. Such evidence must be produced within a reasonable time prior to the final hearing. * * * *

22.7 The fact that the demanded information is adverse to the interest of the party to which the demand is directed is not a valid objection to its production. * * * *

23. Deposition and Testimony by Affidavit

23.1 A deposition of a party or other person may be taken by order of the court. Unless the court orders otherwise, a deposition may be presented as evidence in the record. * * * *

23.4 With written permission of the court, a party may present a written statement of sworn testimony of any person, containing statements in their own words about relevant facts. * * * *

Notes and Questions

1. The ALI/UNIDROIT Transnational Rules seek to strike a compromise between the regimes of broad and narrow discovery. Which of the two extremes is being asked to make the greater sacrifice?

2. Note that these are simply proposed model rules that would need to be adopted into the law of various national systems. To date, no country has adopted these model rules.

3. Is it realistic to suggest that transnational and domestic cases could be litigated under different discovery regimes? Could discovery in domestic litigation in the United States be conducted successfully pursuant to rules similar to the Transnational Rules?

4. In 2018 Congress enacted the Clarifying Lawful Overseas Use of Data Act (CLOUD Act). This Act amends the Stored Communications

Act and provides that "[a service provider] shall comply with the obligations * * * to preserve, backup, or disclose * * * any record or other information pertaining to a customer or subscriber within such provider's possession, custody, or control, regardless of whether [it] is located within or outside of the United States." CLOUD Act § 103(a)(1). But what if the CLOUD Act runs up against the data protection laws of other nations? Should the applicable rule be based on the nationality of the end user whose data is being accessed, the location where the data is stored, or the location of the corporation? The CLOUD Act suggests the location of the data is irrelevant.

5.   The Sedona Conference, a nonprofit think tank based in Phoenix, Ariz., has contributed greatly to developing principles for electronic discovery in the context of cross-border disputes. The Conference issued the following International Principles on Discovery, Disclosure & Data Protection:

> Principle 1:   With regard to data that is subject to preservation, disclosure, or discovery, courts and parties should demonstrate due respect to the Data Protection Laws of any foreign sovereign and the interests of any person who is subject to or benefits from such laws.
>
> Principle 2:   Where full compliance with both Data Protection Laws and preservation, disclosure, and discovery obligations presents a conflict, a party's conduct should be judged by a court or data protection authority under a standard of good faith and reasonableness.
>
> Principle 3:   Preservation or discovery of Protected Data should be limited in scope to that which is relevant and necessary to support any party's claim or defense in order to minimize conflicts of law and impact on the Data Subject.
>
> Principle 4:   Where a conflict exists between Data Protection Laws and preservation, disclosure, or discovery obligations, a stipulation or court order should be employed to protect Protected Data and minimize the conflict. * * * *

6.   Liberal discovery rules in the United States can also be invoked for the *benefit* of foreigners and/or foreign litigation. Section 1782 of Title 28 of the U.S. Code provides that a federal district court "may order" a person "resid[ing]" or "found" in the district to produce documents or provide testimony "for use in a proceeding in a foreign or international tribunal * * * upon application of any interested person." Section 1782 is particularly useful because its requirements are much simpler than the Hague Convention procedures. The essential requirements for assistance under Section 1782 are: (1) the person from whom discovery is sought resides in or is found in the forum where the application is made; (2) the discovery is sought for use before a foreign

or international tribunal; and (3) the application is made by the tribunal or any interested person. Where those requirements are satisfied, the forum court has broad discretion to decide whether to grant the assistance.

The United States Supreme Court has endorsed the broad and aggressive use of Section 1782. In *Intel Corp. v. Advanced Micro Devices, Inc.*, 542 U.S. 241 (2004), the Court defined "interested person" and "foreign or international tribunal" broadly to include an action initiated by a complainant with the Directorate General Competition of the European Communities. Further, the Court held that the proceeding need only be "within reasonable contemplation" to invoke the federal statute. And finally, the Court found no "foreign discoverability" requirement—i.e., the Court held that the evidence sought in the United States forum need not be discoverable in the foreign or international tribunal. Nor would the discovering party need to demonstrate that United States law would allow discovery in domestic litigation analogous to the foreign proceeding. Does Section 1782 encourage foreign countries to emulate the United States' example by providing similar assistance? *See generally* Okezie Chukwumeriie, *International Judicial Assistance: Revitalizing Section 1782*, 37 GEO. WASH. INT'L L. REV. 649 (2005).

Chapter 11

TRIALS AND THE AMERICAN CIVIL JURY

————

This chapter again explores the nexus between a society's culture and its procedural system. Although all procedural systems share certain general characteristics, the dissimilarities—whether trivial or profound—are sometimes traceable to cultural differences. Procedures can both reflect and project a society's values; to study *why* a particular procedural approach has been adopted is usually more significant (and interesting) than merely recording *that* it has been adopted. Accordingly, understanding the values, beliefs, and idiosyncrasies that animate procedural rules is an important part of comparative study. It is also an essential task if one is to consider or advocate transplanting a particular procedure from one system into another.

While scholars have argued for the recent convergence of civil law and common law systems, one fundamental distinction remains. Unlike the common law system, a trial in a civil law system is not a single continuous event. Rather, the court gathers and evaluates evidence over a series of hearings, as many as the circumstances require. Further, while juries are an accepted tradition in common law countries, juries (or more specifically, lay participation) are a far more recent innovation for many other systems. And while *criminal* juries may be found in other English-speaking countries, the broad right to a civil jury is perhaps distinctly an American institution. Today, critiques of the American civil jury as well as the declining number of trials have led civil procedure scholars to question the role of the civil jury.[*]

In his classic study *Democracy in America*, Alexis de Tocqueville touted civil juries as an important judicial and political institution sustaining American democracy. In the article that follows Professor Oscar Chase explores the ideology that underlies this institution.

————

[*] *See, e.g.,* Nora Freeman Engstrom, *The Diminished Trial*, 86 FORDHAM L. REV. 2131 (2018). *But see* ALEXANDRA LAHAV, IN PRAISE OF LITIGATION (2017) (arguing for the importance of civil trials to democratic participation).

How fundamental is the civil jury system to the American experience?

ALEXIS DE TOCQUEVILLE, DEMOCRACY IN AMERICA
(1831)

Trial By Jury in the United States Considered as a Political Institution

Trial by jury, which is one of the instruments of the sovereignty of the people, deserves to be compared with the other laws which establish that sovereignty. * * * *

To look upon the jury as a mere judicial institution is to confine our attention to a very narrow view of it; for however great its influence may be upon the decisions of the law courts, that influence is very subordinate to the powerful effects which it produces on the destinies of the community at large. The jury is above all a political institution, and it must be regarded in this light in order to be duly appreciated.

By the jury I mean a certain number of citizens chosen indiscriminately, and invested with a temporary right of judging. Trial by jury, as applied to the repression of crime, appears to me to introduce an eminently republican element into the government upon the following grounds:

The institution of the jury may be aristocratic or democratic, according to the class of society from which the jurors are selected; but it always preserves its republican character, inasmuch as it places the real direction of society in the hands of the governed, or of a portion of the governed, instead of leaving it under the authority of the Government. Force is never more than a transient element of success; and after force comes the notion of right. A government which should only be able to crush its enemies upon a field of battle would very soon be destroyed. The true sanction of political laws is to be found in penal legislation, and if that sanction be wanting the law will sooner or later lose its cogency. He who punishes infractions of the law is therefore the real master of society. Now the institution of the jury raises the people itself, or at least a class of citizens, to the bench of judicial authority. The institution of the jury consequently invests the people, or that class of citizens, with the direction of society.

In England the jury is returned from the aristocratic portion of the nation; the aristocracy makes the laws, applies the laws, and punishes all infractions of the laws; everything is established upon a consistent footing, and England may with truth be said to constitute an aristocratic republic. In the United States the same system is applied to the whole people. Every American citizen is qualified to be an elector, a juror, and is eligible to office. The system of the jury, as it is understood in America, appears to me to be as direct and as extreme a consequence of the sovereignty of the people as universal suffrage. These institutions are two instruments of equal power, which contribute to the supremacy of the majority. All the sovereigns who have chosen to govern by their own authority, and to direct society instead of obeying its directions, have destroyed or enfeebled the institution of the jury. The monarchs of the House of Tudor sent to prison jurors who refused to convict, and Napoleon caused them to be returned by his agents.

However clear most of these truths may seem to be, they do not command universal assent, and in France, at least, the institution of trial by jury is still very imperfectly understood. If the question arises as to the proper qualification of jurors, it is confined to a discussion of the intelligence and knowledge of the citizens who may be returned, as if the jury was merely a judicial institution. This appears to me to be the least part of the subject. The jury is pre-eminently a political institution; it must be regarded as one form of the sovereignty of the people; when that sovereignty is repudiated, it must be rejected, or it must be adapted to the laws by which that sovereignty is established. The jury is that portion of the nation to which the execution of the laws is entrusted, as the Houses of Parliament constitute that part of the nation which makes the laws; and in order that society may be governed with consistency and uniformity, the list of citizens qualified to serve on juries must increase and diminish with the list of electors. This I hold to be the point of view most worthy of the attention of the legislator, and all that remains is merely accessory.

I am so entirely convinced that the jury is pre-eminently a political institution that I still consider it in this light when it is applied in civil causes. Laws are always unstable unless they are founded upon the manners of a nation; manners are the only durable and resisting power in a people. When the jury is reserved for criminal offences, the people only witnesses its occasional action in certain particular cases; the ordinary course of life goes on without its interference, and it is considered as an instrument, but not as the only instrument, of obtaining justice. This is true a fortiori when the jury is only applied to certain criminal causes.

When, on the contrary, the influence of the jury is extended to civil causes, its application is constantly palpable; it affects all the interests of the community; everyone co-operates in its work: it thus penetrates into all the usages of life, it fashions the human mind to its peculiar forms, and is gradually associated with the idea of justice itself.

The institution of the jury, if confined to criminal causes, is always in danger, but when once it is introduced into civil proceedings it defies the aggressions of time and of man. If it had been as easy to remove the jury from the manners as from the laws of England, it would have perished under Henry VIII, and Elizabeth, and the civil jury did in reality, at that period, save the liberties of the country. In whatever manner the jury be applied, it cannot fail to exercise a powerful influence upon the national character; but this influence is prodigiously increased when it is introduced into civil causes. The jury, and more especially the jury in civil cases, serves to communicate the spirit of the judges to the minds of all the citizens; and this spirit, with the habits which attend it, is the soundest preparation for free institutions. It imbues all classes with a respect for the thing judged, and with the notion of right. If these two elements be removed, the love of independence is reduced to a mere destructive passion. It teaches men to practice equity, every man learns to judge his neighbor as he would himself be judged; and this is especially true of the jury in civil causes, for, whilst the number of persons who have reason to apprehend a criminal prosecution is small, every one is liable to have a civil action brought against him. The jury teaches every man not to recoil before the responsibility of his own actions, and impresses him with that manly confidence without which political virtue cannot exist. It invests each citizen with a kind of magistracy, it makes them all feel the duties which they are bound to discharge towards society, and the part which they take in the Government. By obliging men to turn their attention to affairs which are not exclusively their own, it rubs off that individual egotism which is the rust of society.

The jury contributes most powerfully to form the judgement and to increase the natural intelligence of a people, and this is, in my opinion, its greatest advantage. It may be regarded as a gratuitous public school ever open, in which every juror learns to exercise his rights, enters into daily communication with the most learned and enlightened members of the upper classes, and becomes practically acquainted with the laws of his country, which are brought within the reach of his capacity by the efforts of the bar, the advice of the judge, and even by the passions of the parties. I think that the practical intelligence and political good sense of the Americans are mainly attributable to the long use which they have made of the jury in civil causes. I do not know whether the jury is useful to those who are in litigation; but I am certain it is highly beneficial to those who decide the litigation; and I look upon it as one of the most efficacious means for the education of the people which society can employ.

OSCAR G. CHASE, *AMERICAN "EXCEPTIONALISM" AND COMPARATIVE PROCEDURE*

50 AM. J. COMP. L. 277 (2002)

* * * *

AMERICAN CULTURE

American "exceptionalism" has been observed and remarked upon at least since Alexis de Tocqueville published his observations of American society over one hundred-fifty years ago. "Tocqueville is the first to refer [to] the United States as exceptional—that is, qualitatively different from all other countries." The qualities that struck Tocqueville, such as individualism, egalitarianism, and a readiness to pursue disputes through litigation have persisted over time and been observed by other students of society. A leading modern proponent of the "America as unique" thesis is Seymour Martin Lipset, who recently developed his argument in *American Exceptionalism: A Double Edged Sword*. Because Lipset so successfully captures this standard description of American culture I will center my discussion of it around his work, but the reader should keep in mind that Lipset is only one of many scholars who have identified similar American characteristics. * * * *

According to Lipset, America's "ideology can be described in five words: liberty, egalitarianism, individualism, populism, and laissez-faire." As Lipset notes, egalitarianism in the United States "involves equality of opportunity and respect, not of result or condition." Thus, American egalitarianism is consistent with individualism and laissez-faire. "The emphasis in the American value system, in the American creed, has been on the individual." It is the emphasis on the individual as a person equal in status to all other countrymen that produces populism, rights-orientation and laissez-faire (or anti-statist) attitudes.

Lipset argues that these values explain many distinctive features of American society, including some that are far from admirable, such as high crime rates. More ambiguous effects are those seen in the nature of governmental institutions and practices. He notes the relative weakness of the American central government and its modest involvement in the economy. The Constitution, he observes, "established a divided form of government . . . and reflected a deliberate decision by the country's founders to create a weak and internally conflicted political system." Almost all other modern states have parliamentary systems under which the majority party exercises power that is virtually plenary. As Mirjan Damaska said about American government, "Most astonishing to a foreign eye is the continuing fragmentation and decentralization of authority."[23]

Individualism, liberty and laissez-faire values also explain the comparatively low levels of American economic and social regulation (except for the strangely co-existing Puritanism that explains sex and drug laws). Meager American governmental support of welfare-state projects, be they cultural activities or universal health care—again typically laissez faire and individualist—is reflected even in constitutions. Many in Europe, but not the American, contain provisions that impose welfare-state obligations on the government. According to Mary Ann Glendon, these constitutional differences "are legal manifestations of divergent, and deeply rooted, cultural attitudes toward the state and its functions . . . [C]ontinental Europeans today, whether of the right or the left, are much more likely than Americans to assume that governments have affirmative duties."[26] At the same time, the Bill of Rights incorporates the American ideal of a citizen as possessing the right to be "let alone" by government. As Jerold Auerbach has it, "Law has absorbed and strengthened the competitive, acquisitive values associated with American individualism and capitalism."[27] If this is true of law in general it is more so the case with dispute procedures in particular.

Since American values strongly influence its governmental arrangements, it would be odd if these same values did not also contribute to an American exceptionalism in disputing. * * * *

American individualism and egalitarianism, Lipset also claims, underlies the emphasis on a rights-based legal discourse, and helps explain high rates of litigation compared to other industrialized nations. "In America . . . 'egalitarianism is based on the notion of equal rights of free-standing, rights-asserting individuals.' " The American attachment to courts suggests, perhaps, a weakness in the claim of anti-statism. Courts are governmental institutions and a resort to courts to resolve disputes is unavoidably to invoke governmental authority. While there is a point here, I think that the difference between courts and other governmental institutions is such that the inclination to sue in pursuit of private interest is better understood as of a piece with individualism and laissez-faire.

---

[23] MIRJAN DAMASKA, THE FACES OF JUSTICE AND STATE AUTHORITY: A COMPARATIVE APPROACH TO THE LEGAL PROCESS 233 (1991) [hereinafter "FACES OF JUSTICE"].

[26] Mary Ann Glendon, *Rights in Twentieth Century Constitutions, in* THE BILL OF RIGHTS IN MODERN STATES 521 (Geoffrey R. Stone, Richard A. Epstein & Cass R. Sunstein eds. 1992).

[27] JEROLD AUERBACH, JUSTICE WITHOUT LAW? 138 (1983).

Compared with most governmental institutions, courts are responsive to individualized pursuit of personal claims. Consider that private litigation is for the most part controlled by the litigants, who provide its impetus, its direction and often, its ultimate resolution. (The vast majority of American civil actions are settled before trial.) Courts neither meddle nor rescue unless called upon to do so, and then paradigmatically only for the litigants before them. And, as we shall see in more detail, the values of a distinctly American ideology underlie the forms and structures of disputing in America, and indeed have contributed to an American "exceptionalism" in disputing. * * * *

SOME FEATURES OF AMERICAN PROCEDURAL EXCEPTIONALISM

* * * * The jury is one of America's venerated institutions. It has achieved and maintained an importance in American trials that is unparalleled elsewhere in the world. While the jury retains a lively role in criminal cases in most English-speaking nations (but not in the rest of the world),[64] it is striking that in no other nation has the jury been retained in civil litigation to the degree it has in the United States. The right to a jury trial in civil cases is historic and iconic: it was added to the Federal Constitution by the Seventh Amendment as one of the Bill of Rights ratified in 1791. In 1938, when the Federal Rules of Civil Procedure were promulgated, its drafters thought it desirable to include a provision reminding readers that "The right of trial by jury as declared by the Seventh Amendment to the Constitution or as given by a statute of the United States shall be preserved to the parties inviolate." The Seventh Amendment and the Federal Rules apply only in federal litigation, but the right to a jury in civil cases has been constitutionalized by the states as well. Typical is the provision of the New York Constitution: As adopted in 1777, it provides that the right "shall remain inviolate forever."

Contrariwise, civil juries have never been found in any of the countries that follow Continental procedure. "Truly astonishing in the Continental view was the degree to which decisions of the lay jury—the paradigmatic adjudicator—escaped supervision through regular appellate mechanisms."[69] The United Kingdom, where it originated, has abandoned the civil jury in all but a very few kinds of

---

[64] MIRJAN R. DAMAŠKA, EVIDENCE LAW ADRIFT 28 (1997) (notes that while juries were established in France and elsewhere following the French Revolution, "the Continental love affair with the jury was one of short duration." Juries are used in criminal cases only in Belgium, Switzerland and Denmark. *Id.* at n. 5.

[69] FACES OF JUSTICE, at 219–20. The passage refers to the pre-twentieth century period when "classic civil procedure" was still used in England, including the civil jury.

cases,[70] and most of the countries with legal roots in England * * * have followed suit.[71]

It is not hard to see how the historic American attachment to the jury is bottomed on core American values. It is quintessentially an egalitarian, populist, anti-statist institution. It is "strongly egalitarian" because it gives lay people with no special expertise a factfinding power superior to that of the judge, despite all of his or her training and experience. Although it is true that the judge presiding at the trial may overrule a jury verdict and grant judgment "as a matter of law" against the party favored by the jury, this power is circumscribed. It can be exercised only if "there is no legally sufficient evidentiary basis for a reasonable jury to find for that party . . ."[73] The jury is also egalitarian in that it is a duty of citizenship imposed on all and that every juror has an equal vote regardless of education or social status. Indeed, it is strikingly an institution which plunges people, willy-nilly, into a situation in which communication and cooperation across distinctions of racial, ethnic and wealth are mandatory.

The civil jury is populist, "an avatar of democratic participation in government," because it allows the people to rule directly. A jury can determine, for example that a particular product was designed or manufactured in an unreasonably unsafe manner, thus setting safety standards that might otherwise be governed by statute or regulation. Jurors are well aware of their power to act as a "mini-legislature" in such cases. According to a recent article in the journal of the American Bar Association, "Like no time before, the 12 people seated in the jury box regularly demonstrate an increasing willingness—even a clamoring—to force basic American institutions, such as government, business and even private social organizations, to change the way they operate."[76] The article lists a number of cases in which juries awarded large verdicts in order to "send a message" to the defendant and its industry that certain behavior was not

---

[70] On the decline of the civil jury in the U.K., *see* MARY ANN GLENDON, MICHAEL WALLACE GORDON & CHRISTOPHER OSAKWE, COMPARATIVE LEGAL TRADITIONS 613–27 (2nd ed. 1994). The materials there collected indicate that the atrophy of the civil jury in the U.K. began during the First World War and culminated in 1965 when the Court of Appeal decided that there was no right to a jury trial except where specifically authorized by statute.

[71] Benjamin Kaplan & Kevin Clermont, *England and the United States, in* Chapter 6, ORDINARY PROCEEDINGS IN FIRST INSTANCE, CIVIL PROCEDURE, XVI INTERNATIONAL ENCYCLOPEDIA OF COMPARATIVE LAW (1984) at 3, 29 n. 265 (reports that there is some variation among the provinces of Canada and Australia but that in general the jury is seldom used in civil cases in those countries).

[73] FED. R. CIV. PROC. 50(a). The judge can also set the verdict aside if it is "against the weight of the evidence," but in such case there is a new trial before a new jury.

[76] Mark Curriden, *Power of 12*, ABA J. 36 (August 2000).

acceptable. Although the civil jury is of course an organ of government, it nonetheless has an anti-statist quality because it allows the people to decide matters differently than the other institutions of government might wish. Both in the civil and criminal spheres, this is no mere theoretical matter, as demonstrated by the debate over jury nullification, the sometimes-claimed power of the jury to ignore the law as a way of "doing justice" that continues to the present.[77]

The jury's connection to American individualism is not as obvious as its egalitarian and populist qualities. In some sense it is anti-individualist because the jury operates as a collectivity. Moreover, people do not volunteer to serve as jurors but are compelled by force of law to do so. On the other hand, the role of the individual is apparent because the number of persons on each jury is small, twelve or less, and as few as six in some jurisdictions. Where, as is traditional, a verdict depends on unanimity, a single hold-out can abort the trial and effectively command a new one.[78] But the American individualism as a value that underlies the civil jury is better appreciated when we introduce the point of view of the litigants. For the individual citizen whose liberty or property is in its hands, the jury is seen as a protector of the rights in a way that the judge, an official of the state, is not.

The synchronic development of an egalitarian American ethos and the jury as a device for protecting individual rights exemplifies the reciprocally constitutive role of cultural values and dispute institutions. The iconic status of the jury in American life emerged at the same time as the American people took on their "exceptionalist" values. It was in the period around the time of the American revolution that the jury became "so deeply embedded in American democratic ethos."[79] By the mid-eighteenth century, as Americans increasingly distinguished themselves as a separate people, juries had become a means of resisting the Crown's control over colonial affairs and British attempts to circumscribe jury powers were seen as a further cause of grievance. Tales of courageous jurors who stood up to tyrannical English government have ever since been an important part of the American self-image: "Most American history books hail the trial of [John Peter] Zenger for seditious libel in 1735 as the leading case for freedom of the press and as an example of a

---

[77] Jeffrey Abramson, WE, THE JURY 57–95 (1994). Several examples of juries' refusal to convict despite overwhelming evidence of guilt are presented.

[78] Unanimity is not required in all jurisdictions. In New York, for example, a verdict of five-sixths is sufficient in civil cases, see N.Y. Civil Practice Law and Rules 4113(a).

[79] VALERIE P. HANS & NEIL VIDMAR, JUDGING THE JURY (1986) at 32.

victory of the people over an aristocracy." Zenger, the publisher of a New York newspaper, was prosecuted because of the journal's sharp criticism of the appointed English governor of the colony. Andrew Hamilton, who defended Zenger, wove together a substantive claim— the right of the people to criticize their government—and the procedural point that the jurors had the power to protect that right.

> Jurymen are to see with their own eyes, to hear with their own ears, and to make use of their own consciences and understandings in judging of the lives, liberties or estates of their fellow subjects.

Although the hagiography surrounding the Zenger case has arguably idealized the participants, the case did help to establish unique American views on the jury and its place between law and those governed. The jury's continuing role in the construction of the American ethos was observed by Jefferson, who called jury service the "school by which [the] people learn the exercise of civic duties as well as rights" and by Tocqueville: "The jury, and more especially the civil jury, ... is the soundest preparation for free institutions. . . ." Modern scholars contend that the jury continues to serve as an influence on the moral reasoning of participants. A recent example of the jury/values connection is provided by the acquittal of John DeLorean, the entrepreneur who claimed that police entrapment had led to the charge of drug-dealing. One juror explained the verdict: ". . . there is a message here. . . . It's that our citizens will not let our government go too far. . . . It was like the book Nineteen Eighty-Four. They set one trap after another for DeLorean. . . ."

It is telling that George Priest links the right to vote and the jury trial as the two institutions of American democracy that it "seems simply unthinkable to criticize."[88] Both are icons of American values. The attachment to the jury is not, *pace* Professor Priest, shared by all Americans, and its place in the legal system is not static.[89] Like the culture in which it is found, it is contested and dynamic; its powers have ebbed and flowed in response to changes in social life. In one sense the story has been one of diminution, both in the frequency in which civil cases are tried to a jury and in its power in respect to the judge.[90] In another, as we have seen, jurors are

---

[88] *See* FACES OF JUSTICE, at 20–21.

[89] A thoughtful critical assessment of the civil jury was made by Jerome Frank in COURTS ON TRIAL 110–25 (1949). For an argument that the popular conception of the jury in America has undergone changes over the life of the country, see Abramson, *The Jury and Popular Culture,* 50 DEPAUL L. REV. 497 (2000).

[90] VALERIE P. HANS & NEIL VIDMAR, JUDGING THE JURY (1986) at 31–46. In 1999, less than two percent of all civil actions brought in federal courts were resolved by a jury trial, see New York Times, March 2, 2001, p. 1.

currently willing and eager to exercise their broad powers when they have a chance. Whether the American civil jury will, like its British ancestor, atrophy to irrelevance depends in large part on the continued viability of those ingredients of the collective American psyche that have sustained it so far.[92] Surveys of attorneys, judges, and the general public show that the civil jury continues to enjoy very wide support in the United States.[93]

In the preceding article, Chase asks whether the American civil jury will "atrophy to irrelevance" like the British civil jury. In *The Decline of Anglo-American Civil Jury Trial Practice*, Professor William Dorsaneo lays out the legislative decline of the British civil jury. As you read, consider whether a similar decline might occur in the United States. In what ways might the unique political and cultural context in America prevent the development of laws such as the ones Dorsaneo describes? Alternatively, under what circumstances can you imagine these sorts of laws being enacted in the United States?

WILLIAM V. DORSANEO III, *THE DECLINE OF ANGLO-AMERICAN CIVIL JURY PRACTICE*
71 SMU L. REV. 353 (2018)

* * * *

By the middle of the twentieth century, the English civil jury trial had virtually disappeared. Jury trials are available in only a handful of civil cases.

Lord Patrick Devlin's monograph describes the method of trying civil cases to juries before its virtual abandonment in England. With certain exceptions, this method very strongly resembled the methods used today in conventional trials in American courts. Devlin's monograph also summarized the decline and demise of jury trial in civil cases in England in the nineteenth and twentieth centuries.

---

[92] Stephen Yeazell argues that the different fates of the British and American juries reflect more pervasive differences between the two cultures, most notably different attitudes about the concentration of governmental power: "The persistence of the civil jury in the United States reflects a distrust of concentrated governmental power." Yeazell, *The New Jury and the Ancient Jury Conflict*, 1990 U. CHI. LAW FORUM 87, 106 (1990).

[93] See the surveys collected in Hans, *Attitudes Toward the Civil Jury: A Crisis of Confidence?*, in VERDICT (Robert E. Litan ed., 1993) at 248. An "ambitious national survey" conducted in 1978 found that eighty per cent of the respondents rated the right of trial by jury as "extremely important" and most of the others rated it as "important." *Id.* at 255.

• **1854, Common Law Procedure Act**. For centuries, trial by jury was the only form of trial used in any common law action in the King's courts. But in 1854, the enactment of the Common Law Procedure Act provided that trial by judge alone could be had by consent of both parties. The same Act empowered the trial judge to refer matters of account for determination by a judge or referee in such cases.

• **1873, Judicature Act**. As a result of the enactment of the 1873 Judicature Act, which also enacted complete fusion of law and equity for actions in the King's courts, so-called "prolonged examination cases" could be referred to a referee for "matters requiring prolonged examination of documents or accounts of any scientific or local investigation."

• **1883 (R.S.C. Ord. 36)**. In 1883, in "libel, slander, malicious prosecution, false imprisonment, seduction and breach of promise of marriage" cases, "trial by jury continued to be obtainable as a matter of course, but in all other cases it had to be specially asked for. . . . Later, the procedure was tightened by requiring the application for a jury to be made within a fixed time limit."

• **1918, Juries Act**. "In 1918, the right to jury was abolished except in seven cases, . . . the six cases previously enumerated together with cases of fraud; in all other cases trial by jury was made discretionary." This "emergency legislation [was] designed to expire six months after the end of the war, but when it did expire, it was replaced by another Act [(Administration of Justice Act), which was] intended to be permanent." As explained by Lord Devlin, toward the end of the Great War of 1914–1918, "jurors were no longer easily available."

• **1920, Administration of Justice Act.** In 1920, the Administration of Justice Act replaced the Juries Act of 1918. The Administration of Justice Act made the provisions of the 1918 Juries Act permanent. Lord Devlin explains that "[a]s a permanent alteration [widespread abolition of jury trial in most civil cases] was not well received; indeed, it was critic[z]ed so severely that in 1925 Parliament" reversed course and restored the right to jury trial as an option in all cases if "specially asked for" by a party."

- **1925, Supreme Court of Judicature (Consolidation) Act.** "[I]n 1925, Parliament restored the *status quo ante* 1918. But the restoration was not long lived."

- **1933, Administration of Justice Act.** "In 1933, as part of a drive for cheaper litigation, Parliament substantially re-enacted the 1920 [Administration of Justice] Act," which curtailed the use of juries in civil cases, with the exception of cases of libel, slander, malicious prosecution, false imprisonment, seduction, the breach of the promise of marriage, and fraud. Lord Devlin explains that the chief alteration made by the 1933 Act was "that the right to a jury in cases of fraud was granted only to the party charged." In other cases, the Administration of Justice Act of 1933 granted trial judges discretion to grant jury trials under a rule of civil procedure.

- ***Ward v. James*, All ER 563.** Until the Court of Appeal's 1965 decision in *Ward v. James*, the trial court's discretion was regarded as more or less unfettered. But in *Ward v. James*,[32] the Court of Appeal decided that absent "extraordinary circumstances," personal injury cases should be decided by judges without the existence of a jury. Lord Denning (Master of the Rolls) reasoned that having judges rather than jurors assess damages improved the uniformity and predictability of damage awards. Subsequent decisions usually followed the same analysis.

- **The Supreme Court Act of 1981.** Ultimately the Supreme Court Act of 1981 "permits a right to jury trial only in cases of defamation, malicious prosecution, fraud, and false imprisonment."

Most recently, Parliament promulgated the Defamation Act of 2013, declaring that for a defamation cause of action there will be a trial "without a jury unless the court orders otherwise." Defamation Act 2013, c. 26, § 11 (Eng.).

In the article below, Professor Valerie Hans outlines the approaches various countries have used in carving out space for lay citizens to participate in the legal decision-making process, predominately in criminal cases. These approaches range from all-citizen juries to mixed systems or collaborative court models. As you

---

[32] *Ward v. James* [1965] 1 All ER 563 at 568–70 (Eng.).

read, consider the cultural and/or political reasons for a particular approach to the use of juries. Do all of the approaches serve the same function in equal measure, or are some approaches "better" at fulfilling the purported role of a jury (i.e. civic education, legitimacy, reflection of communal values, etc.)? Why is there reluctance to extend the jury system to the civil context? Is the role of the jury different in a criminal, as opposed to a civil, case?

VALERIE P. HANS, *JURY SYSTEMS AROUND THE WORLD*

4 ANN. REV. L & SOC. SCI. 276 (2008)

TYPES OF LAY PARTICIPATION SYSTEMS

Many countries use the term "juror" for any layperson who participates in legal decision making, even though the systems for using lay people vary significantly. In their survey of law participation in countries that are members of the Council of Europe, Jackson and Kovalev usefully differentiate five distinct approaches to lay legal decision making. It is worthwhile to begin our review by describing these five models, as they highlight important differences in how countries use lay citizens in legal decision making.

Jackson & Kovalev label the first approach the continent jury model, the all-citizen jury based on English tradition, which allocates to the jury an exclusive function to determine the defendant's guilt. Great Britain, the United States, Canada, Australia, New Zealand, and more than 40 other nations employ juries of citizens drawn from the general population who decide cases collectively. Many countries that were once part of the British Empire inherited the English legal system, including its jury. After independence from Britain, although a number of former colonies abandoned the jury because of its association with an oppressive imperial regime, others retained it and made it a permanent part of the legal system. Although juries are more frequently found in common law systems, some civil law countries such as Spain and Austria employ all-citizen juries. Criminal juries typically decide on the verdict only. The major exception is U.S. capital cases, for which juries are constitutionally required to determine, at a minimum, whether the offense is eligible for a death sentence. Although the jury is carefully insulated from the judge during the deliberation, judges still play a significant role by presiding over jury trials, ruling on admissibility of evidence, providing legal rules for the jury, and in some jurisdictions guiding fact finding by commenting on the evidence or directing special verdicts.

Civil law countries characteristically employ mixed decision-making bodies of lay citizens and law-trained judges to decide cases. They are most often called mixed tribunals or mixed juries; Jackson & Kovalev label them collaborative court models. Usually, mixed tribunals decide both guilt and sentence in criminal cases.

Jackson & Kovalev distinguish three distinct variants of collaborative courts. The classic German or *Schöffen* collaborative court model features a professional judge and two lay assessors, although the number and composition vary depending on the seriousness of the case and the potential punishment. The French collaborative court model also includes professional judges deciding cases with citizens, but the ratio of lay to professional judges is much greater than in the German model. So, for example, in the French *cour d'assises*, which hears serious criminal cases, three professional judges deliberate together with nine jurors to determine the guilt of the accused. Remarkably, a French jury court of appeal, *cour d'assises d'appel*, with 12 jurors and 3 professional judges, was recently introduced. The jury court of appeal which operates by majority rule, conducts a fresh examination of the evidence in the case.

The German and French models differ in the selection and treatment of the lay participants. In the German model, citizens are appointed as members of the court and sit at the head of the courtroom with the professional judge. By contrast, in France lay members are randomly selected from the population to be jurors. They do not become members of the court as the German *Schöffen* do. During their period of service, French jurors sit separately from the judges, coming together for the deliberation.

Another approach to a mixed court noted by Jackson & Kovalev is the expert assessor collaborative court model, an interesting variant. Here, members of the community with special expertise thought to be relevant to a case sit with one or more law-trained judges to decide the outcome. For example, in Croatia, lay judges in mixed courts that decide the cases of juvenile defendants must be teachers, professors, or other persons with relevant experience in juvenile education.

A parallel can be drawn between the expert assessor collaborative court and the special jury, in which citizens with relevant background and expertise are chosen from the public to decide the case. Special all-women juries of matrons served in early English and American trials. The earliest jury of any sort in Australia was reportedly a jury of matrons. A woman facing the death penalty might claim she was pregnant and "plead her belly," requesting a delay in execution until the child could be born. The jury of matrons examined the defendant and used their personal knowledge to determine the veracity of the claim and whether a delay in her execution could be justified. The practice waned as medical specialists took over the task of assessing pregnancy claims.

Early on, special juries were also used in cases of substantial social and political importance. Sometimes that required that jurors have particular domains of expertise, but more often it simply meant that jurors were selected from elite members of the society, such as those with major property holdings or advanced education. As the idea of the representative jury gained ascendance in the latter half of the twentieth century, however, the use of the special jury declined. Nonetheless, the idea of drawing on community members with particular expertise continues to attract supporters, as evidenced by calls for specialized medical courts today.

The expert collaborative court approach has some appeal even in nations that do not have a strong tradition of citizen participation in law. For example, * * * in Thailand, a predominantly civil law country with no history of lay participation, three specialty courts have laypersons with expertise in the court's domain decide cases together with professional judges.

A final approach identified by Jackson & Kovalev is the pure lay judge model, in which lay judges without formal legal training sit either individually or in small groups to decide the outcomes of legal cases. They operate in various countries as lay judges, justices of the peace, or lay magistrates. Lay judges are used most frequently in lower courts and minor cases. Lay judges perform their work as an occupation or during substantial terms of service. * * * *

Jackson & Kovalev's effort is one of the few attempts at systematic categorization of different types of contemporary lay participation systems; their ambitious project examines members of the Council of Europe but deserves to be expanded to non-European nations. * * * * [N]o single source has comprehensively surveyed and described all lay participation systems worldwide. That straightforward descriptive task is an important first step for comparative analysis that in time will produce a richer understanding of the phenomenon of citizen involvement in legal decision making.

Notes and Questions

1.   Why might the civil jury "continue[ ] to enjoy very wide support in the United States" while the number of civil cases that go to trial continues to decline? How might you explain such a phenomenon?

2.   The Preface to the Transnational Rules of Civil Procedure includes the following statement: "We conclude that a system of procedure acceptable generally throughout the world could not require a jury trial. * * * * This in turn has led us to conclude that the scope of the proposed Transnational Civil Rules and Principles is limited to commercial disputes and excludes categories of litigation such as personal-injury and wrongful death actions, because barring jury trial in such cases would be unacceptable in the United States." Why would the elimination of jury trials in commercial cases be more acceptable than the elimination of jury trials in tort cases? (Can you use the five values— liberty, egalitarianism, individualism, populism, and laissez-faire—to explain this?)

3.   Professor Hans identifies mixed juries, what Jackson & Kovalev refer to as "collaborative court models." What are some of the benefits that might accompany juries with both professional and lay judges? Pitfalls? It may be helpful to consider how decisions by an all-layperson jury might differ from those delivered by a mixed jury.

4.   In *Deliberative Democracy and the American Civil Jury,* Valerie Hans et al. note that jury service generally may encourage deliberative democracy because the process requires citizens to work together to "resolve important social and political disputes." Is it likely that all forms of jury service equally "encourage deliberative democracy"? Are some approaches listed in *Jury Systems around the World* better suited to fully realize the investment in citizens described by Tocqueville?

5.   For juries to fulfill their role as institutions of deliberative democracy and lay participation, jurors must be drawn from a broad cross-section of society. Yet, in the United States a variety of laws and procedural mechanisms have historically limited the ability of women and people of color to serve on juries. And while the use of peremptory challenges to strike jurors on the basis of race was held unconstitutional in *Batson v. Kentucky*, 476 U.S. 79 (1986), it has not ended racial discrimination in jury selection.

Chapter 12

INTERNATIONAL ARBITRATION

Parties to a transnational contract might sometimes be concerned about using the laws or courts of either party's home country to resolve disputes arising under that contract. Instead, they may opt for arbitration, which allows the dispute to be decided by a "neutral" forum agreed upon by the parties; that is, by a multinational tribunal applying international arbitration rules in a mutually acceptable venue. As a general matter, if parties agree to arbitrate without specifying any rules or procedures, the default procedure for the appointment of the tribunal and the conduct of the arbitration will be that provided by the law of the seat of the arbitration. Many countries have arbitration laws that provide a legal framework for the conduct of arbitrations. Thus, if the seat of the arbitration is in the United States, then the arbitration may be governed by Chapter 1 of the United States Arbitration Act ("Federal Arbitration Act", "FAA").

Parties may also specify a particular institution for arbitration, each with its own set of rules. One of the oldest and most respected is The International Court of Arbitration of the International Chamber of Commerce (ICC), established in 1923 and based in Paris. *See* www.iccwbo.org. Others include the London House of International Arbitration (LCIA); The International Centre for Dispute Resolution (ICDR) (a part of the American Arbitration Association); The Hong Kong International Arbitration Centre (HKIAC); and The Singapore International Arbitration Centre (SIAC). The rules of each of these institutions are substantially the same, but the institutions vary in their fee structures, the degree of involvement of the arbitrators, and the degree of scrutiny that arbitral awards are given.

The UNCITRAL Arbitration Rules (developed by the United Nations Commission on International Trade Law) (as revised in 2013) provide a widely used set of rules for both general commercial transactions and arbitrations between States and individuals. If the UNCITRAL Arbitration Rules are selected, the parties may also designate an institution to administer the arbitration (under the UNCITRAL Arbitration Rules) or to act as an "appointing authority" to appoint the arbitrator(s) if the system of party appointments breaks down, or if there are any other challenges.

Below is a sample of the UNCITRAL Arbitration Rules, focusing on sections 1 and 3, Introductory Rules and Arbitral Proceedings respectively. As you read the excerpt, consider the degree to which these rules try to address possible concerns about neutrality, efficiency, and equality. Is international arbitration more protected from possible bias? Do these rules seem to accord with ideals of neutrality and equality?

UNCITRAL ARBITRATION RULES
United Nations Commission on International Trade Law, 2013

Section I.   Introductory rules

Article I

1.   Where parties have agreed that disputes between them in respect of a defined legal relationship, whether contractual or not, shall be referred to arbitration under the UNCITRAL Arbitration Rules, then such disputes shall be settled in accordance with these Rules subject to such modification as the parties may agree. * * * *

3.   These Rules shall govern the arbitration except that where any of these Rules is in conflict with a provision of the law applicable to the arbitration from which the parties cannot derogate, that provision shall prevail.

Section II.   Composition of the arbitral tribunal

Number of arbitrators

Article 7

1.   If the parties have not previously agreed on the number of arbitrators, and if within 30 days after the receipt by the respondent of the notice of arbitration the parties have not agreed that there shall be only one arbitrator, three arbitrators shall be appointed.

2.   Notwithstanding paragraph 1, if no other parties have responded to a party's proposal to appoint a sole arbitrator within the time limit provided for in paragraph 1 and the party or parties concerned have failed to appoint a second arbitrator in accordance with article 9 or 10, the appointing authority may, at the request of a party, appoint a sole arbitrator pursuant to the procedure provided for in article 8, paragraph 2, if it determines that, in view of the circumstances for the case, this is more appropriate.

Appointment of arbitrators (articles 8 to 10)

Article 8

1. If the parties have agreed that a sole arbitrator is to be appointed and if within 30 days after receipt by all other parties of a proposal for the appointment of a sole arbitrator the parties have not reached agreement thereon, a sole arbitrator shall, at the request of a party, be appointed by the appointing authority.

2. The appointing authority shall appoint the sole arbitrator as promptly as possible. In making the appointment, the appointing authority shall use the following list-procedure, unless the parties agree that the list-procedure should not be used or unless the appointing authority determines in its discretion that the use of the list-procedure is not appropriate for the case:

   (a) The appointing authority shall communicate to each of the parties an identical list containing at least three names;

   (b) Within 15 days after the receipt of this list, each party may return the list to the appointing authority after having deleted the name or names to which it objects and numbered the remaining names on the list in order of its preference;

   (c) After the expiration of the above period of time the appointing authority shall appoint the sole arbitrator from among the names approved on the lists returned to it and in accordance with the order of preference indicated by the parties;

   (d) If for any reason the appointment cannot be made according to this procedure, the appointing authority may exercise its discretion in appointing the sole arbitrator.

Section III. Arbitral proceedings

General provisions

Article 17

1. Subject to these Rules, the arbitral tribunal may conduct the arbitration in such manner as it considers appropriate, provided that the parties are treated with equality and that at an appropriate stage of the proceedings each party is given a reasonable opportunity of presenting its case. The arbitral tribunal, in exercising its discretion, shall conduct the proceedings so as to avoid unnecessary delay and expense and to provide a fair and efficient process for resolving the parties' dispute.

2. As soon as practicable after its constitution and after inviting the parties to express their views, the arbitral tribunal shall

establish the provision timetable of the arbitration. The arbitral tribunal may, at any time, after inviting the parties to express their views, extend or abridge any period of time prescribed under these Rules or agreed by the parties.

3.   If at an appropriate stage of the proceedings any part so requests, the arbitral tribunal shall hold hearings for the presentation of evidence by witnesses, including expert witnesses, or for oral argument. In the absence of such a request, the arbitral tribunal shall decide whether to hold such hearings or whether the proceedings shall be conducted on the basis of documents and other materials.

4.   All communications to the arbitral tribunal by one party shall be communicated by that party to all other parties. Such communications shall be made at the same time, except as otherwise permitted by the arbitral tribunal if it may do so under applicable law.

5.   The arbitral tribunal may, at the request of any party, allow one or more third persons to be joined in the arbitration as a party provided such person is a party to the arbitration agreement, unless the arbitral tribunal finds, after giving all parties, including the person or persons to be joined, the opportunity to be heard, that joinder should not be permitted because of prejudice to any of those parties. The arbitral tribunal may make a single award or several awards in respect of all parties so involved in the arbitration.

Here is a sample arbitration clause under UNCITRAL:

"Any dispute, controversy or claim arising out of or relating to this contract, or the breach, termination or invalidity thereof, shall be settled by arbitration in accordance with the UNCITRAL Arbitration Rules.

Note: Parties should consider adding: (a) The appointing authority shall be . . . [name of institution or person]; (b) The number of arbitrators shall be . . . [one or three]; (c) The place of arbitration shall be . . . [town and country]; (d) The language to be used in the arbitral proceedings shall be . . . ."

In choosing the seat of the arbitration, the parties are not only selecting the procedural law that applies but also the law for enforcing the resulting award. One of the key instruments in enforcement of international arbitration awards is the Convention on the Recognition and Enforcement of Foreign Arbitral Awards, also known as the "New York Arbitration Convention" or the "New York Convention." Another is the 1975 Inter-American Convention on International Arbitrations ("Panama Convention"). The New York Convention applies to the recognition and enforcement of foreign arbitral awards and the referral by a court to arbitration. By becoming party to the Convention, each of the States has agreed, subject to limited grounds of refusal, to enforce commercial arbitral awards made in other States party to the New York Convention. Accordingly, by selecting a State that is party to the New York Convention as the seat for any arbitration, parties provide considerable scope for enforcement of their awards.

A key objective of the New York Convention was uniformity; the New York Convention's drafters sought to establish a single set of international legal standards for the enforcement of arbitration agreements and awards. In all contracting states, the New York Convention is implemented through national legislation, and generally agreements and awards are enforced either under this Convention or through national law or another treaty, whichever is more favorable. As of 2020, 162 nations have ratified the Convention.

As you read the excerpt from the New York Convention below, consider how these rules may present their own legal challenges in terms of enforcement and applicability of relevant law. What aspects of the New York Convention seem most susceptible to dispute or confusion?

CONVENTION ON THE RECOGNITION AND ENFORCEMENT OF FOREIGN ARBITRAL AWARDS ("NEW YORK CONVENTION")

June 10, 1958, 21 U.S.T. 2517

Article I

1.   This Convention shall apply to the recognition and enforcement of arbitral awards made in the territory of a State other than the State where the recognition and enforcement of such awards are sought, and arising out of differences between persons, whether physical or legal. It shall also apply to arbitral awards not considered as domestic awards in the State where their recognition and enforcement are sought.

2.   The term "arbitral awards" shall include not only awards made by arbitrators appointed for each case but also those made by permanent arbitral bodies to which the parties have submitted.

3. When signing, ratifying or acceding to this Convention, or notifying extension under article X hereof, any State may on the basis of reciprocity declare that it will apply the Convention to the recognition and enforcement of awards made only in the territory of another Contracting State. It may also declare that it will apply the Convention only to differences arising out of legal relationships, whether contractual or not, which are considered as commercial under the national law of the State making such declaration.

Article II

1. Each Contracting State shall recognize an agreement in writing under which the parties undertake to submit to arbitration all or any differences which have arisen or which may arise between them in respect of a defined legal relationship, whether contractual or not, concerning a subject matter capable of settlement by arbitration.

2. The term "agreement in writing" shall include an arbitral clause in a contract or an arbitration agreement, signed by the parties or contained in an exchange of letters or telegrams.

3. The court of a Contracting State, when seized of an action in a matter in respect of which the parties have made an agreement within the meaning of this article, shall, at the request of one of the parties, refer the parties to arbitration, unless it finds that the said agreement is null and void, inoperative or incapable of being performed.

Article III

Each Contracting State shall recognize arbitral awards as binding and enforce them in accordance with the rules of procedure of the territory where the award is relied upon, under the conditions laid down in the following articles. There shall not be imposed substantially more onerous conditions or higher fees or charges on the recognition or enforcement of arbitral awards to which this Convention applies than are imposed on the recognition or enforcement of domestic arbitral awards.

Article IV

1. To obtain the recognition and enforcement mentioned in the preceding article, the party applying for recognition and enforcement shall, at the time of the application, supply:

(a) The duly authenticated original award or a duly certified copy thereof;

(b) The original agreement referred to in article II or a duly certified copy thereof.

2.   If the said award or agreement is not made in an official language of the country in which the award is relied upon, the party applying for recognition and enforcement of the award shall produce a translation of these documents into such language. The translation shall be certified by an official or sworn translator or by a diplomatic or consular agent.

Article V

1.   Recognition and enforcement of the award may be refused, at the request of the party against whom it is invoked, only if that party furnishes to the competent authority where the recognition and enforcement is sought, proof that:

(a)   The parties to the agreement referred to in article II were, under the law applicable to them, under some incapacity, or the said agreement is not valid under the law to which the parties have subjected it or, failing any indication thereon, under the law of the country where the award was made; or

(b)   The party against whom the award is invoked was not given proper notice of the appointment of the arbitrator or of the arbitration proceedings or was otherwise unable to present his case; or

(c)   The award deals with a difference not contemplated by or not falling within the terms of the submission to arbitration, or it contains decisions on matters beyond the scope of the submission to arbitration, provided that, if the decisions on matters submitted to arbitration can be separated from those not so submitted, that part of the award which contains decisions on matters submitted to arbitration may be recognized and enforced; or

(d)   The composition of the arbitral authority or the arbitral procedure was not in accordance with the agreement of the parties, or, failing such agreement, was not in accordance with the law of the country where the arbitration took place; or

(e)   The award has not yet become binding on the parties, or has been set aside or suspended by a competent authority of the country in which, or under the law of which, that award was made.

2.   Recognition and enforcement of an arbitral award may also be refused if the competent authority in the country where recognition and enforcement is sought finds that:

(a)   The subject matter of the difference is not capable of settlement by arbitration under the law of that country; or

(b) The recognition or enforcement of the award would be contrary to the public policy of that country.

The New York Convention is implemented through national legislation. In the United States, Chapter 2 of the United States Arbitration Act ("Federal Arbitration Act", "FAA") enforces the New York Convention. *See* 9 U.S.C.A. §§ 201–208 (West). The FAA also goes beyond the New York Convention and imposes additional requirements, changing how the treaty is implemented in the United States.

Chapter 1 (9 USC § 1 *et seq*) codifies the FAA and sets forth general provisions applicable to arbitration agreements involving maritime, interstate or foreign commerce. While Chapter 2 enforces the New York Convention, Chapter 3 (9 USC § 301 *et seq*) implements the Panama Convention. Note how the line between domestic and international often gets blurred. For example, what about arbitral awards rendered in the United States in cases that have an international element, *e.g.,* a non-U.S. party, property located outside the United States, or performance outside the United States?

UNITED STATES ARBITRATION ACT ("FEDERAL ARBITRATION ACT")

9 U.S. Code CHAPTER 1—GENERAL PROVISIONS

9 U.S.C. § 2. Validity, irrevocability, and enforcement of agreements to arbitrate

A written provision in any maritime transaction or a contract evidencing a transaction involving commerce to settle by arbitration a controversy thereafter arising out of such contract or transaction, or the refusal to perform the whole or any part thereof, or an agreement in writing to submit to arbitration an existing controversy arising out of such a contract, transaction, or refusal, shall be valid, irrevocable, and enforceable, save upon such grounds as exist at law or in equity for the revocation of any contract.

9 U.S.C. § 5. Appointment of arbitrators or umpire

If in the agreement provision be made for a method of naming or appointing an arbitrator or arbitrators or an umpire, such method shall be followed; but if no method be provided therein, or if a method be provided and any party thereto shall fail to avail himself of such method, or if for any other reason there shall be a lapse in the naming of an arbitrator or arbitrators or umpire, or in filling a vacancy, then upon the application of either party to the controversy the court shall designate and appoint an arbitrator or arbitrators or umpire, as the case may require, who shall act under the said agreement with the same force and effect as if he or they had been specifically named therein; and unless otherwise provided in the agreement the arbitration shall be by a single arbitrator.

9 U.S.C. §7. Witnesses before arbitrators; fees; compelling attendance

The arbitrators selected either as prescribed in this title or otherwise, or a majority of them, may summon in writing any person to attend before them or any of them as a witness and in a proper case to bring with him or them any book, record, document, or paper which may be deemed material as evidence in the case. The fees for such attendance shall be the same as the fees of witnesses before masters of the United States court * * *.

9 U.S.C. § 9. Award of arbitrators; confirmation; jurisdiction; procedure

If the parties in their agreement have agreed that a judgment of the court shall be entered upon the award made pursuant to the arbitration, and shall specify the court, then at any time within one year after the award is made any party to the arbitration may apply to the court so specified for an order confirming the award, and thereupon the court must grant such an order unless the award is vacated, modified, or corrected as prescribed in sections 10 and 11 of this title. If no court is specified in the agreement of the parties, then such application may be made to the United States court in and for the district within which such award was made * * *.

9 U.S.C. § 10. Same; vacation; grounds; rehearing

(a) In any of the following cases the United States court in and for the district wherein the award was made may make an order vacating the award upon the application of any party to the arbitration—

(1) where the award was procured by corruption, fraud, or undue means;

(2) where there was evident partiality or corruption in the arbitrators, or either of them;

(3) where the arbitrators were guilty of misconduct in refusing to postpone the hearing, upon sufficient cause shown, or in refusing to hear evidence pertinent and material to the controversy; or of any other misbehavior by which the rights of any party have been prejudiced; or

(4) where the arbitrators exceeded their powers, or so imperfectly executed them that a mutual, final, and definite award upon the subject matter submitted was not made.

(b) If an award is vacated and the time within which the agreement required the award to be made has not expired, the court may, in its discretion, direct a rehearing by the arbitrators * * *.

9 U.S. Code CHAPTER 2—CONVENTION ON THE RECOGNITION AND ENFORCEMENT OF FOREIGN ARBITRAL AWARDS

9 U.S.C. § 201. Enforcement of Convention

The Convention on the Recognition and Enforcement of Foreign Arbitral Awards of June 10, 1958, shall be enforced in United States courts in accordance with this chapter.

9 U.S.C. § 202. Agreement or award falling under the Convention

An arbitration agreement or arbitral award arising out of a legal relationship, whether contractual or not, which is considered as commercial, including a transaction, contract, or agreement described in section 2 of this title, falls under the Convention. An agreement or award arising out of such a relationship which is entirely between citizens of the United States shall be deemed not to fall under the Convention unless that relationship involves property located abroad, envisages performance or enforcement abroad, or has some other reasonable relation with one or more foreign states. For the purpose of this section a corporation is a citizen of the United States if it is incorporated or has its principal place of business in the United States.

9 U.S.C. § 206. Order to compel arbitration; appointment of arbitrators

A court having jurisdiction under this chapter may direct that arbitration be held in accordance with the agreement at any place therein provided for, whether that place is within or without the United States. Such court may also appoint arbitrators in accordance with the provisions of the agreement.

9 U.S.C. § 207. Award of arbitrators; confirmation; jurisdiction; proceeding

Within three years after an arbitral award falling under the Convention is made, any party to the arbitration may apply to any court having jurisdiction under this chapter for an order confirming the award as against any other party to the arbitration. The court shall confirm the award unless it finds one of the grounds for refusal or deferral of recognition or enforcement of the award specified in the said Convention.

Notes and Questions

1.   Under 28 U.S.C. § 1782, a United States District Court "may order" a person residing or found in the district to give testimony or produce documents "for use in a proceeding in a foreign or international tribunal * * * upon the application of any interested person." Two recent appellate court decisions have held, for the first time, that a private international arbitration panel constitutes a "foreign or international tribunal" and that Section 1782 therefore permits taking discovery for use in private commercial arbitrations. *See Abdul Latif Jameel Transp. Co. v. FedEx Corp.* (In re Application to Obtain Discovery for Use in Foreign Proceedings), 939 F.3d 710, 723 (6th Cir. 2019); *Servotronics, Inc. v. Boeing Co.*, 954 F.3d 209 (4th Cir. 2020).

2.   In addition, courts grapple with whether some types of disputes should not be arbitrable, or the degree to which other U.S. procedural doctrines, such as personal jurisdiction, should apply to the enforcement of arbitral awards. Consider the following case.

FRONTERA RESOURCES AZERBAIJAN CORP. V. STATE OIL CO. OF AZERBAIJAN REPUBLIC

United States Court of Appeals for the Second Circuit, 2009
582 F.3d 393

WALKER, JR., CIRCUIT JUDGE:

* * * * Frontera and SOCAR [State Oil Co. of Azerbaijan Republic] are two companies in the oil industry. Frontera is based in the Cayman Islands, and SOCAR is based in and owned by the Republic of Azerbaijan ("Azerbaijan"). In November 1998, the parties entered into a written agreement (the "Agreement") under which Frontera developed and managed oil deposits in Azerbaijan and delivered oil to SOCAR. In 2000, a dispute arose over SOCAR's refusal to pay for some of this oil * * *.

* * * * After Frontera and SOCAR were unable to settle their dispute amicably, Frontera served SOCAR in July 2003 with a request for arbitration as per the Agreement. In January 2006, after a hearing on the merits with full participation by both parties, a Swedish arbitral tribunal awarded Frontera approximately $1.24 million plus interest.

On February 14, 2006, Frontera filed a petition in the Southern District of New York to confirm the award pursuant to Article II (2) of the Convention on the Recognition and Enforcement of Foreign

Arbitral Awards ("New York Convention"). The district court dismissed the petition for lack of personal jurisdiction, on the basis that SOCAR had insufficient contacts with the United States to meet the Due Process Clause's requirements for the assertion of personal jurisdiction. * * * * The district court also declined to find quasi in rem jurisdiction over SOCAR, because Frontera had not identified specific SOCAR assets within the court's jurisdiction. The district court denied jurisdictional discovery and dismissed Frontera's petition. This appeal followed.

* * * * Frontera argues that a district court does not need personal jurisdiction over a respondent to confirm a foreign arbitral award against that party. * * * * [In particular,] Frontera contends that * * * there is no "positive statutory or treaty basis" for such a jurisdictional requirement. The federal statute that implements the New York Convention requires a court to confirm an award "unless it finds one of the grounds for refusal or deferral of recognition of enforcement of the award specified in the said Convention." 9 U.S.C. § 207. Article VI of the New York Convention "provides the exclusive grounds for refusing confirmation," *Yusuf Ahmed Alghanim & Sons, W.L.L. v. Toys "R" Us, Inc.*, 126 F.3d 15, 20 (2d Cir. 1997), and specifies seven grounds for refusing to enforce an arbitral award, none of which include a lack of jurisdiction over the respondent or the respondent's property, *see* New York Convention at art. 5, 21 U.S.T. at 2517. Frontera accordingly argues that we cannot impose a jurisdictional requirement if the Convention does not already have one. We disagree.

Unlike, "state courts[,][which] are courts of general jurisdiction[,] . . . federal courts are courts of limited jurisdiction which thus require a specific grant of jurisdiction." *Foxhall Realty Law Offices, Inc. v. Telecomm. Premium Servs., Ltd.*, 156 F.3d 432, 435 (2d Cir. 1998) (citing *Sheldon v. Sill*, 49 U.S. (8 How.) 441, 449 (1850)). "The validity of an order of a federal court depends upon that court's having jurisdiction over both the subject matter and the parties." *Ins. Corp. of Ir., Ltd. v. Compagnie des Bauxites de Guinee*, 456 U.S. 694, 701 (1982). While the requirement of subject matter jurisdiction "functions as a restriction on federal power," *id.* at 702, the need for personal jurisdiction is fundamental to "the court's power to exercise control over the parties," *Leroy v. Great W. United Corp.*, 443 U.S. 173, 180 (1979). "Some basis must be shown, whether arising from the respondent's residence, his conduct, his consent, the location of his property or otherwise, to justify his being subject to the court's power." *Glencore Grain*, 284 F.3d at 1122.

Because of the primacy of jurisdiction, "jurisdictional questions ordinarily must precede merits determinations in dispositional order." *Sinochem Int'l Co. v. Malay. Int'l Shipping Corp.,* 549 U.S. 422, 431, 127 S. Ct. 1184, 167 L. Ed.2d 15 (2007). "[T]he items listed in Article V as the exclusive defenses . . . pertain to *substantive* matters rather than to procedure. *Monegasque De Reassurances S.A.M. v. Nak Naftogaz of Ukr.,* 311 F.3d 488, 496 (2d Cir. 2002) (emphasis added). Article V's exclusivity limits the ways in which one can challenge a request for confirmation, but it does nothing to alter the fundamental requirement of jurisdiction over the party against whom enforcement is being sought. * * * *

We therefore hold that the district court did not err by treating jurisdiction over either SOCAR or SOCAR's property as a prerequisite to the enforcement of Frontera's petition. * * * *

Notes and Questions

1. The Second Circuit inserts domestic constitutional due process requirements into the enforcement of arbitral awards. Do these requirements undermine the goals of the Convention?

2. Is the judgment of the Second Circuit one the drafters of the New York Convention would likely have expected? Is it one they should have expected?

3. What if the Convention had explicitly stated that procedural doctrines under domestic law do not create adequate grounds to refuse enforcement? Should such a clause in a treaty override a constitutionally-based requirement, such as personal jurisdiction?

4. In considering how domestic law applies to arbitration agreements falling under the New York Convention, it is important to consider the purpose of having international arbitral agreements in the first place. As articulated by the U.S. Supreme Court, "[t]he goal of the Convention was to encourage the recognition and enforcement of commercial arbitration agreements in international contracts and to unify the standards by which agreements to arbitrate are observed and arbitral awards are enforced in the signatory countries." *Scherk v. Alberto-Culver Co.,* 417 U.S. 506, 520 n.15 (1974). In theory, enforcing arbitration agreements promotes "international comity [and] respect for the capacities of foreign and transnational tribunals." *Mitsubishi Motors v. Soler Chrysler-Plymouth,* 473 U.S. 614, 629 (1985). Moreover, because of the complexity of international transactions, certainty and uniformity of enforcement are particularly critical. *See id.* (citing "the need of the international commercial system for predictability in the resolution of disputes"). Beyond that, the dangers of forum shopping based on perceived home-court advantage are especially acute when parties hale from different countries. When both parties are sophisticated commercial actors and the agreements are part of true arms-length contracts, there is accordingly little reason not to enforce them.

5.   On the other hand, domestic legal systems tend to guard important doctrines from being eroded through international agreements. Thus, judges may feel the need to interpose core constitutional due process doctrines such as personal jurisdiction. How does this compare to the decision not to enforce the *Yahoo!* decision, which was discussed in Chapter One? If the French judgment had been an international arbitral decision, would the outcome have been different? Should the court have been less likely to interpose First Amendment concerns in the arbitral context? Should the enforcement of foreign court judgments be less automatic than the enforcement of arbitral decisions?

6.   What about other, non-constitutional, domestic law doctrines, whether state or federal? Are they also applicable in a case implicating the New York Convention? Consider the following case:

GE ENERGY POWER CONVERSION FRANCE SAS, CORP. V. OUTOKUMPU STAINLESS USA, LLC

Supreme Court of the United States, 2020
140 S. Ct. 1637

THOMAS, J.

* * * * In 2007, ThyssenKrupp Stainless USA, LLC, entered into three contracts with F. L. Industries, Inc., for the construction of cold rolling mills at ThyssenKrupp's steel manufacturing plant in Alabama. Each of the contracts contained an identical arbitration clause. The clause provided that "[a]ll disputes arising between both parties in connection with or in the performances of the Contract . . . shall be submitted to arbitration for settlement." App. 171. After executing these agreements, F. L. Industries, Inc., entered into a subcontractor agreement with petitioner GE Energy Power Conversion France SAS, Corp. (GE Energy), then known as Converteam SAS. Under that agreement, GE Energy agreed to design, manufacture, and supply motors for the cold rolling mills. Between 2011 and 2012, GE Energy delivered nine motors to the Alabama plant for installation. Soon thereafter, respondent Outokumpu Stainless USA, LLC, acquired ownership of the plant from ThyssenKrupp.

According to Outokumpu, GE Energy's motors failed by the summer of 2015, resulting in substantial damages. In 2016, Outokumpu and its insurers filed suit against GE Energy in Alabama state court. GE Energy removed the case to federal court under 9 U. S. C. § 205, which authorizes the removal of an action from state to federal court if the action "relates to an arbitration agreement . . . falling under the Convention [on the Recognition and Enforcement of Foreign Arbitral Awards]." GE Energy then moved to dismiss and compel arbitration, relying on the arbitration clauses in the contracts between F. L. Industries, Inc., and ThyssenKrupp.

The District Court granted GE Energy's motion to dismiss and compel arbitration with Outokumpu and Sompo Japan Insurance Company of America. The court held that GE Energy qualified as a party under the arbitration clauses because the contracts defined the terms "Seller" and "Parties" to include subcontractors. Because the court concluded that both Outokumpu and GE Energy were parties to the agreements, it declined to address GE Energy's argument that the agreement was enforceable under equitable estoppel.

The Eleventh Circuit reversed the District Court's order compelling arbitration. The court interpreted the Convention on the Recognition and Enforcement of Foreign Arbitral Awards (New York Convention or Convention) to include a "requirement that the parties actually sign an agreement to arbitrate their disputes in order to compel arbitration." The court concluded that this requirement was not satisfied because "GE Energy is undeniably not a signatory to the Contracts." It then held that GE Energy could not rely on state-law equitable estoppel doctrines to enforce the arbitration agreement as a nonsignatory because, in the court's view, equitable estoppel conflicts with the Convention's signatory requirement. * * * *

Chapter 1 of the Federal Arbitration Act (FAA) permits courts to apply state-law doctrines related to the enforcement of arbitration agreements. Section 2 of that chapter provides that an arbitration agreement in writing "shall be ... enforceable, save upon such grounds as exist at law or in equity for the revocation of any contract." 9 U. S. C. § 2. As we have explained, this provision requires federal courts to "place [arbitration] agreements "upon the same footing as other contracts." *Volt Information Sciences, Inc. v. Board of Trustees of Leland Stanford Junior Univ.*, 489 U.S. 468, 474 (1989). But it does not "alter background principles of state contract law regarding the scope of agreements (including the question of who is bound by them)." *Arthur Andersen LLP v. Carlisle*, 556 U.S. 624, 630 (2009).

The "traditional principles of state law" that apply under Chapter 1 include doctrines that authorize the enforcement of a contract by a nonsignatory. *Id.* at 631 (internal quotation marks omitted). For example, we have recognized that arbitration agreements may be enforced by nonsignatories through " 'assumption, piercing the corporate veil, alter ego, incorporation by reference, third-party beneficiary theories, waiver and estoppel.' " *Id.* (quoting 21 R. Lord, Williston on Contracts § 57:19, p. 183 (4th ed. 2001)). * * * *

The New York Convention is a multilateral treaty that addresses international arbitration. 21 U.S.T. 2517, T. I. A. S. No. 6997. It focuses almost entirely on arbitral awards. Article I(1) describes the Convention as applying only to "the recognition and enforcement of arbitral awards." *Id.*, at 2519. Articles III, IV, and V contain recognition and enforcement obligations related to arbitral awards for contracting states and for parties seeking the enforcement of arbitral awards. *Id.*, at 2519–2520. Article VI addresses when an award can be set aside or suspended. *Id.*, at 2520. And Article VII(1) states that the "Convention shall not . . . deprive any interested party of any right he may have to avail himself of an arbitral award in the manner and to the extent allowed by the law or the treaties of the country where such award is sought to be relied upon." *Id.*, at 2520–2521.

Only one article of the Convention addresses arbitration agreements—Article II. That article contains only three provisions, each one sentence long. Article II(1) requires "[e]ach Contracting State [to] recognize an agreement in writing under which the parties undertake to submit to arbitration all or any differences which have arisen or which may arise between them in respect of a defined legal relationship, whether contractual or not, concerning a subject matter capable of settlement by arbitration." *Id.* at 2519. Article II(2) provides that "[t]he term 'agreement in writing' shall include an arbitral clause in a contract or an arbitration agreement, signed by the parties or contained in an exchange of letters or telegrams." *Ibid.* Finally, Article II(3) states that "[t]he court of a Contracting State, when seized of an action in a matter in respect of which the parties have made an agreement within the meaning of this article, shall, at the request of one of the parties, refer the parties to arbitration, unless it finds that the said agreement is null and void, inoperative or incapable of being performed." *Ibid.* * * * *

The text of the New York Convention does not address whether nonsignatories may enforce arbitration agreements under domestic doctrines such as equitable estoppel. The Convention is simply silent on the issue of nonsignatory enforcement, and in general, "a matter not covered is to be treated as not covered"—a principle "so obvious that it seems absurd to recite it," A. SCALIA & B. GARNER, READING LAW: THE INTERPRETATION OF LEGAL TEXTS 93 (2012).

This silence is dispositive here because nothing in the text of the Convention could be read to otherwise prohibit the application of domestic equitable estoppel doctrines. Only one Article of the Convention addresses arbitration agreements—Article II—and only one provision of Article II addresses the enforcement of those agreements—Article II(3). The text of Article II(3) states that courts of a contracting state "shall . . . refer the parties to arbitration" when the parties to an action entered into a written agreement to arbitrate and one of the parties requests referral to arbitration. The provision, however, does not restrict contracting states from applying domestic law to refer parties to arbitration in other circumstances. That is, Article II(3) provides that arbitration agreements must be enforced in certain circumstances, but it does not prevent the application of domestic laws that are more generous in enforcing arbitration agreements. Article II(3) contains no exclusionary language; it does not state that arbitration agreements shall be enforced *only* in the identified circumstances. Given that the Convention was drafted against the backdrop of domestic law, it would be unnatural to read Article II(3) to displace domestic doctrines in the absence of exclusionary language. * * * *

SOTOMAYOR, J., concurring.

I agree with the Court that the Convention on the Recognition and Enforcement of Foreign Arbitral Awards, June 10, 1958, 21 U.S.T. 2517, T.I.A.S. No. 6997 (New York Convention), does not categorically prohibit the application of domestic doctrines, such as equitable estoppel, that may permit nonsignatories to enforce arbitration agreements. I note, however, that the application of such domestic doctrines is subject to an important limitation: Any applicable domestic doctrines must be rooted in the principle of consent to arbitrate.

This limitation is part and parcel of the Federal Arbitration Act (FAA) itself. It is a "basic precept," *Stolt-Nielsen S. A. v. AnimalFeeds Int'l Corp.*, 559 U.S. 662, 681 (2010), that "[a]rbitration under the [FAA] is a matter of consent, not coercion," *Volt Information Sciences, Inc. v. Board of Trustees of Leland Stanford Junior Univ.*, 489 U.S. 468, 479 (1989); see also, e.g., *Lamps Plus, Inc. v. Varela*, 587 U.S. ___, ___ (2019) (slip op., at 7) ("Consent is essential under the FAA"); *Granite Rock Co. v. Teamsters*, 561 U.S. 287, 299 (2010) ("[T]he first principle that underscores all of our arbitration decisions" is that "[a]rbitration is strictly 'a matter of consent' "). "We have emphasized th[is] 'foundational FAA principle' many times," *Lamps Plus*, 587 U.S., at ___ (slip op., at 7) (quoting *Stolt-Nielsen*, 559 U.S., at 684) (citing cases), and even the parties find common ground on the point. Because this consent principle governs the FAA on the whole, it constrains any domestic doctrines under Chapter 1 of the FAA that might "appl[y]" to Convention proceedings (to the extent they do not "conflict with" the Convention). 9 U. S. C. § 208; cf. *ante*, at 5–6. Parties seeking to enforce arbitration agreements under Article II of the Convention thus may not rely on domestic nonsignatory doctrines that fail to reflect consent to arbitrate. While the FAA's consent principle itself is crystalline, it is admittedly difficult to articulate a bright-line test for determining whether a particular domestic nonsignatory doctrine reflects consent to arbitrate. That is in no small part because some domestic nonsignatory doctrines vary from jurisdiction to jurisdiction. With equitable estoppel, for instance, one formulation of the doctrine may account for a party's consent to arbitrate while another does not. *Cf.* Brief for Respondents 45 (maintaining that courts have applied at least "three different versions" of GE Energy's equitable-estoppel theory, including one that allegedly "allows a non-party to force arbitration even of claims wholly unconnected to the agreement"). Lower courts must therefore determine, on a case-by-case basis, whether applying a domestic nonsignatory doctrine would violate the FAA's inherent consent restriction.*

Article II of the Convention leaves much to the contracting states to resolve on their own, and the FAA imposes few restrictions. Nevertheless, courts applying domestic nonsignatory doctrines to enforce arbitration agreements under the Convention must strictly adhere to "the foundational FAA principle that arbitration is a matter of consent." *Stolt-Nielsen*, 559 U.S., at 684. Because the Court's opinion is consistent with this limitation, I join it in full.

Notes and Questions

1. Professor Roger Perlstadt highlights the tension between the role of Article III judges and arbitrators in settling disputes:

> Because arbitration is not simply a glorified form of settlement, and arbitrators bindingly resolve disputes by applying law to facts they determine, arbitrators exercise judicial power. Further, to the extent arbitrators exercise such judicial power over disputes falling within the coverage of Article III, they are exercising the judicial power of the United States, which Article III assigns exclusively to life-tenured and salary-protected judges. Thus, resolution of such disputes by arbitrators pursuant to the FAA is in tension with the literal mandate of Article III.

Roger J. Perlstadt, *Article III Judicial Power and the Federal Arbitration Act*, 62 AM. U. L. REV. 201, 227 (2012). Are the advantages of arbitration sufficient to overcome such a tension? Does the enforcement of

---

* In this case, however, I am skeptical that any domestic nonsignatory doctrines need come into play at all, because Outokumpu appears to have expressly agreed to arbitrate disputes under the relevant contract with subcontractors like GE Energy. The contract provided that disputes arising between the buyer and seller in connection with the contract were subject to arbitration. It also specified that the seller in the contract "shall be understood" to include "[s]ub-contractors." And it appended a list of potential subcontractors, one of which was GE Energy's predecessor, Converteam.

international arbitration further complicate the relationship between arbitrators and Article III judges? International arbitration may involve international agreements and relationships among various nations. Do such additional factors suggest that international arbitration enforcement by U.S. courts may be more palatable than strictly domestic arbitration enforcement in the eyes of those opposed to arbitration in the first place?

2.   According to 9 U.S.C. § 202, "[a]n agreement or award arising out of such a relationship which is entirely between citizens of the United States shall be deemed not to fall under the Convention unless that relationship involves property located abroad, envisages performance or enforcement abroad, or has some other reasonable relation with one or more foreign states." Suppose two American citizens, A and B, have agreed to settle any disputes by arbitration. The subject of a dispute between A and B involves B's substantial property holdings in a country that is both outside the United States and a member of the New York Convention. How might the parties use the cited provisions *supra* to devise a plan for arbitration? Must the parties consider substantive law under each of the countries?

3.   One of the justifications for enforcing arbitration agreements is that doing so promotes international comity and respect for the capacities of foreign and transnational tribunals. Do you agree?

4.   Writing for the majority, Justice Thomas makes it clear that nonsignatories may enforce an arbitration agreement according to common law doctrines such as assumption and third-party beneficiary theories. In her concurrence, Justice Sotomayor emphatically points out that a nonsignatory's enforcement of an arbitration agreement must conform to "the foundational FAA principle that arbitration is a matter of consent." What do you think inspired Justice Sotomayor to author this concurrence? In what ways does a federal system pose particular problems with regard to the enforcement of *international* arbitration agreements? Given that parties sometimes agree to arbitrate to avoid application of domestic law, might litigants be more reluctant to attempt to enforce arbitral awards in the United States in light of the *GE Energy Power Conversion* opinion above?

Chapter 13

INTERSYSTEMIC PRECLUSION AND JUDGMENT RECOGNITION

Should a case or issue that has already been litigated in another country be enforced in the United States? From one perspective, it may be inefficient or unfair to allow parties to relitigate what has already been adjudicated elsewhere. Recognition and enforcement of foreign judgments also fosters stability and collaboration among participants in a global community where an increasing number of social and economic activities have multinational contacts. By recognizing and enforcing judgments entered elsewhere, a country anticipates that others will return the courtesy. Nevertheless, it may sometimes be difficult for a court to recognize and enforce a judgment rendered by a legal system whose procedures or substantive law is strongly contrary to conceptions of justice in the enforcing court's own jurisdiction.

Treaties offer one solution for contracting states united in their desire to harmonize their domestic laws on the enforcement of judgments. The Brussels I Regulation, for example, provides rules for the recognition and enforcement of the judgments of Member States within the European Union, as part of an effort to promote trade and further integrate the various domestic systems. The Rules are brief and rather straightforward. Provided that the Member State's court proceedings from which the judgment emanated fall within the definition of civil and commercial matters, there are few exceptions to the general proposition that the judgment of another contracting state must be recognized or enforced. According to Article 45 of the Regulation, a judgment shall not be recognized:

(a) if such recognition is manifestly contrary to public policy in the Member State addressed;

(b) where the judgment was given in default of appearance, if the defendant was not served with the document which instituted the proceedings or with an equivalent document in sufficient time and in such a way as to enable him to arrange for his defense unless the defendant failed to commence proceedings to challenge the judgment when it was possible for him to do so;

(c)   if the judgment is irreconcilable with a judgment given between the same parties in the Member State addressed;

(d) if the judgment is irreconcilable with an earlier judgment given in another Member State or in a third State involving the same cause of action and between the same parties, provided that the earlier judgment fulfils the conditions necessary for its recognition in the Member State addressed.

In the United States, the Full Faith and Credit Clause of the U.S. Constitution is even more exacting. Whereas Article 45(a) of the Brussels I Regulation allows the enforcing state to refuse recognition of a judgment that is "manifestly contrary to public policy," the U.S. Supreme Court has made clear that a state may *not* interpose public policy as a reason to deny enforcement to another state's judgment. *See Baker v. General Motors*, 522 U.S. 222, 233 (1998). Indeed, even a judgment of a foreign state based on an incorrect understanding of the enforcing state's law must still be enforced. *See Fauntleroy v. Lum*, 210 U.S. 230, 237 (1908).

Automatic judgment recognition on a transnational scale is obviously more complicated. Yet, even in this context most judgments issued abroad are routinely enforced by U.S. courts. As discussed in the previous chapter, with regard to foreign arbitration decisions the United States has ratified and implemented the United Nations Convention on the Recognition and Enforcement of Foreign Arbitral Awards. *See* 9 U.S.C. §§ 201–208 (Federal Arbitration Act). The Convention, often referred to as the New York Convention, is the primary legal basis for enforcing international commercial arbitration awards. In international commercial arbitration, there is a strong presumption that arbitrations are valid and the award should be enforced. The New York Convention's "pro-enforcement bias" prevents courts from reviewing the merits of the underlying dispute when the prevailing party seeks to convert the arbitral award into a court judgment. Adhered to by nearly half of the world's states, including almost all of the major trading states and all of the principal centers of international arbitration, the New York Convention gives arbitral awards greater currency even than formal judgments of courts. Although the Convention identifies a few specific and limited grounds upon which an arbitral award may be denied recognition, the pro-enforcement bias is very strong.

With regard to court judgments (as opposed to arbitral decisions), there is no such comprehensive treaty (despite many years of efforts). Nevertheless, even if not obligated by a treaty, a country might *choose* to recognize and enforce the judgments of other countries. Indeed, the United States has long been among the countries in the world most receptive to the recognition and enforcement of foreign judgments, notwithstanding the fact that the United States has not been a party to any comprehensive bilateral or multilateral treaty concerning such matters. Strikingly, this receptiveness is the product not of Congressional legislation, but rather a coordinated effort among the states to adopt a common analytical framework.

To that end, 31 states and the District of Columbia have adopted some version of the Uniform Foreign Money Judgments Recognition Act. However, because not all states have adopted the Uniform Act, and because the Uniform Act is limited to money judgments, a second and similar analytical framework also serves an important function in recognition and enforcement practice in the United States. The Restatement (Third) of Foreign Relations Law, summarizes the prevailing common and statutory law of the states of the United States.

RESTATEMENT (THIRD) OF FOREIGN RELATIONS LAW
AM. LAW. INST. 1987

§ 481.   Recognition and Enforcement of Foreign Judgment. Except as provided in § 482, a final judgment of a court of a foreign state granting or denying recovery of a sum of money, establishing or confirming the status of a person, or determining interests in property, is conclusive between the parties, and is entitled to recognition in courts in the United States. * * * *

Comment:

* * * c.   Effect of foreign judgment. A foreign judgment is generally entitled to recognition by courts in the United States to the same extent as a judgment of a court of one State in the courts of another State. As in the case of a sister-State judgment, a judgment of a foreign country ordinarily has no greater effect in the United States than in the country where the judgment was rendered. * * * *

d.   Reciprocity in enforcement of foreign judgments. A judgment otherwise entitled to recognition will not be denied recognition or enforcement because courts in the rendering state might not enforce a judgment of a court in the United States if the circumstances were reversed. *Hilton v. Guyot,* 159 U.S. 113 (1895), declared a limited reciprocity requirement applicable when the judgment creditor is a national of the state in which the judgment was rendered and the judgment debtor is a national of the United States. Though that holding has not been formally overruled, it is no longer followed in the great majority of State and federal courts in the United States. * * * *

g.   Proceedings to enforce foreign judgments in the United States. In many States, including those that have adopted the Uniform Foreign Money Judgments Recognition Act, * * * an action to enforce a foreign money judgment may be initiated through expedited procedures, such as a motion for summary judgment in lieu of a complaint. Enforcement of a foreign judgment may also be pursued by counterclaim, cross-claim, or affirmative defense.

§ 482   Grounds for Nonrecognition of Foreign Judgments.

(1)   A court in the United States may not recognize a judgment of the court of a foreign state if:

(a)   the judgment was rendered under a judicial system that does not provide impartial tribunals or procedures compatible with due process of law; or

(b)   the court that rendered the judgment did not have [personal] jurisdiction over the defendant * * *.

(2)   A court in the United States need not recognize a judgment of the court of a foreign state if:

(a)   the court that rendered the judgment did not have jurisdiction of the subject matter of the action;

(b)   the defendant did not receive notice of the proceedings in sufficient time to enable him to defend;

(c)   the judgment was obtained by fraud;

(d)   the cause of action on which the judgment was based, or the judgment itself, is repugnant to the public policy of the United States or of the State where recognition is sought;

(e)   the judgment conflicts with another final judgment that is entitled to recognition;

(f)   the proceeding in the foreign court was contrary to an agreement between the parties to submit the controversy on which the judgment is based to another forum.

Notes and Questions

1.   Note that if one of the defenses listed in Paragraph (1) of Section 482 is established, the court where recognition is sought is

required to deny recognition. If one of the defenses listed in Paragraph
(2) is established, the court has the discretion to deny recognition.

2.   By equating foreign judgments to sister-state judgments, the
statement in § 481 cmt. c establishes a strong policy in favor of
recognizing and enforcing foreign judgments. Article IV Section 1 of the
United States Constitution requires that "Full Faith and Credit shall be
given in each State to the public Acts, Records, and judicial Proceedings
of every other State."

3.   The reference to *Hilton v. Guyot* in § 481 cmt. D deserves
special attention. That case, decided in 1895, is the United States
Supreme Court's only guidance about standards for the recognition and
enforcement of foreign judgments. In that case, Justice Gray, writing for
a 5-member majority, embraced principles of comity and expressed
respect for the diversity of approaches in foreign systems, but ultimately
adopted reciprocity as a touchstone for resolving questions about the
recognition and enforcement of foreign judgments. The Court refused to
enforce the French judgment obtained by French plaintiffs against an
American defendant because, were the roles reversed, the French court
would not have enforced the American judgment. The legacy of that
opinion rests not in its holding (common law that bound only federal
courts sitting in diversity until 1938, when general federal common law
was extinguished), but rather in its articulation of the need for comity
and deference to foreign legal systems.

4.   Reciprocity requirements still are a fundamental component of
the recognition and enforcement practices of many countries. On one
hand, adoption of a reciprocity requirement indicates that a country is
open to enforcing the judgments of other countries that are willing to do
the same in return. But on the other hand, it forces the "other" country
to act first—to establish a record of enforcing the judgments of the
country that has the reciprocity requirement. If both (or all) countries
have a reciprocity requirement, who acts first? Does a policy that
punishes non-cooperation ultimately encourage cooperation? Is there
another more effective, yet equally cautious, method of demonstrating a
receptiveness to enforcing foreign judgments provided the same courtesy
is returned?

BRIDGEWAY CORP. V. CITIBANK

United States Court of Appeals for the Second Circuit, 2000
201 F.3d 134

CALABRESI, CIRCUIT JUDGE:

Bridgeway Corp. ("Bridgeway"), a Liberian corporation seeking
to enforce a final judgment rendered by the Supreme Court of
Liberia, appeals from the district court's decision denying
Bridgeway's motion for summary judgment and granting, *sua sponte*,

summary judgment in favor of the nonmoving party, Citibank. The district court held, first, that Citibank was not judicially estopped from challenging the fairness of the Liberian judicial system simply because it had participated voluntarily in litigation in Liberia and, second, that the evidence in the record established, as a matter of law, that the Liberian judicial system was not "a system that . . . provide[s] impartial tribunals or procedures compatible with the requirements of due process." We affirm.

I. BACKGROUND

A. Overview of Liberian History

This appeal derives from an action by Bridgeway to enforce a money judgment against Citibank entered by the Supreme Court of Liberia on July 28, 1995. Because the merits of this case turn on the events surrounding the Liberian civil war during the first half of the 1990s, it is helpful to provide a brief overview of those circumstances before proceeding to discuss the case. The following facts are drawn from the district court's thoughtful opinion and are not traversed in the record before us.

Liberia was founded in 1817 to resettle freed American slaves, and in 1847 it became an independent republic. The original 1847 Constitution, amended in 1976 and again in 1986, established a government modeled on that of the United States. Under the 1986 Constitution, for example, the judicial powers of the Liberian government are vested in a Supreme Court and such subordinate courts as the Legislature may establish. The Supreme Court is composed of one chief justice and four associate justices. Justices and judges are nominated by the President and confirmed by the Senate and have life tenure unless impeached.

From 1980 to 1989, Samuel Kanyon Doe headed a Liberian government marked by corruption and human rights abuses, as well as by rampant inflation. In 1989, a group of dissidents seized power and, in 1990, executed Doe. Doe's death marked the beginning of a violent seven-year civil war. By 1991, Liberia was in effect ruled by two governments: one controlled Monrovia, the capital, while the other controlled the remainder of the country. Following several short-lived cease fires, a formal peace accord was signed in August 1995. After another outbreak of violence in 1996, elections were held in July 1997. In August 1997, Charles Taylor was inaugurated, and the 1986 Constitution was reinstated.

Throughout the period of civil war, Liberia's judicial system was in a state of disarray and the provisions of the Constitution concerning the judiciary were no longer followed. Instead, under an agreement worked out among the warring parties in 1992, the Supreme Court was reorganized, with various factions each unilaterally appointing a specified number of justices. The United States State Department Country Reports for Liberia during this period paint a bleak picture of the Liberian judiciary. The 1994 Report observed that "corruption and incompetent handling of cases remained a recurrent problem." The 1996 Report stated that, "the judicial system, already hampered by inefficiency and corruption, collapsed for six months following the outbreak of fighting in April."

In 1997, before elections were held, the leaders of the various factions acknowledged that the integrity of the Supreme Court had been compromised by factional loyalties since 1992 and agreed that the Court would have to be reconstituted so that it might gain the legitimacy that would enable it to resolve successfully disputes that might arise concerning the elections. The members of the Court were therefore dismissed, and new members were appointed based on the recommendations of the Liberian National Bar Association.

B. This Case

Plaintiff-appellant Bridgeway is a Liberian corporation with its principal place of business in Monrovia, Liberia. Defendant-appellee, Citibank, is a United States banking corporation with its principal place of business in New York. For many years Citibank maintained a branch in Monrovia, but it closed that branch in January 1992 and completely withdrew from Liberia by 1995. As required by Liberian law, Citibank, before withdrawing, formulated a plan of liquidation, which was approved by the National Bank of Liberia. According to this plan, funds were to be remitted by Citibank to Meridian Bank Liberia Ltd., in order to meet Citibank's obligations to depositors. Citibank alerted its customers to its plans so that they could withdraw their funds. On April 21, 1995, the National Bank of Liberia indicated by letter that Citibank had satisfactorily completed the liquidation plan and was no longer licensed to do business in Liberia.

Bridgeway had an account at Citibank's Liberian branch with a balance of $189,376.66. In November 1992, Bridgeway brought suit in Liberia against Citibank, seeking a declaration that Citibank was obligated to pay Bridgeway its balance in United States (rather than Liberian) dollars. In August 1993, the trial court ruled in favor of Citibank. The court found that, under Liberian law, a person may not refuse to accept Liberian dollars for the discharge of an obligation unless there is an express agreement to the contrary and that Liberian law gives the Liberian dollar a par value equal to the value of the United States dollar. The trial court also found that under

Bridgeway's contract with Citibank, the latter had the right to decide the currency in which a withdrawal would be paid. Bridgeway appealed to the Liberian Supreme Court, which reversed the lower court's decision and entered judgment for Bridgeway.

Bridgeway filed suit in New York state court to enforce the Liberian Supreme Court judgment, and Citibank removed the case to the federal district court. When it became apparent that Citibank was going to defend itself by challenging the legitimacy of the Liberian judicial system, Bridgeway moved for summary judgment—arguing that Citibank was estopped from questioning the fairness of the Liberian judiciary. But the district court denied that motion and, *sua sponte*, granted summary judgment for Citibank. Specifically, the court found that, as a matter of law, Liberia's courts did not constitute "a system of jurisprudence likely to secure an impartial administration of justice" and that, as a result, the Liberian judgment was unenforceable in the United States. Bridgeway now appeals.

II. DISCUSSION

* * * * [A]. Judicial Estoppel

Bridgeway * * * argues that because Citibank voluntarily participated in litigation in Liberian courts, it was judicially estopped from raising any question as to the impartiality of those courts in the instant case. Bridgeway observes that Citibank has taken part in at least a dozen civil cases in Liberia since 1992. And in several of those cases, Citibank appeared as a plaintiff. Having availed itself of Liberia's courts without there raising any objections to the fairness of Liberian justice, Citibank should now be estopped, Bridgeway argues, from calling into question the validity of Liberian judgments. Citibank responds by arguing that its participation in Liberian litigation did not amount to an admission of the fairness of Liberian courts. Moreover, it argues that it could not have raised its objections to Liberia's judicial system in Liberia, because Liberian courts routinely sanction lawyers who question the Liberian judicial system. The district court agreed with Citibank.

Judicial estoppel "prevents a party from asserting a factual position in a legal proceeding that is contrary to a position previously taken by [the party] in a prior legal proceeding." In this Circuit, "[a] party invoking judicial estoppel must show that (1) the party against whom the estoppel is asserted took an inconsistent position in a prior proceeding and (2) that position was adopted by the first tribunal in some manner." We have described the type of inconsistency required as a "clear inconsistency between [the party's] present and former positions."

In order for Bridgeway to prevail, we must conclude that voluntarily participating in litigation in a foreign tribunal is fundamentally inconsistent with the belief that the tribunal is unlikely to provide an impartial forum or one that comports with notions of due process. Such a position is without merit. Defending a suit where one has been haled into court, and suing where jurisdiction and venue readily exist do not constitute assertions that the relevant courts are fair and impartial. Accordingly, we do not view Citibank's voluntary participation in Liberian litigation, even as a plaintiff, as clearly contradictory to its present position.

[B].   Fairness of Liberian Courts[1]

i.   Burden

The parties strenuously dispute who bears the ultimate burden of proof with respect to the fairness of the Liberian judicial system. Although there are cases in which the question of the burden might be significant, it does not ultimately matter here. Accordingly, we express no opinion on it. Even if Citibank were to bear both the burden of production and that of persuasion, it has come forward with sufficiently powerful and uncontradicted documentary evidence describing the chaos within the Liberian judicial system during the period of interest to this case to have met those burdens and to be entitled to judgment as a matter of law. Thus, the United States State Department Country Reports presented by Citibank indicate that the Liberian judicial system was in a state of disarray, as do, more subtly, the affidavits by Citibank's Liberian counsel, H. Varney G. Sherman.

The only evidence Bridgeway has introduced in support of its position are three statements by Liberian attorneys: (1) an affidavit of James E. Pierre, Esq., a member of the Liberian Bar, stating that the procedural rules of Liberia are modeled on those of New York State courts; (2) an affidavit introduced by Citibank, in which H. Varney G. Sherman, Citibank's Liberian counsel, states that "the Liberian Government is patterned after the state governments of the United States of America;" and (3) an affidavit of N. Oswald Tweh, former Vice President of the Liberian National Bar Association, that "Liberia's judicial system was and is structured and administered to afford party-litigants therein impartial justice." The first statement concerns the design of the Liberian judicial system, but says nothing

---

[1]   In granting summary judgment, the district court reflexively applied New York law. Citibank argues that federal law should apply. Because of the similarity of the New York and federal standards concerning the enforcement of foreign judgments, however, the district court's application of New York law did not affect the outcome. * * * * We therefore express no view on whether the district court was correct.

about its practice during the period in question.[2] The second, in addition to suffering from the same defect as the first, does not even discuss the Liberian judicial system directly. And the third is purely conclusory.

ii. Evidence

Summary judgment cannot be granted on the basis of inadmissible evidence. *See* Fed. R. Civ. P. 56(e). And Bridgeway raises many objections to the evidence relied upon by the district court in determining that Liberia's courts were, as a matter of law, unlikely to render impartial justice. Although the parties argue over a variety of different pieces of evidence, in the absence of any proof supporting Bridgeway's position, we need only consider whether Citibank adduced admissible evidence in sufficient amount to make the district court's decision regarding the performance of the Liberian judiciary during the civil war be supportable as well as uncontroverted. In fact, all of the district court's conclusions concerning this issue can be derived from just two sources: the affidavits of H. Varney G. Sherman ("Sherman affidavits") and the U.S. State Department Country Reports for Liberia for the years 1994–1997 ("Country Reports" or "Reports").

Bridgeway does not object to the admissibility of the Sherman affidavits (except on the ground that they support an argument that Bridgeway alleges Citibank is estopped from making). Indeed, in its brief, Bridgeway cites statements derived from these very affidavits in support of its own position. We will therefore assume that the Sherman material was properly relied upon by the district court.[3]

The district court also relied quite heavily on the Country Reports. Bridgeway argues that these Reports constitute excludable

---

[2] Evidence concerning the design of a judicial system might be sufficient, in the absence of countervailing evidence. But where a party presents evidence concerning the actual practice of a judicial system, evidence about design is not likely to create a genuine issue of material fact.

[3] Sherman's affidavits contain much of the information on the basis of which the district court made its decision and wrote its opinion: the history of the Liberian governmental system, the history of the civil war, and some of the effects of the civil war on the Liberian judicial system. Although Sherman was somewhat restrained in his description, he did indicate that during the civil war the constitutional provisions governing the appointment of Supreme Court justices were not followed, members of the Supreme Court served at the "will and pleasure of the appointing powers," and, when elections were finally called, the parties acknowledged that "membership on the Supreme Court had been based on factional appointment and with factional loyalties." *Cf.* RESTATEMENT (THIRD) OF FOREIGN RELATIONS LAW § 482 cmt. b. (1987) ("Evidence that the judiciary was dominated by the political branches of government . . . would support a conclusion that the legal system was one whose judgments are not entitled to recognition."). He concluded that "between July, 1990 and August, 1997, the Supreme Court was not organized in keeping with the 1986 Constitution."

hearsay. Citibank replies that the Reports are admissible under Fed. R. Evid. 803(8)(C), which allows the admission of "factual findings resulting from an investigation made pursuant to authority granted by law, unless the sources of information or other circumstances indicate lack of trustworthiness." * * * *

In this case, there is little doubt that the Country Reports constitute "factual findings." Moreover, the Reports are certainly gathered pursuant to legal authority: federal law requires that the State Department submit the Reports annually to Congress, see 22 U.S.C. §§ 2151n(d), 2304(b) (1994 & Supp. 1999). They are therefore presumptively admissible.

Bridgeway attempts to rebut this presumption by arguing that the Reports are untrustworthy, and it points to language in the State Department's description of their preparation. The State Department says that "[w]e have given particular attention to attaining a high standard of consistency despite the multiplicity of sources and the obvious problems related to varying degrees of access to information, structural differences in political and social systems, and trends in world opinion regarding human rights practices in specific countries." Although this constitutes a frank recognition of the shortcomings intrinsic in any historical investigation, it does not amount (as Bridgeway argues) to an admission of the lack of trustworthiness required to reject the admissibility of these documents.

When evaluating the trustworthiness of a factual report, we look to (a) the timeliness of the investigation, (b) the special skills or experience of the official, (c) whether a hearing was held and the level at which it was conducted, and (d) possible motivation problems. *See* Fed. R. Evid. 803(8)(C) advisory committee's note. With the exception of (c), which is not determinative by itself, *cf. id.* ([T]he rule . . . assumes admissibility in the first instance but with ample provision for escape if *sufficient negative factors* are present, (emphasis added)), nothing about the Reports calls into question their reliability with respect to these factors. The Reports are submitted annually, and are therefore investigated in a timely manner. They are prepared by area specialists at the State Department. And nothing in the record or in Bridgeway's briefs indicates any motive for misrepresenting the facts concerning Liberia's civil war or its effect on the judicial system there.[4]

---

[4] One could certainly imagine situations in which motivational problems might plausibly be present (*e.g.*, a country report on an avowed enemy or a significant ally of the United States), but Bridgeway has raised no such doubts here. Accordingly, we express no views on the admissibility of country reports in those circumstances.

In addition to its reliance on the Sherman affidavits and the Country Reports, the district court took judicial notice of historical facts drawn from a variety of sources. Bridgeway objects to this. Even if we agreed with Bridgeway's objection, we would affirm the district court's decision because the facts of which the district court took judicial notice were merely background history and of no moment to the ultimate determination of the fairness of Liberia's courts during the period of the civil war. The information in the district court's opinion concerning the functioning of the Liberian courts during the war is drawn (or could easily be drawn) entirely from the Sherman affidavits and the Country Reports, both of which were clearly admissible.

Having found all of Bridgeway's contentions to be without merit, we affirm the judgment of the district court.

Notes and Questions

1.   Why wasn't Citibank's prior voluntary participation (as a plaintiff) in the judicial system of Liberia sufficient to demonstrate that system's fundamental impartiality and fairness?

2.   In Liberia Citibank prevailed at the trial court but lost on appeal. Does this make it harder or easier for Citibank to argue that it was denied meaningful process?

3.   Upon consideration of whether to enforce the Liberian judgment, should the American court review the procedural protections of the Liberian appellate process, the trial process, or both?

4.   After *Bridgeway*, are all Liberian judgments (during the relevant time period) unenforceable? In other words, is Liberia now a country that is deemed to be lacking a commitment to the rule of law and to the norms of due process? Or might it vary on a case-by-case basis? (But vary based on what?)

5.   How can a court adequately assess whether a foreign legal system is sufficiently fair so as to justify enforcement? After all, there are unfair aspects of every legal system, either in their structure or their practice, or both. How does a court appropriately differentiate a sufficiently fair system from an unfair one? Should the State Department maintain a definitive list for such purposes?

DEJORIA V. MAGHREB PETROLEUM EXPLORATION, SA

United States Court of Appeals for the Fifth Circuit, 2015
804 F.3d 373

STEWART, CHIEF JUDGE:

* * * * John Paul DeJoria ("DeJoria") was a major investor in an American company called Skidmore Energy, Inc. ("Skidmore"), which was engaged in oil exploration and technology projects in Morocco. In pursuit of its goals, Skidmore formed and capitalized a Moroccan corporation, Lone Star Energy Corporation ("Lone Star") (now Maghreb Petroleum Exploration, S.A., or "MPE"). Corporations established under Moroccan law are required to have a "local" shareholder. For Lone Star, that local shareholder was Mediholding, S.A., owned by Prince Moulay Abdallah Alaoui, a first cousin of the Moroccan King, King Mohammed VI.

In March 2000, Lone Star entered into an "Investment Agreement" obligating it to invest in hydrocarbon exploration in Morocco. King Mohammed assured DeJoria that he would line up additional investors for the project to ensure adequate funding. Armadillo Holdings ("Armadillo") (now Mideast Fund for Morocco, or "MFM"), a Liechtenstein-based company, agreed to make significant investments in Lone Star. In the negotiations leading up to this agreement, Skidmore represented to Armadillo that Skidmore previously invested $27.5 million in Lone Star and that Lone Star's market value was roughly $175.75 million.

On August 20, 2000, King Mohammed gave a nationally televised speech to announce the discovery of "copious and high-quality oil" in Morocco. Three days later, then-Moroccan Minister of Energy Youssef Tahiri, accompanied by DeJoria and DeJoria's business partner Michael Gustin, traveled to the site and held a press conference claiming that the discovered oil reserves would fulfill Morocco's energy needs for decades. Moroccans celebrated this significant news, as the King's announcement was the only stimulus likely to revive Morocco's sluggish economy. The Moroccan stock market soared.

There was one major problem: the oil reserves were not as plentiful as announced. The "rosy picture" of Moroccan energy independence did not materialize, damaging both the Moroccan government's credibility and Lone Star's viability. As a result, the business relationship between MFM and Skidmore/DeJoria suffered. Lone Star replaced DeJoria and Gustin on Lone Star's Board of

Directors. DeJoria has not been to Morocco since 2000 and claims that his life would have been endangered had he returned.

Unhappy with the return on its initial investment in Lone Star, MFM sued Skidmore, DeJoria, Gustin, and a number of other Skidmore officers in their individual capacities in Moroccan court. MFM asserted that Skidmore fraudulently induced its investment by misrepresenting Skidmore's actual investment in Lone Star. MPE later joined as a plaintiff in the suit and claimed that Skidmore's fraudulent misrepresentations deprived Lone Star of necessary capital. * * * *

After nearly seven years of considering MPE and MFM's suit, the Moroccan court ruled against DeJoria and Gustin but absolved five of their co-defendants—including Skidmore—of liability. The court entered judgment in favor of MPE and MFM for approximately $122.9 million. DeJoria sued MPE and MFM in Texas state court, challenging domestic recognition of the Moroccan judgment * * * *.

Because federal jurisdiction in this case is based on diversity of citizenship, we apply Texas law regarding the recognition and enforcement of foreign judgments. * * * * In Texas, the recognition of foreign judgments is governed by the Texas Recognition Act. Tex. Civ. Prac. & Rem.Code Ann. §§ 36.001–36.008. Under the Act, unless a ground for non-recognition applies, the judgment of a foreign country is "conclusive between the parties" and "enforceable in the same manner as a judgment of a sister state that is entitled to full faith and credit." *Id.* § 36.004. The ten statutory grounds for non-recognition are the only defenses available to a judgment debtor.

The party seeking to avoid recognition of a foreign judgment has the burden of establishing one of these statutory grounds for non-recognition. * * * *

DeJoria contends that the Moroccan judgment is unenforceable because the Moroccan judicial system does not meet due process standards. Under the Texas Recognition Act, a foreign judgment is not conclusive and is thus unenforceable if "the judgment was rendered under a system that does not provide impartial tribunals or procedures compatible with the requirements of due process of law." Tex. Civ. Prac. & Rem.Code Ann. § 36.005(a)(1). "[T]he statute requires only the use of procedures *compatible* with the requirements of due process. [T]he foreign proceedings need not comply with the traditional rigors of American due process to meet the requirements of enforceability under the statute." *Soc'y of Lloyd's v. Turner,* 303 F.3d 325, 330 (5th Cir.2002) (internal quotations omitted). That is, the foreign judicial system must only be "fundamentally fair" and "not offend against basic fairness." *Id.* (internal quotations omitted). This concept sets a high bar for non-recognition.

The court's inquiry under Section 36.005(a)(1) focuses on the fairness of the foreign judicial system as a whole, and we do not parse the particular judgment challenged. The plain language of the Texas Recognition Act requires that the foreign judgment be "rendered [only] under a *system* that provides impartial tribunals and procedures compatible with due process." *Id.* (internal quotations omitted). Accordingly, we now consider whether Morocco's judicial system as a whole is "fundamentally fair" and inoffensive to basic notions of fairness.

To justify non-recognition of the Moroccan judgment, DeJoria argues that Morocco's judiciary is made up of judges beholden to the King and therefore lacks independence. Under the Moroccan Constitution, Morocco is an executive monarchy headed by a King who serves as the supreme leader. As described in a 2003 World Bank publication (the "World Bank Report"), the King has the final authority over the appointment of judges. A United States Agency for International Development report (the "USAID Report") observes that the Moroccan judicial system is "permeable to political influence" and that judges are "vulnerable to political retribution." State Department Country Reports also question the independence of the Moroccan judiciary. For example, the 2009 State Department Country Report explains that "in practice the judiciary . . . was not fully independent and was subject to influence, particularly in sensitive cases." Moroccan courts also battle a public perception of ineffectiveness. In 2012, nearly 1,000 Moroccan judges protested for "greater independence for the judiciary." Though this evidence led the district court to find that Morocco's judicial system was not compatible with the requirements of due process, we conclude that it does not present the entire picture.

Azzedine Kabbaj, a Moroccan attorney who has been practicing for thirty-five years, testified that Moroccan judges must pass an admissions test and complete two years of judge-specific training. Kabbaj noted that the Moroccan system "places great emphasis" on providing "actual notice" of lawsuits to defendants, allows for numerous challenges to the appointments of experts, and gives defendants a de novo appeal after an initial judgment. Abed Awad, an adjunct professor at Rutgers University School of Law, further explained that the procedures followed in Moroccan commercial courts resemble those followed in United States courts. The law firm of DeJoria's expert advertised Morocco's judicial system as "adher[ing] to international standards." The same USAID Report cited by DeJoria notes that the King's government "has made judicial reform one of its key objectives," explains that the "rule of law" is a "critical factor" in Morocco's development, and observes that the Moroccan government "is making strides" toward building a state reliant on the rule of law. The USAID Report, while acknowledging fundamental concerns about judicial independence, concludes that the "Monarchy's interest in reforming the justice sector is a positive sign." The World Bank Report describes the advances in Morocco's judicial system as "indisputable" and recognizes Morocco's "enhanced drive toward an independent judiciary." Finally, the State Department has recognized that the Moroccan government has implemented reforms intended to increase judicial independence and impartiality.

The Texas Recognition Act does not require that the foreign judicial system be perfect. Instead, a judgment debtor must meet the high burden of showing that the foreign judicial system as a whole is so lacking in impartial tribunals or procedures compatible with due process so as to justify routine non-recognition of the foreign judgments. DeJoria has not met this burden. Based on the evidence in the record, we cannot agree that the Moroccan judicial system lacks sufficient independence such that fair litigation in Morocco is impossible.[9] The due process requirement is not "intended to bar the enforcement of all judgments of any foreign legal system that does not conform its procedural doctrines to the latest twist and turn of our courts." *Society of Lloyd's v. Ashenden*, 233 F.3d 473, 476 (7th Cir. 2000). Thus, the record here does not establish that any judgment rendered by a Moroccan court is to be disregarded as a matter of course.

Even under DeJoria's characterization, the Moroccan judicial system would still contrast sharply with the judicial systems of foreign countries that have failed to meet due process standards. For example, in *Bank Melli Iran v. Pahlavi,* the Ninth Circuit refused to enforce an Iranian judgment and concluded that the Iranian judicial system did not comport with due process standards. 58 F.3d 1406, 1411–13 (9th Cir.1995). The court relied on official reports advising Americans against traveling to Iran during the relevant time period and identifying Iran as an official state sponsor of terror. *Id.* at 1411. Further, the court noted that Iranian trials were private, politicized proceedings, and recognized that the Iranian government itself did

---

[9] Although our inquiry focuses on Morocco's judicial *system*, we also observe that the record does not establish that the King actually exerted any improper influence on the Moroccan court in this case. For example, the Moroccan court (1) appointed experts, (2) took seven years to reach a decision, (3) awarded a lesser judgment than the expert recommended, and (4) absolved five defendants—including DeJoria's company Skidmore—of liability.

not "believe in the independence of the judiciary." *Id.* at 1412. Judges were subject to continuing scrutiny and potential sanction and could not be expected to be impartial to American citizens. *Id.* Further, "revolutionary courts" had the power to usurp and overrule decisions of the Iranian civil courts. *Id.* Attorneys were also warned against "representing politically undesirable interests." *Id.* Based on this evidence, the court concluded that the Iranian judicial system simply could not produce fair proceedings.

Similarly, in *Bridgeway Corp. v. Citibank,* the Second Circuit declined to recognize a Liberian judgment rendered during the Liberian Civil War. 201 F.3d 134, 144 (2d Cir.2000). There, the court observed that, during the relevant time period, "Liberia's judicial system was in a state of disarray and the provisions of the Constitution concerning the judiciary were no longer followed." *Id.* at 138. Further, official State Department Country Reports noted that the Liberian judicial system—already marred by "corruption and incompetent handling of cases"—completely "collapsed" following the outbreak of fighting. *Id.* Because the court concluded that there was "sufficiently powerful and uncontradicted documentary evidence describing the chaos within the Liberian judicial system during the period of interest," it refused to enforce the Liberian judgment. *Id.* at 141–42.

Pahlavi and *Bridgeway* thus exemplify how a foreign judicial system can be so fundamentally flawed as to offend basic notions of fairness. Unlike the Iranian system in *Pahlavi,* there is simply no indication that it would be impossible for an American to receive due process or impartial tribunals in Morocco. In further contrast with *Pahlavi,* there is no record evidence of a demonstrable anti-American sentiment in Morocco; in fact, American law firms do business in Morocco. While the judgment debtor in *Pahlavi* could not have retained representation in Iran, Skidmore—a co-defendant in the Moroccan case—did briefly retain Moroccan attorney Azzedine Kettani until a conflict of interest forced his withdrawal. One expert opined that it is "not at all uncommon" for Moroccan attorneys to represent unpopular figures in Moroccan courts. *Bridgeway* presents an even more stark contrast. Morocco's judicial system is not in a state of complete collapse, and there is no evidence that Moroccan courts or the Moroccan government routinely disregard constitutional provisions or the rule of law. Because Morocco's judicial system is not in such a dire situation, it does not present the unusual case of a foreign judicial system that "offend[s] against basic fairness." *Turner,* 303 F.3d at 330 (internal quotations omitted).

* * * *

As alternative grounds for non-recognition, DeJoria asserts that Morocco does not recognize judgments rendered by Texas courts * * *.

* * * *

Under the Texas Recognition Act, a court may refuse to enforce a foreign judgment if "it is established that the foreign country in which the judgment was rendered does not recognize judgments rendered in this state that, but for the fact that they are rendered in this state, conform to the definition of 'foreign country judgment.'" Tex. Civ. Prac. & Rem.Code Ann. § 36.005(b)(7). This "reciprocity" ground for non-recognition is discretionary. Even if reciprocity is lacking, a reviewing court may still elect to recognize the foreign judgment. * * * *

MPE and MFM have identified the relevant statutory provisions under Moroccan law and offered expert testimony that Moroccan courts would recognize American judgments and have routinely recognized other foreign judgments. * * * * Further, Moroccan law specifically allows for the recognition of foreign judgments. Article 430 of the Morocco Code of Civil Procedure provides that, in order to enforce a foreign judgment, a Moroccan court "shall determine the judgment is genuine and that the foreign court that issued the judgment had jurisdiction, and shall verify that no part of the judgment violates Moroccan public policy." On its face, Article 430 seems to answer the reciprocity question; however, DeJoria insists that it is uncertain whether Article 430 would actually allow recognition of a United States judgment. DeJoria's expert, Kettani, observed "that there is no certainty as to how . . . the statutory criteria of 'public order' . . . would be used in practice to deny enforcement." Such speculation is insufficient to justify non-enforcement. The statutory criteria for non-enforcement under Article 430, lack of jurisdiction and violation of public policy, are no different than three of the grounds for non-recognition under the Texas Recognition Act. See Tex. Civ. Prac. & Rem.Code Ann. § 36.005(a)(2), (a)(3), (b)(3). * * * *

Finally, DeJoria challenges his amenability to jurisdiction. * * * * Courts generally apply the standards of the rendering court to determine jurisdiction.

DeJoria argues that the Moroccan court lacked jurisdiction because no curator was appointed. Under Article 39 of the Morocco Code of Civil Procedure, "[i]n all cases where the domicile and residence of a party are unknown, the judge appoints, in the capacity as curator, an officer of the court to whom the summons is notified." Expert testimony revealed that under Moroccan law, the failure to appoint a curator where required violates due process and can result in nullification of a judgment. However, expert testimony further clarified that a "Moroccan court would never appoint a curator for a defendant with a known address." The Moroccan court was not required to appoint a curator, because DeJoria's domicile and residence were known. In fact, DeJoria was served with process at his home and was later served with the judgment in Texas. Accordingly, we conclude that Article 39 is not applicable to this case.

Under Moroccan law, if the defendant is not domiciled in Morocco, jurisdiction is proper at the domicile or place of residence of the plaintiff. Article 27 of the Morocco Code of Civil Procedure provides: "If the defendant has no domicile or residence in Morocco, [a suit] may be brought before the court of the domicile or residence of the applicant or one of them if there are several." Thus, jurisdiction was proper in Morocco, where MPE was domiciled.

Further, jurisdiction is proper even under the stricter requirements of American due process. "Texas courts may exercise personal jurisdiction over a nonresident if (1) the Texas long-arm statute authorizes the exercise of jurisdiction, and (2) the exercise of jurisdiction is consistent with federal and state constitutional due-process guarantees." *Moncrief Oil Int'l, Inc. v. OAO Gazprom,* 414 S.W.3d 142, 149 (Tex.2013) (internal quotations omitted). * * * *

Applying the Texas standard as if it were the standard applied by Moroccan courts, we conclude that Morocco obtained personal jurisdiction over DeJoria. "[A]llegations that a tort was committed in [the forum] satisfy [the] long-arm statute. . . ." *Id.* at 149. Here, MPE and MFM alleged that DeJoria committed torts in Morocco related to his investment in Skidmore and its relationship with Lone Star. Specifically, MFM alleges that DeJoria made fraudulent misrepresentations regarding his investment in Lone Star, and MPE alleges that DeJoria's misrepresentations deprived it of necessary capital. These allegations are sufficient to satisfy the long-arm statute.

"A defendant establishes minimum contacts with a state when it 'purposefully avails itself of the privilege of conducting activities within the forum state, thus invoking the benefits and protections of its laws.'" *Retamco Operating, Inc. v. Republic Drilling Co.,* 278 S.W.3d 333, 338 (Tex. 2009) (quoting *Hanson v. Denckla,* 357 U.S. 235, 253, 78 S.Ct. 1228, 2 L.Ed.2d 1283 (1958)). DeJoria voluntarily started a Moroccan corporation to explore for oil reserves in Morocco through Lone Star. DeJoria's investment activity was in Morocco. DeJoria visited Morocco in connection with his relationship with Lone Star, including a visit to a drilling site with Morocco's then-Energy Minister. Nearly all of the alleged acts and omissions in the underlying case occurred in Morocco. DeJoria thus has sufficient, purposeful contacts with Morocco to render jurisdiction reasonable.

"In addition to minimum contacts, due process requires the exercise of personal jurisdiction to comply with traditional notions of fair play and substantial justice." *Moncrief Oil,* 414 S.W.3d at 154. "If a nonresident has minimum contacts with the forum, rarely will the exercise of jurisdiction over the nonresident not comport with traditional notions of fair play and substantial justice." *Id.* at 154–55. While litigation in Morocco would have imposed a burden on DeJoria, that burden would not be so heavy as to render jurisdiction unreasonable. Moroccan courts do not require that the defendant appear personally, and DeJoria could have litigated entirely through counsel without returning to Morocco. When weighed against Morocco's substantial interest in adjudicating a dispute involving a Moroccan corporation and Moroccan resources, DeJoria's burden of litigating in Morocco would not have been unfair in relation to his contacts with the forum. Because DeJoria voluntarily engaged in purposeful contacts with Morocco, the exercise of jurisdiction does not offend "traditional notions of fair play and substantial justice." *Id.* at 154.

* * * *

Notes and Questions

1. The court emphasizes that it looks to the fairness of the legal system as a whole, rather than the fairness of this particular judgment. Does that make sense? What if the system is fair in most cases, but the King had exerted unfair influence in this particular case? Should the resulting judgment be enforced abroad?

2. Are the court's efforts to distinguish Iran and Liberia from Morocco convincing? What facts does the court rely upon? Are these distinctions that judges are competent to make?

3. Should reciprocity matter in a recognition decision? After all, if a foreign judgment accords with due process, should it be denied enforcement just because the foreign country does not enforce U.S. judgments? Isn't that a diplomatic question between the two countries that is independent of the question of fairness as between the particular parties to the suit?

4. The court analyzes whether the Moroccan court had personal jurisdiction over DeJoria under both Moroccan and Texas/US jurisdiction law. But which is the appropriate standard? What if the Moroccan court had followed Moroccan jurisdiction law, but that assertion of jurisdiction would not be permissible under the U.S. Supreme Court's minimum contacts test? For example, consider the

Zuid-Chemie case from Chapter Three. There, the European Court of Justice permitted the assertion of jurisdiction over a defendant on grounds that might well violate the U.S. Supreme Court's precedent in *World-Wide Volkswagen Corp. v. Woodson*, 444 U.S. 286 (1980). If the defendant in that case had been a U.S. corporation, should the subsequent judgment be deemed unenforceable just because the assertion of jurisdiction did not satisfy U.S. standards? On the other hand, what if the foreign jurisdictional law is deemed wildly unfair to defendants under the U.S. minimum contacts framework? Should the resulting judgment be enforced just because the foreign law had been properly followed? Or should courts apply some generalized due process test of jurisdiction that is perhaps different from either the specific foreign standard or the U.S. one?

Chapter 14

CLASS ACTIONS AND AGGREGATE LITIGATION

Class actions have long been associated with the United States legal system. However, that has changed in recent decades. During this period, courts in the United States have cut back on the ability of plaintiffs to successfully pursue class actions, just as other legal systems around the world have begun opening the door to various forms of aggregate or group litigation.

In this chapter, we will look at class actions from both a comparative and transnational perspective. As a comparative matter, we present an overview of trends in court systems around the world. Then, we address transnational problems raised in class actions, particularly when members of a putative class are citizens of multiple different countries.

A. COMPARATIVE CLASS ACTION DOCTRINE

DEBORAH R. HENSLER, *THE GLOBALIZATION OF CLASS ACTIONS: AN OVERVIEW*

622 ANNALS AM. ACAD. POL. & SOC. SCI. 7 (2009)

* * * * Around the world, individuals, nongovernmental organizations (NGOs), and public officials are turning to courts for remedies for mass harms: mass injuries caused by defective products or environmental exposure to toxic chemicals, mass financial losses resulting from violations of antitrust (anticompetition) law, securities law, consumer protection statutes, and historical and contemporaneous civil rights and human rights abuses. While some of this litigation is brought by public officials on behalf of citizens of their jurisdictions, an increasing fraction of the litigation is initiated by private parties. In some instances, the litigation comprises large numbers of similarly situated individuals or entities whose individual lawsuits have been combined: so-called aggregate litigation. In other instances, the harms are perceived as having been visited on a group of people with shared interests, not all of whom are individually identifiable at the onset of litigation-consumers,

workers, women, victims of genocide, or indigenous peoples-and the lawsuit is commenced by a party who claims to represent this group: what is commonly called a *class action*. In the first instance, all of the parties are formally before the court and formally in control of their own lawsuits, although individual claimants may in fact have little control over what transpires in the litigation. In the second instance, all or most of the class members are absent from court and control over the litigation is formally assigned to the class representative(s) and class counsel. Both aggregate and class litigation reflect an escalating trend in private civil litigation: what were once viewed as singular disputes between individuals or between an individual and a corporation, not all of which deserved legal redress, are now viewed increasingly as group struggles against multinational corporations and other global institutions, properly resolvable in court.

In many respects, the United States has led the way in these developments: the 1970s "rights revolution" in the United States created the statutory framework for asserting civil rights, demanding protection from environmental harms, and claiming compensation for losses resulting from anti-consumer business practices; and the adoption of a revised federal class action rule in 1966 (rapidly duplicated by state courts) made it easier for individuals to come forward to claim remedies, including money damages, on behalf of large groups of similarly situated individuals. Public interest lawyers used the procedure to obtain injunctive relief from governments: elimination of racial and other discriminatory practices and education, prison, and welfare reform, among other goals. Private sector lawyers used the procedure to obtain monetary compensation for victims of consumer fraud, violations of security regulations, product-related injuries, and environmental damage. The rise of an entrepreneurial plaintiffs bar (in part a response to the new procedural rule) provided the engine to power class actions for money damages, and a media-centric mass culture created an environment in which such litigation could flourish.

While on the surface the adoption of a class action procedure may appear to be a technical matter of interest only to lawyers, the social, economic, and political consequences of permitting class actions are potentially vast. Because the type of class action procedure adopted by the U.S. federal judiciary in 1966 and elaborated on since empowers individuals with relatively modest claims that would be impractical to litigate individually to join forces and seek redress, its availability within a legal regime dramatically shifts the balance of power between legal "haves" and "have-nots." Because this type of class action procedure permits one or a few individuals or entities to litigate on behalf of people who may not be aware that they have viable legal claims, its availability within a legal regime has the potential to increase substantially the frequency of litigation. And because the type of class action procedure that the United States adopted permits class representatives to claim monetary damages on behalf of all those who fit the definition of the class as long as the latter do not come forward and decline to participate—that is, opt out—its availability within a legal regime has the potential to increase substantially the breadth of civil litigation as well. Taken together, these consequences have enormous potential to deter institutional and corporate wrongdoing and to shift the balance of power between citizens and their governments, employees and employers, and consumers and manufacturers and service providers. Because private litigation may be widely dispersed—especially in federal and decentralized regimes such as the United States—it can be much more difficult for powerful groups within society to constrain by comparison with the executive and legislative branches, which are highly susceptible to lobbying by those seeking to protect and extend their own interests.

At first blush, aggregate litigation comprising large numbers of individual lawsuits arising out of the same harm—personal injury, property damage, financial loss, human rights abuse—does not appear to pose the same challenges to powerful public institutions and private corporations. To secure legal representation, individuals must either have the financial wherewithal to pay lawyers' hourly fees and expenses (and, in a legal regime where losers are liable for winners' expenses, assume the risk of adverse costs), or their claims must have sufficient expected monetary value to secure the services of a contingent fee lawyer (in a regime that permits as such). Hence, aggregate nonclass litigation always involves individual claims of some considerable monetary value. Individuals must believe that they have been harmed, attribute the harm to another's fault, and think that the law affords them redress before they will seek out lawyers to represent them. As a result, the rate of litigation, relative to the extent of harm, is likely to be limited. By definition, all aggregate nonclass litigation is opt in.

Despite these differences between class and nonclass aggregate litigation, nonclass aggregate litigation has proved capable of shifting the balance of power between "haves" and "have-nots" and facilitating expansion of litigation. By agreeing to represent hundreds or thousands of individuals in separate lawsuits and then bundling those lawsuits together during the pretrial development process and during settlement negotiations, plaintiff attorneys have been able to achieve huge economies of scale, which enhances the benefit-risk ratio of this type of litigation to them—and its attractiveness. By consolidating cases for pre-trial management using * * * *group litigation procedures* * * *, judges in pursuit of case processing efficiency have further reduced the cost per lawsuit of aggregate litigation for plaintiff attorneys and increased the risks attendant on defendants should plaintiffs prevail. In a settlement-oriented legal culture such as the United States, consolidation of claims also opens the doors to vast numbers of claims of questionable or small value seeking a free (or at least inexpensive) ride to the settlement fund. As a consequence, aggregate litigation is likely to settle for a substantially larger amount of money in total than would have been expended to settle claims had individual litigation prevailed.

Not surprisingly, the potential consequences of "U.S.-style" class actions have evoked great controversy, both in the United States, where the procedure first took root in modern times, and in countries around the world where the adoption of such a procedure has been debated in recent years. Class litigation may impose costs on economic actors that are larger than any benefit it creates, thereby diminishing social welfare. Placing responsibility for social reform and public policy in appointed judicial decision makers (much less lay jurors) rather than elected legislators may produce outcomes that are not supported by the majority of citizens. Permitting lawyer-entrepreneurs to bring vast lawsuits that enrich themselves more than they benefit any individual class member may bring the legal system into disrepute and ultimately erode the rule of law. To date, no credible analysis of the actual benefit-cost ratio has been conducted in any jurisdiction that has adopted a class action procedure, so the actual consequences are unknown.

Today, in the United States, there is vigorous debate about the costs and benefits of class litigation, and efforts have been made at the federal and state level to rein in the litigation, by statute and court decision. But as the tide has turned (perhaps just temporarily) *against* class actions in the United States, class actions and other group litigation procedures have attracted support in other parts of the world. On virtually every continent, one or more nations—including both common law and civil law regimes—have adopted some sort of representative litigation procedure. Some jurisdictions that have rejected representative litigation for now have instituted group litigation procedures to manage aggregate litigation.

Notes and Questions

1.   What do you see as the potential advantages and disadvantages of class actions? If you were a member of a legislature would you vote to create such a remedy? Why or why not?

2.   Note that some class action suits seek an injunction—meaning that they are demanding that the defendant do something or refrain from doing something—whereas other class actions seek money damages. In the United States the best-known examples of injunction class actions are civil rights suits seeking broad institutional changes by governmental or corporate defendants. In contrast, damages class actions seek monetary compensation for wrongs committed. As Hensler points out, sometimes such claims for monetary damages are for claims so small that no single litigant would have sufficient incentive to bring suit individually. Other times they may be mass tort actions when a single defendant is alleged to have similarly harmed many people. Does the rationale for class actions vary depending on what kind of claim is involved?

3.   On June 30, 2020, the European Commission endorsed an agreement that, if adopted by the European Parliament, would make collective redress actions available across the European Union, covering a broad range of areas, from financial services to passenger rights, from telecommunications to energy. Although the proposal creates the possibility for cross-border class action type adjudication, the proposed agreement differs from U.S. class action practice in significant respects. For example, only "qualified entities," such as officially designated consumer organizations will be able to launch an action. Such entities will also have strict obligations of transparency regarding the source of their funding, including the funds used to launch a specific collective action. Finally, putative class members in Europe will need to affirmatively opt in to the class, in contrast with the United States class action mechanism, which places members into the class unless they opt out.

B.   TRANSNATIONAL CLASS ACTIONS

CURRIE V. MCDONALD'S RESTAURANTS OF CANADA LTD.

Court of Appeal for Ontario, 2005
74 O.R. 3d 321

SHARPE, J.A.

The plaintiff Greg Currie brings a proposed class action alleging wrongdoing in relation to promotional games offered to customers of McDonald's Restaurants of Canada Ltd. ("McDonald's Canada"). He is met with an Illinois judgment approving the settlement of a class action brought on behalf of an American and international class of McDonald's customers, including the customers of McDonald's Canada (the "Boland judgment"). The Illinois court directed that notice of the class action to Canadian class members be given by means of an advertisement in Maclean's magazine. Currie did not participate in the Illinois proceedings, but Preston Parsons, the named plaintiff in another Ontario class proceeding, represented by the same law firm and purporting to represent the same class, appeared in the Illinois court to challenge the settlement.

The central issue on this appeal is whether the Boland judgment is binding so as to preclude Currie's proposed class action in Ontario.

In the period between January 1, 1995 and December 31, 2001— and earlier—McDonald's sponsored numerous promotional games, or contests, of chance—or chance and skill—at its restaurants in North America. Some, but not all, of these were made available in the Canadian restaurants. Prizes of different kinds and amounts were to be awarded. Participation in the games was, to a large extent, tied to the purchase of food at the restaurants. Simon Marketing Inc.—a corporation based in California that provided businesses with marketing services involving the provision and operation of promotional games—was retained for that purpose by McDonald's.

On August 21, 2001, Jerome Jacobson—a senior employee of Simon Marketing—and a number of other individuals were indicted for embezzling prizes allocated to McDonald's games.

The proceedings in Boland were commenced on the following day. The class-action complaint, alleg[ing] that Jacobson had directed prizes to specific individuals, * * * claimed damages against McDonald's and Simon Marketing Inc. for consumer fraud and unjust enrichment. The plaintiffs sued on behalf of themselves and "all customers of McDonald's who paid money for McDonald's food products in order to receive a subject contest game piece for subject contest promotions between 1995 and the present". Settlement discussions in the Boland action were conducted from October 2001 and culminated in a settlement agreement between the plaintiffs and McDonald's on April 19, 2002.

The settlement agreement provided that the parties would apply to the Circuit Court of Cook County, Illinois for preliminary certification of the proceedings as a class action and for preliminary approval of the settlement as "fair, reasonable and adequate to the class and to members of the public." Further orders were to be requested to approve the terms of a notice to class members—and the manner in which it was to be disseminated—to provide class members with an opportunity to opt out of the class and the settlement by a date to be specified and to make the settlement—and the releases to be provided to McDonald's and its subsidiaries— binding on those who did not do so. The terms of the releases were broad. They covered all claims—referred to in the settlement agreement as "Released Claims"—relating to McDonald's promotional games under common law or statute, and specifically for breach of the consumer protection laws of any jurisdiction, contract, unjust enrichment, fraud, negligent misrepresentation, breach of fiduciary duty, strict liability and unfair or deceptive trade practices. The Released Claims would have covered each of the claims subsequently pleaded in the Parsons and Currie actions even though not all of the material facts on which they were based had been pleaded in Boland. * * * *

On May 8, 2002, the application for the above orders was heard by Judge Stephen Schiller in Chicago and, on June 6, 2002, he granted the preliminary relief requested with some modifications to the proposed notice to class members. August 28, 2002 was designated as the final date for members to opt out and a final fairness hearing was to be held on September 17, 2002.

The manner in which notice was to be given to customers in Canada was specifically addressed at the preliminary hearing on May 8, 2002, and the order of the court provided for the approved form of notice to be published in each of three French-language newspapers in Quebec on July 15, 2002 and in *Maclean's* magazine on July 15 and July 22 as well as in two U.S. publications that had circulation in Canada. * * * *

After a U.S. attorney had notified the firm of Paliare Roland in Toronto, the firm placed information about the U.S. proceedings on its website and was subsequently contacted by the plaintiff, Preston Parsons. The Parsons action was commenced by statement of claim on September 13, 2002. * * * * On September 16, 2002, a group of Canadians, including Mr. Parsons, moved for leave to intervene in the Boland proceedings to object to the settlement of that action. The documents filed in the court in Illinois named Paliare Roland as solicitors for Mr. Parsons although members of the firm did not—and could not—represent him in proceedings in that jurisdiction. * * * *

The Currie action was commenced on October 28, 2002, with Paliare Roland as solicitors of record.

On January 3, 2003, Judge Schiller released his decision dismissing the objections of the Canadian objectors. The terms of the settlement were given final approval and the certification order was made final. On April 8, 2003, the formal order of the court was entered containing, among other things, the release of McDonald's and its subsidiaries by the members of the class and a declaration that all members of the class who had not opted out were bound by the terms of the order.

* * * *

The following issues arise on this appeal.

(1) Should the Ontario courts recognize and enforce the *Boland* judgment against Currie and the * * * Canadian class members he seeks to represent?

(2) Did the notice to the Canadian class members satisfy the requirements of natural justice?

(3) Is Currie precluded by the doctrines of res judicata or abuse of process from prosecuting his claim in Ontario?

ANALYSIS

1.   Should the Ontario courts recognize and enforce the *Boland* judgment against Currie and the * * * Canadian class members he seeks to represent?

It is common ground on this appeal that if the *Boland* judgment should be recognized in Ontario under the applicable conflict of laws principles, Currie and the members of the class he seeks to represent are bound by it and that Currie's proposed class action would be precluded. * * * *

In *Morguard Investments Ltd. v. De Savoye*, [1990] 3 S.C.R. 1077, [1990] S.C.J. No. 135, the Supreme Court of Canada identified the twin principles of "order and fairness" and "real and substantial connection" for the assessment of the propriety of * * * jurisdiction. * * * *

The "real and substantial connection" test * * * is described variously in *Morguard*, at pp. 1104–09, as a connection "between the subject-matter of the action and the territory where the action is brought", "between the jurisdiction and the wrongdoing", "between the damages suffered and the jurisdiction", "between the defendant and the forum province", "with the transaction or the parties", and "with the action". The real and substantial connection test is a flexible one, * * * and there is no strict or rigid test to be applied.

Morguard dealt with the recognition and enforcement of inter-provincial judgments. [Subsequently,] those same principles were adapted and applied to international judgments. * * * * The novel point raised on this appeal is the application of the real and substantial connection test and the principles of order and fairness to unnamed, non-resident plaintiffs in international class actions.

Ontario residents frequently engage in cross-border activities that may become the subject of class action litigation in Ontario, in another province or in a foreign jurisdiction. * * * * There are strong policy reasons favouring the fair and efficient resolution of interprovincial and international class action litigation. Conflict of law rules should recognize, in appropriate cases, the importance of having claims finally resolved in one jurisdiction. In some cases, Ontario courts will render judgments affecting the rights of non-residents and in other cases, Ontario residents will be affected by class action proceedings elsewhere. Ontario expects its judgments to be recognized and enforced, provided its courts assert jurisdiction in a proper manner, and comity requires that, in appropriate cases, Ontario law should give effect to foreign class action judgments.

Recognition and enforcement rules should take into account certain unique features of class action proceedings. In this case, we must consider the situation of the unnamed, non-resident class plaintiff. In a traditional non-class action suit, there is no question as to the jurisdiction of the foreign court to bind the plaintiff. As the party initiating proceedings, the plaintiff will have invoked the jurisdiction of the foreign court and thereby will have attorned to the foreign court's jurisdiction. The issue relating to recognition and enforcement that typically arises is whether the foreign judgment can be enforced against the defendant.

Here, the tables are turned. It is the defendant who is seeking to enforce the judgment against the unnamed, non-resident plaintiffs. The settling defendants, plainly bound by the judgment, seek to enforce it as widely and as broadly as possible in order to preclude further litigation against them. * * * * Before enforcing a foreign class action judgment against Ontario residents, we should ensure that the foreign court had a proper basis for the assertion of jurisdiction and that the interests of Ontario residents were adequately protected.

To determine whether the assumption of jurisdiction by the foreign court satisfies the real and substantial connection test and the principles of order and fairness, it is necessary to consider the situation from the perspective of the party against whom enforcement is sought. * * * * The principal connecting factors linking the cause of action asserted in Currie's proposed class action to the state of Illinois are that the alleged wrong occurred in the United States and Illinois is the site of McDonald's head office. The alleged wrongful conduct, manipulating the "random" selection of winners of "high value" prizes to ensure that no such prizes would be awarded to contestants in Canada, occurred in the United States. This factor is a "real and substantial connection" in favour of Illinois jurisdiction. * * * * On the other hand, the principles of "order and fairness" require that careful attention be paid to the situation of ordinary McDonald's customers whose rights are at stake. These non-resident class members would have no reason to expect that any legal claim they may wish to assert against McDonald's Canada as result of visiting the restaurant in Ontario would be adjudicated in the United States. The consumer transactions giving rise to the claims took place entirely within Ontario. The consumers are residents of Canada, and McDonald's Canada is a corporation that conducts its business in Canada. Damages from the alleged wrong were suffered in Ontario. The *Currie* plaintiffs themselves did nothing that could provide a basis for the assertion of Illinois jurisdiction, while McDonald's Canada invited the jurisdiction of the courts of Ontario by carrying on business here.

To address the concern for fairness, it is helpful to consider the adequacy of the procedural rights afforded the unnamed non-resident class members in the *Boland* action. * * * * Given the substantial connection between the alleged wrong and Illinois, and given the small stake of each individual class member, it seems to me that the principles of order and fairness could be satisfied if the interests of the non-resident class members were adequately represented and if it were clearly brought home to them that their rights could be affected in the foreign proceedings if they failed to take appropriate steps to be removed from those proceedings. * * * *

The right to opt out is an important procedural protection afforded to unnamed class action plaintiffs. Taking appropriate steps to opt out and remove themselves from the action allows unnamed class action plaintiffs to preserve legal rights that would otherwise be determined or compromised in the class proceeding. * * * * It is obvious, however, that if the right to opt out is to be meaningful, the unnamed plaintiff must know about it and that, in turn, implicates the adequacy of the notice afforded to the unnamed plaintiff. * * * * [Here, because] the unnamed plaintiffs were not afforded adequate notice of the *Boland* proceedings, the Ontario courts should not recognize and enforce the *Boland* judgment against Currie and the * * * Canadian class members he seeks to represent.

I would add this observation. Even if the *Boland* judgment is not accorded recognition and enforcement, it may still have some impact upon Currie's proposed class action in Ontario because of the principle against double recovery. As a result of the *Boland* judgment, certain benefits were conferred upon Canadian McDonald's patrons. If the *Currie* action succeeds on the merits, then the trial judge will likely take into account the benefits already received by the plaintiff class in order to determine the appropriate remedy and prevent over-compensation.

2.   Did the notice to the Canadian class members satisfy the requirements of natural justice?

In the *Boland* action, the Illinois court ordered that notice be given in Canada by means of two advertisements in *Maclean's* magazine for English Canada and in *La Presse, Le Journal de Québec* and *Le Journal de Montréal* for Quebec. Notice was also published in three U.S. publications with circulation in Canada, *People Magazine, USA Today* and four copies of *TV Guide.* * * * *

It was [within the trial judge's discretion] to conclude that the wording of the notice was so technical and obscure that the ordinary class member would have difficulty understanding the implications of the proposed settlement on their legal rights in Canada or that they had the right to opt out. As I have already indicated, that right is of vital importance to the jurisdiction of the foreign court in international class action litigation. The right to opt out must be made clear and plain to the non-resident class members and I see no basis upon which to disagree with the motion judge's assessment of this notice.

Nor would I interfere with the [trial] judge's finding that the mode of notice was inadequate. The appellants opted to publish the notice in a publication that is not ordinarily used in English-Canada for such purposes, and there was evidence that this notice reached only a small proportion of the members of the plaintiff class. * * * *

3.   Is Currie precluded by the doctrines of res judicata or abuse of process from prosecuting his claim in Ontario?

The appellants argue that Currie should be bound by the *Boland* judgment on the basis that he is in the same interest as or a privy to Parsons. * * * * The allegations in the *Currie* action are the same as those advanced by Parsons. The *Currie* action was brought as a protective measure to preserve the right to bring an action in Canada on behalf of the same class of plaintiffs in the event of an adverse ruling against Parsons in Illinois. The same law firm that represented Parsons commenced the Currie action after Parsons' appearance in the Illinois court.

* * * * Currie and Parsons are, the appellants submit, alter egos of each other, neither having any significant personal interest in their claims and both making the same allegations. The real plaintiff, and the only entity with a real stake in the claim, is the law firm that represents both Currie and Parsons. The appellants urge us to look to the practical realities of class actions. We are asked to focus on the centrality of the lawyers to a process in which the representative plaintiffs play what is at best a nominal role.

I am not persuaded that res judicata applies here * * *. The parties are not the same—Currie took no part in the *Boland* proceedings and McDonald's Canada was not named as a defendant in that action. Further, Currie's allegations specifically related to the Canadian patrons were made by Parsons in objecting to the settlement, but they did not form part of the claim advanced by the representative plaintiff in *Boland*. * * * * There was no evidence that Currie was even aware of the proceedings in the United States until shortly before his own action was commenced. * * * * I reject the submission of the appellants that we should analyze this issue on the basis that the law firm was the real litigant, or that the link provided by the law firm to both Parsons and Currie was sufficient to make them privies. No doubt from a purely financial perspective, the law firm had a greater stake in the outcome than Parsons, Currie or any individual member of the proposed class. However, the financial stake of the class as a whole exceeded that of the law firm. In any event, I am not persuaded that the legal rights of the parties are to be assessed on the basis of their lawyers' pecuniary interest in the outcome. The legal claims that are being advanced belong to Parsons, Currie and to the members of the proposed class, not to the law firm. * * * *

For these reasons, I would dismiss the appeal.

Notes and Questions

1.   Class actions always raise important due process concerns because by definition some people who are members of the class but not controlling the litigation will have their rights adjudicated without being a meaningful part of the suit. As a result, all class action rules include safeguards to protect the rights of absent class members. In the United States, Federal Rule of Civil Procedure 23 contains numerous requirements for class actions that do not exist for non-class litigation. Rule 23(a) requires a judge to certify that a litigation is appropriate for class resolution at the beginning of the litigation. That certification includes various inquiries designed to ensure that the interests of all class members will be adequately represented. In addition, for class actions seeking monetary damages, the class representatives must provide adequate notice to all class members and an opportunity for them to opt out of the class. Finally, if a class action suit settles, the settlement arrangement is subjected to a fairness hearing before the supervising judge, in which class members are permitted to object to the settlement. As this case suggests, all of those inquiries are complicated by the possibility that some class members may be citizens of a different country and therefore potentially subject to different class action and due process standards.

2.   As this case suggests, although courts usually assume that they have jurisdiction over plaintiffs because the plaintiffs have voluntarily submitted to the court's authority, that may not be true with regard to members of a class. The U.S. Supreme Court has ruled that, at least with regard to damages classes, providing adequate notice and opt-out rights is also sufficient to satisfy concerns about jurisdiction. *See Phillips Petroleum v. Shutts*, 472 U.S. 797 (1985).

3.   Does the Canadian court apply Canadian due process standards to the Illinois class settlement or U.S. standards? Although those standards may not meaningfully differ in this instance, they could in theory vary substantially. For example, if under U.S. law the notice to Currie was deemed adequate, should the Canadian court defer to that judgment? Or is the whole point that if Currie did not receive adequate notice under Canadian law then the U.S. judgment is not entitled to preclusive effect in Canada?

4.   The court rejects the argument that Currie should be precluded from bringing suit simply because his law firm also represented another party raising the same arguments. The idea is that the parties are distinct even if the law firm is the same. U.S. courts have generally taken a similar view of preclusion. *See, e.g., Hardy v. Johns-Manville Sales Corp.*, 681 F.2d 334 (5th Cir. 1982).

5.   As in this case, transnational class actions raise the possibility that a case resolved in one country will not ultimately be deemed to resolve the claims of plaintiffs in other countries. This undermines, to some degree, the rationale for class actions, which is to provide a "bill of peace" that once and for all resolves all claims stemming from a single incident. Should the named plaintiffs in a transnational class action be required to both provide notice and establish jurisdiction in ways that would be satisfactory in each of the various countries where plaintiffs are located?

6.   Would an international solution be preferable? Some scholars have proposed creating an International Court of Civil Justice to adjudicate transnational mass tort cases. *See, e.g.,* Maya Steinitz & Paul Gowder, *Transnational Litigation as a Prisoner's* Dilemma, 94 N.C. L. REV. 751 (2016). Is that a better solution? Even if so, is it reasonable to think enough countries around the world will agree on the procedural rules such a court would use?

Index

References are to Pages
